IMAGES
of America

ATLANTIC

I0901115

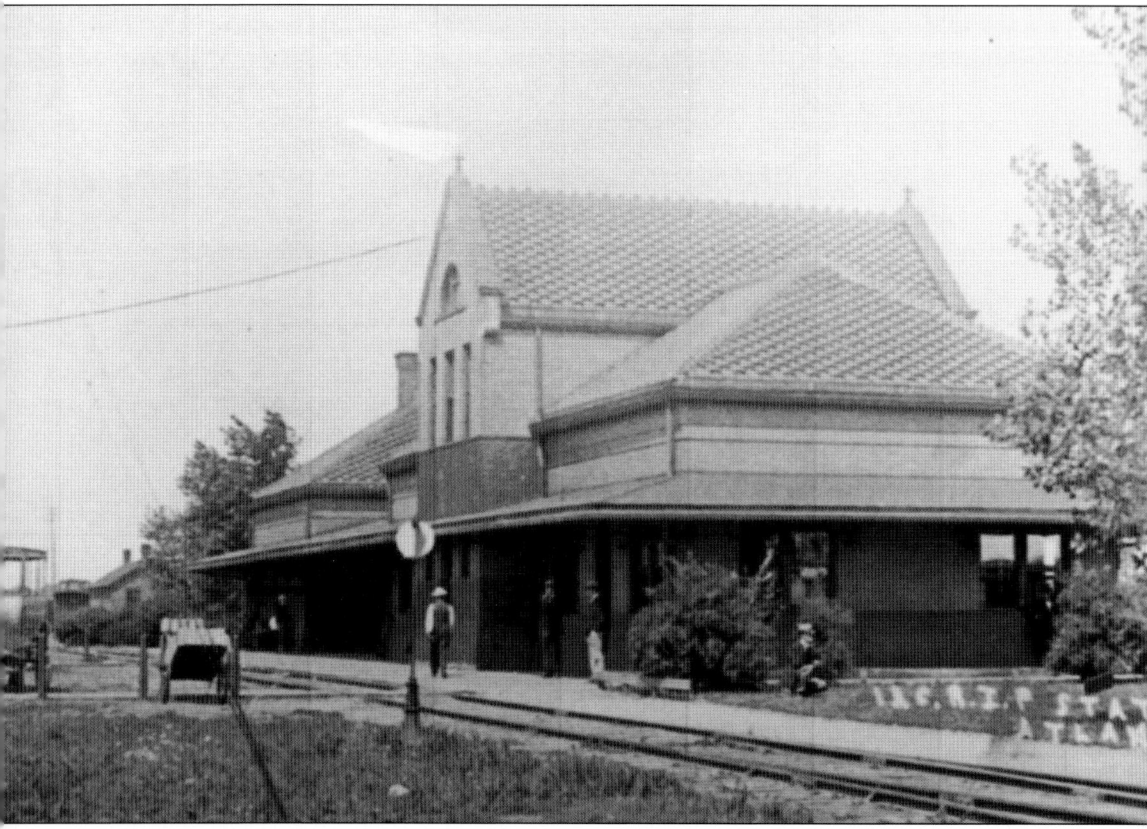

Atlantic is one of many early Iowa towns that can trace their beginnings to the railroad. In 1868, Franklin H. Whitney was hired to survey land for the Chicago, Rock Island, and Pacific Railroad, which was being constructed across Iowa. With an eye toward development of a new town, he negotiated with the railway for the location of the Atlantic depot. The first depot was built of rough native lumber, and William Reynolds was appointed as the first agent in January 1871. The attractive brick depot, which is the symbol of Atlantic, was completed in 1898. Its imposing position at the wide northern end of Chestnut Street is a testament to Whitney's foresight.

On the Cover: Costas Papathakos, the proud owner of Costas Confectionery, stands behind the counter. Chris Yeanos is sitting in a booth with Mary Lianos Papathakos, Costas's wife. Near the center, a Coca-Cola sign hangs from a trellis with paper greenery. Several times a year, a Coca-Cola salesman supplying five-gallon cans of fountain syrup would visit and decorate the store free of charge. The Papathakos's daughter, Jane, still resides in Atlantic in 2010. (Courtesy of Jane Papathakos.)

IMAGES
of America

ATLANTIC

Lila Hoogeveen and Shiona Putnam

ARCADIA
PUBLISHING

Copyright © 2010 by Lila Hoogeveen and Shiona Putnam
ISBN 978-0-7385-8429-4

Published by Arcadia Publishing
Charleston SC, Chicago IL, Portsmouth NH, San Francisco CA

Printed in the United States of America

Library of Congress Control Number: 2010922962

For all general information contact Arcadia Publishing at:
Telephone 843-853-2070
Fax 843-853-0044
E-mail sales@arcadiapublishing.com
For customer service and orders:
Toll-Free 1-888-313-2665

Visit us on the Internet at www.arcadiapublishing.com

This book is dedicated to the visionary pioneers of Atlantic and to Jay and Jerry for unwavering support and encouragement.

Contents

Acknowledgments 6

Introduction 7

1. Following a Dream 9
2. Establishing a Settlement 21
3. Investing in a Town 51
4. Building a City 79
5. Enjoying the Social Scene 95
6. Dealing with Adversity 113
7. Coming of Age 123

ACKNOWLEDGMENTS

The information in this book is a result of hours of research from old manuscripts, letters, newspapers, books, interviews, and many a delightful conversation with those who share our love of history. We extend special thanks to Norma Landon for patience and excellent technical support. We want to thank Deb Herbert, Jane Papathakos, Phil and Trina Chintz, Roger Steffen, Margaret Slepsky, Louise Hunt, and Richard and Pat MacCauley for their willingness to share Atlantic stories. Others who have graciously shared photographs, time, and information include Lloyd and Sharon Roberts, Ken Moorman, Robert and Judy Camblin, and Jim Carey, of the Cass County Genealogical Society. We are grateful to Connie Collins, publisher of the *Atlantic News-Telegraph*, Sue Fischer at Fischer Photography, the staff of the Atlantic Public Library, Dennis Stuetelberg of Rex Pharmacy, the Cass County Historical Museum in Griswold, the staff of the Library Archives at the State Historical Society of Iowa in Des Moines, and Ann McCurdy of the Atlantic Chamber of Commerce. Unless otherwise noted, images are courtesy of the Cass County Historical Society.

Introduction

What would the world be like without the dreamers and the visionaries? What would it be like without those men and women who by sheer force of personality left a lasting mark on the face of the earth? The pioneers who created the city of Atlantic were such people. They came out of the broad, rich prairies of America's heartland, and they had dreams fueled by spirit that were advanced by perseverance. Great history is the story of human achievement, and it is the stories of those who make history that draw generations to seek, to learn, and to appreciate the fruits of previous labors. Ultimately these stories fuel a desire to preserve history and to cherish it. For Atlantic and Cass County, the story began eons ago in the Paleozoic era when animal life first appeared. The land did not look like it does now but was covered by a vast, shallow sea. Limestone deposits developed from the shells and bones of sea life that abounded in the waters. The sea gave way to land that was eventually covered with swamps, ferns, and tropical foliage. Over time, this led to the formation of Iowa's mineral wealth: coal, zinc, lead, and gypsum. During the Mesozoic era, dinosaurs and great reptiles roamed freely. With the dawn of the Cenozoic era, great glaciers formed and spread across the land: the Nebraskan, the Kansan, the Illinoian, and the Wisconsin—the first two being the only ones that extended into Cass County. As these glaciers retreated, huge rocks and boulders were ground up to form the incredibly rich glacial drift that defines Iowa.

The first people known to inhabit the area were American Indians. While there were many tribes, the one most closely associated with Cass County was the Potawatomi. From the region around Lake Michigan, they were moved, by treaty and intrusion, ever westward from their land as a clash of cultures expanded across the continent. In the mid-1800s, there were many proponents of Manifest Destiny, the view that justified the white settlement of the North American continent in the belief that such expansion was not only ethical as a means of bringing civilization to the wilderness but was predestined for the rapidly developing nation. What the white man saw as settlement and progress, the Indians often saw as destruction of the land as they watched the virgin prairies plowed and the dense forests cut. The white man's way of life was diametrically opposed to the culture of the American Indian who saw the land as belonging to no one but bestowed to every being as a gift of the Great Spirit. They used the land for hunting and gathering, taking only what was needed for sustenance. With the coming of the white man, this way of life ended as the Indians joined forces with the trappers and traders and hunted animals, not for food, but for the goods that could be had in exchange for the animal pelts. In June 1846, the Potawatomi sold their lands in western Iowa to the federal government for $850,000, and by 1848 they had moved westward to Kansas Territory.

At this same time, the Mormons were fleeing from religious persecution in New York, Ohio, Illinois, and Missouri. They were on a great migration to the far West seeking a place where they could live according to their beliefs without fear of retribution. One of their trails crossed southwestern Iowa. Brigham Young realized that his people were in need of food and funds, so he made an unusual deal with the U.S. government. At war with Mexico, the country needed recruits, and Young needed cash. Capt. James Allen met a group of Mormons near the Nodaway River. He was to take 500 recruits back with him in exchange for their wages, which were to be delivered in gold to Brigham Young. This group was called the Mormon Battalion. They ended up in California but never saw action.

Pres. James Polk declared Iowa the 29th state in the Union on December 28, 1846. Poor communications at the time created an oddity in this story. Ansel Briggs, Iowa's first governor, had already been inaugurated on December 3, 1846—25 days before statehood was declared. Statehood brought a rush of settlers seeking a chance to build a new life in a new place. Yet moving westward was daunting for men and women alike. Louise Morrow Hunt, a descendant of Atlantic's early settlers and a lifelong resident of the city, described the quiet anguish of the women who trekked through the Great Plains in search of a new home in a new land when she wrote this poem:

> Listen, they whisper!
> Women's ghosts, walking, walking again over rough prairie, up hills, across rivers, to the frozen moment of mountains.
> Long gray skirts lift dust puffs behind them . . . small streams on the ripple of time.
> From my ribbon of concrete, I imagine rocks cutting their shoes on uncharted paths.
> They lift babies, kiss tired toddlers' skinned knees, bind wounds from snakes, and guns, treat disease, help with birthing, comfort the dying . . . no shelter from wind or rain, or dust choking the dying, whose wooden crosses were markers for the wolves.
> Screams pierce the years from that aloof lady, frozen erect in the wagon, clutching her box of dishes from home, as the river swept her away.

As early as 1856, a group of men, led by J. R. Kirk, surveyed and platted the settlement they named Grove City. This site was located three miles east of modern Atlantic. For about 12 years, Grove City grew and thrived, but a man of incredible energy, vision, and determination was to be its downfall. Franklin H. Whitney was a man among men. His accomplishments were legendary. Whitney established towns, built banks, encouraged settlement, served on boards, held civic offices, and bought and sold businesses with seeming abandon. He worked for the Rock Island Railroad as a surveyor and saw the opportunity to create a new city—if the company approved his suggestion for the placement of the depot. Whitney suggested the site of present-day Atlantic. When his recommendation was accepted, the boom was on. The people of Grove City could see the inevitable, and most of them moved to Atlantic as soon as housing could be secured. A mere decade after the founding of Atlantic, there was not a single business and very few houses left in Grove City. The Atlantic Town Company, led by Whitney, was established to promote the new city, and promote it did. The company took out advertisements in eastern newspapers encouraging people to settle in Atlantic, wrested the county seat designation from Lewis, and built a prosperous railroad center that drew visitors from across the nation.

George Washington claimed that perseverance and spirit could do wonders; the story of the settlement, development, and maturing of the proud city of Atlantic, Iowa, would seem to confirm the wisdom of our country's preeminent founding father.

One

Following a Dream

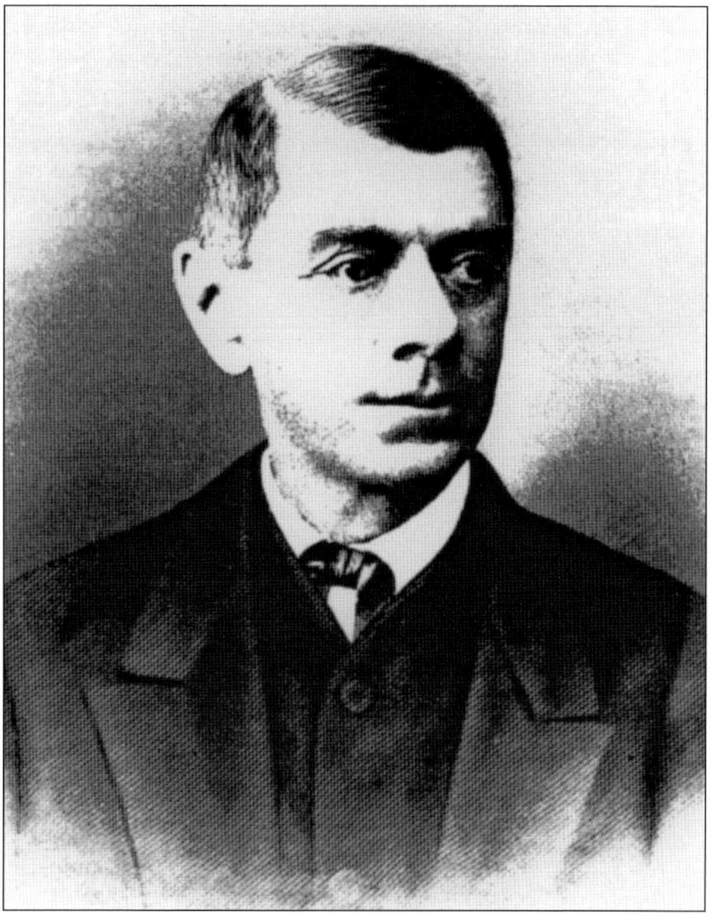

Atlantic was the dream of Franklin H. Whitney, an entrepreneur extraordinaire. Whitney came from New York in 1856 and laid out the town of Whitneyville in southeastern Cass County. In 1862, he moved to Cass Township. He founded the Atlantic Town Company in 1868 and was instrumental in laying out the present city of Atlantic. Whitney was trained as a surveyor and assisted in the plotting of the Chicago, Rock Island, and Pacific Railroad route. He arranged for the train station to be located in Atlantic, a designation that insured it would become a thriving community as well as the seat of Cass County.

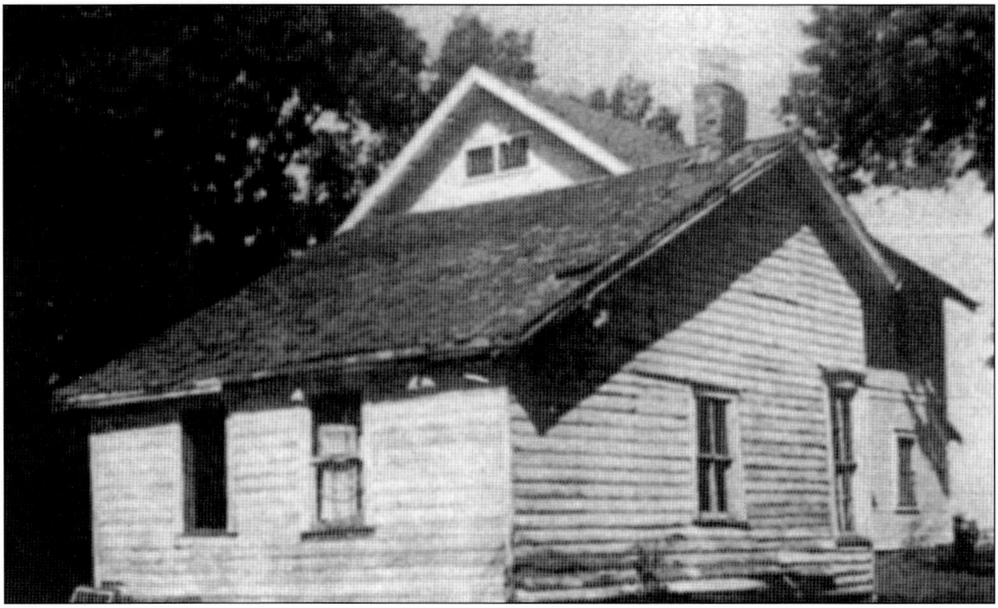

In most instances, men were given the credit for establishing homes on the frontier and building new towns and cities. Ella Graham Whitney, Franklin H. Whitney's wife, exemplified the hardy pioneer woman. When Franklin was busy encouraging settlement of the area and building his many enterprises, Ella was doing her share. Their first home in Cass County served as a stagecoach station, and it was not unusual for Ella to use 50 pounds of flour a week making bread to feed pioneers stopping by on their way west.

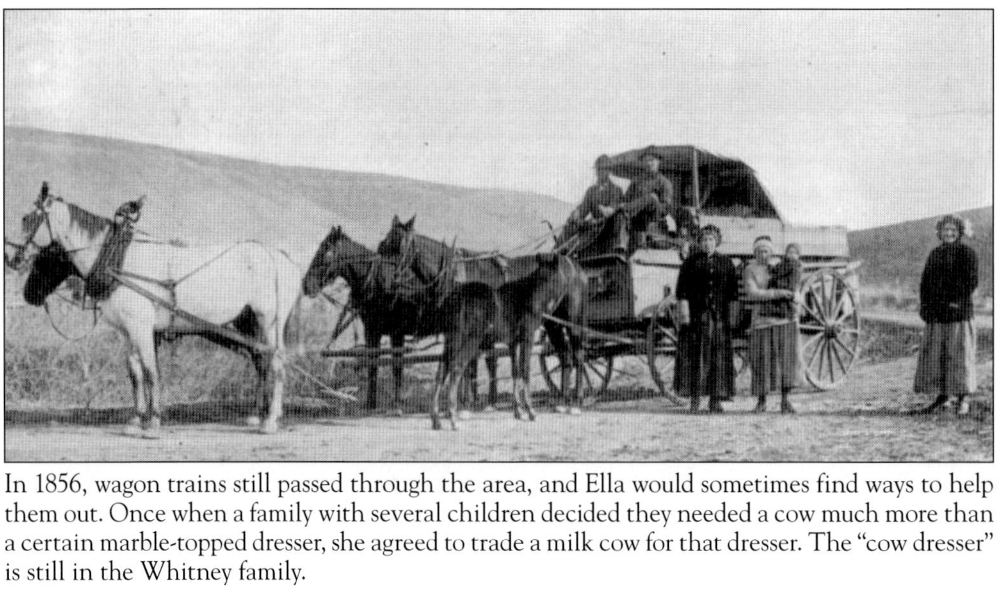

In 1856, wagon trains still passed through the area, and Ella would sometimes find ways to help them out. Once when a family with several children decided they needed a cow much more than a certain marble-topped dresser, she agreed to trade a milk cow for that dresser. The "cow dresser" is still in the Whitney family.

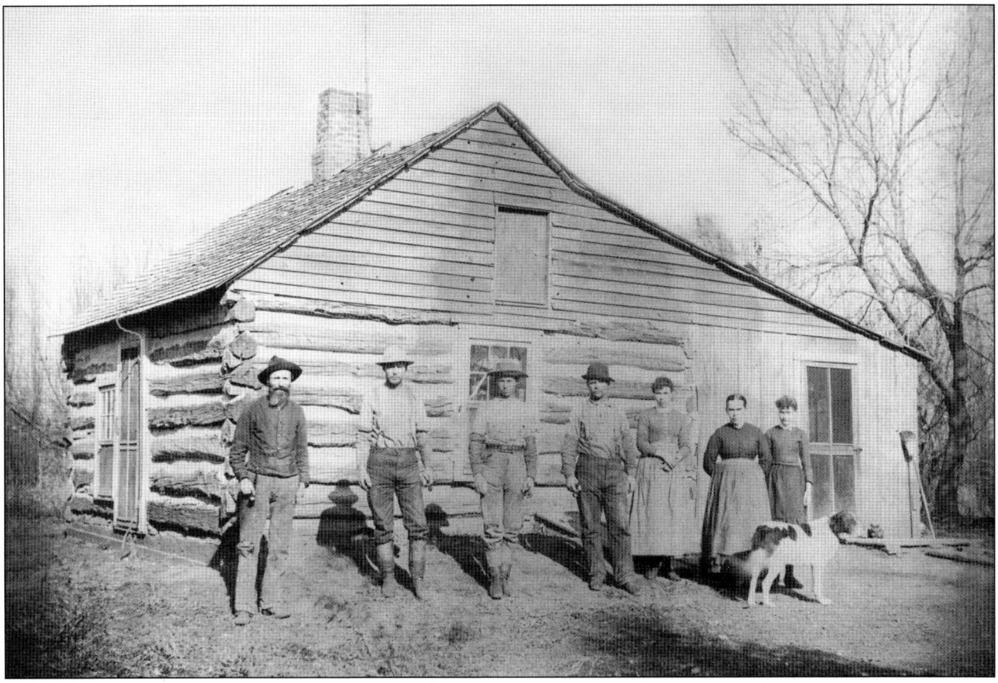

Franklin H. Whitney was successful in attracting settlers to the area through advertisements in East Coast newspapers. On December 16, 1869, he wrote, "To the toiling poor of the East and the men of little means who are willing to work, Atlantic now holds out an inviting hand and says, 'Come, where our prairies, broad, smiling, and beautiful, will welcome you to their midst. Come, and cultivate and improve them, and unite your fortunes with the country, where no proud aristocracy can lord it over you. Come, where you can fill your granaries with corn and your pockets with greenbacks, and make for yourselves what you can never do in the East, a home and a name among men.' " This is a 1870s photograph of the Iowa relatives of Sue Fischer of Atlantic. (Courtesy of Sue Fischer Photography.)

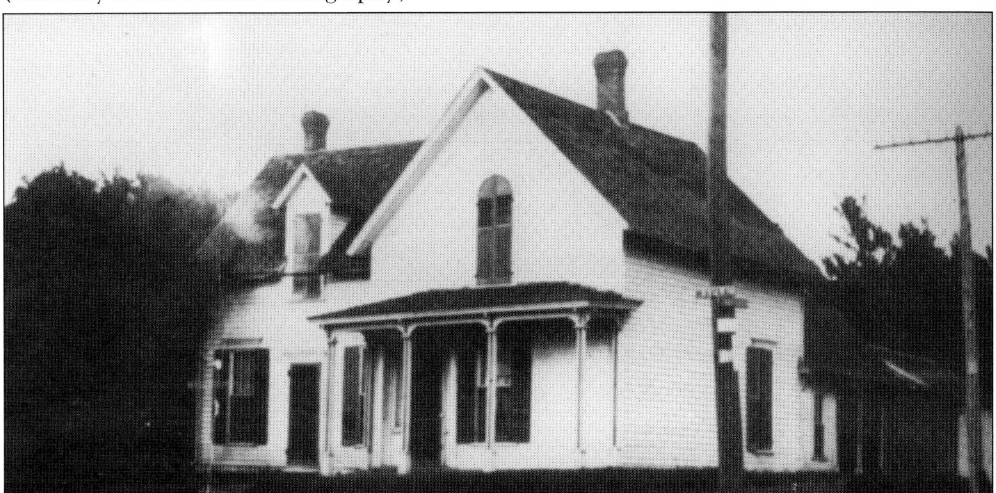

The Whitneys lived at this home at 610 Maple Street. Whitney's empire grew rapidly with enterprises in Chicago, Des Moines, Omaha, Kansas City, and Birmingham, Alabama, where he purchased the Mudd estate. He owned several silver mines in Colorado.

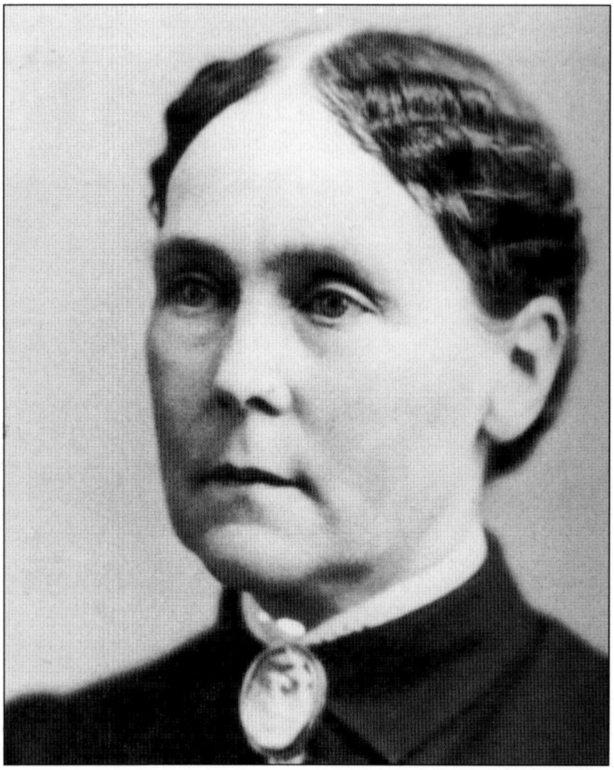

Ella Graham Whitney was born November 28, 1838, in Mexico, New York, where both she and her husband, Franklin, were reared. In her youth, she learned tailoring and studied music, and her wedding gift from Franklin was a melodeon. Ella was a partner in her husband's early enterprises. After his death, she remained in the home on Maple Street in Atlantic, where she died on February 6, 1919.

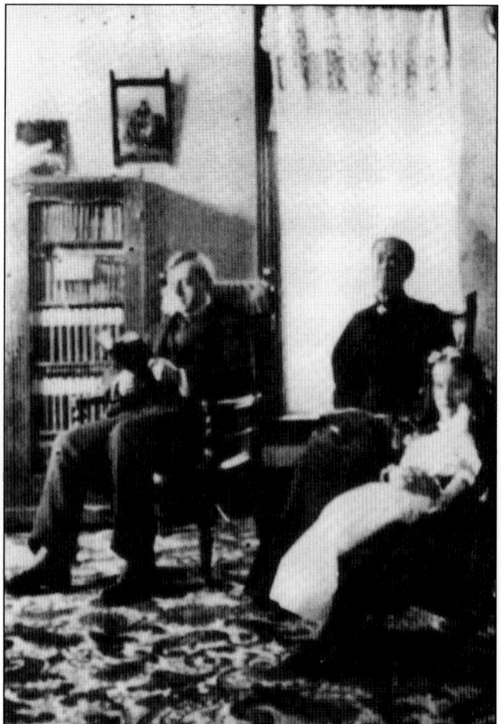

Pictured in this 1897 photograph at the Whitney home are, from left to right, Thomas Hayes Whitney, Ella Whitney, and granddaughter Marie Whitney. After Franklin H. Whitney died on October 11, 1896, his funeral was the largest ever in Atlantic. Flags flew at half-mast and all businesses closed. The Congregational Church was overflowing as city officials and the fire department escorted the coffin to the Atlantic cemetery with the Atlantic band playing funeral marches. Whitney's obituary recalls his energy and his devotion to the town where he had started churches, businesses, and schools and organized fire companies and served as mayor.

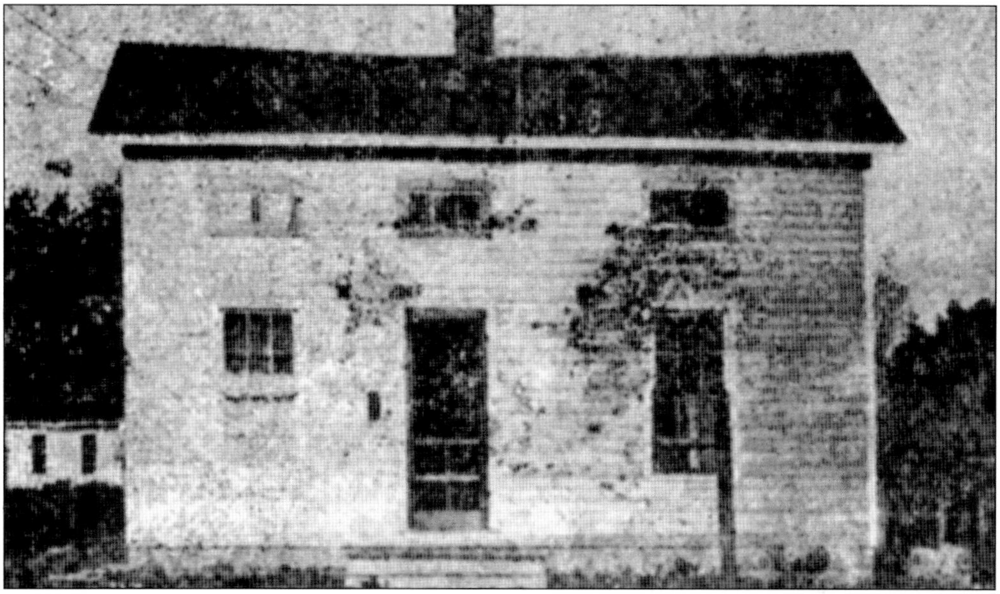

Henry Miller built the first house in Atlantic, at Sixth and Chestnut Streets, on September 9, 1868. It measured 16 feet by 24 feet, was two stories high, and was completed in exactly six days. The Miller house became the eating and living space for many pioneers who grabbed a chance to make their fortunes in the newly established community.

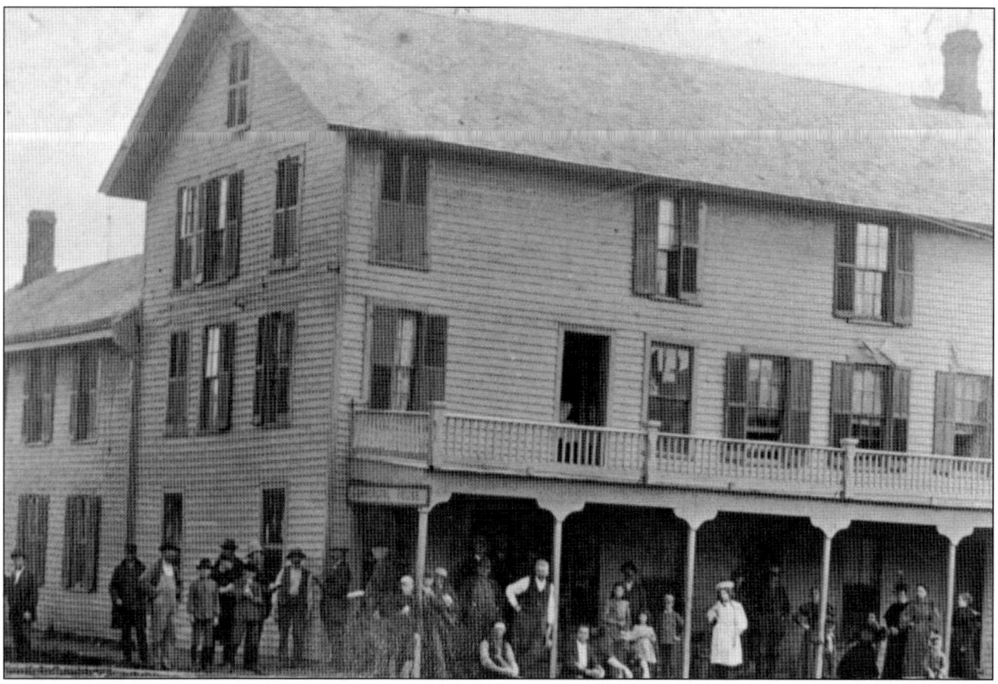

Six days after Miller completed the first home, he started construction on Atlantic's first hotel, the Atlantic House. Hired by the newly formed Atlantic Town Company, led by Franklin H. Whitney, Miller employed 20 men on the project. Naturally they boarded at the Miller house. The hotel was completed in 42 days. When it opened on November 1, 1868, two hundred people were waiting for rooms.

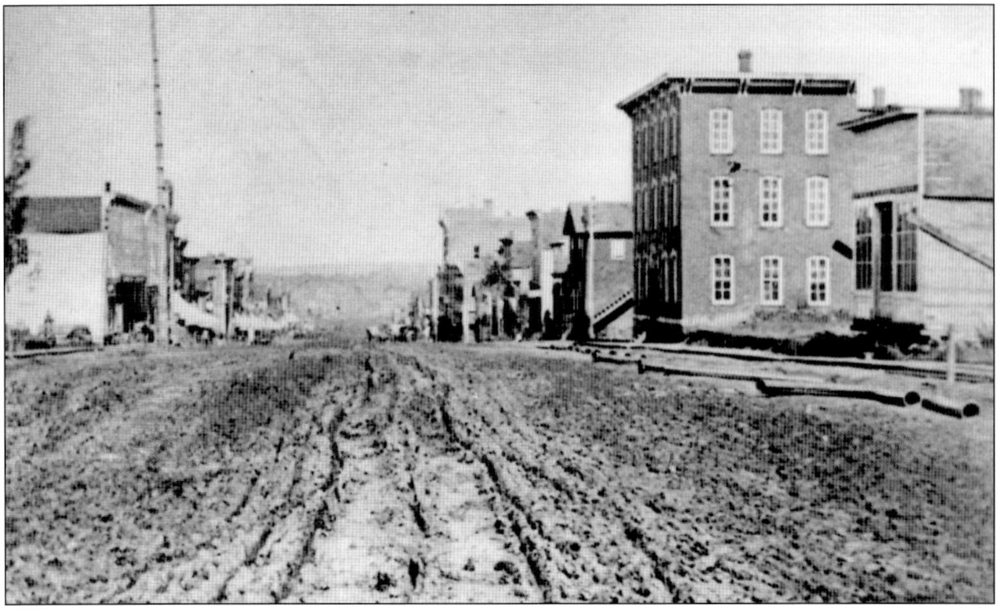

When Henry Miller was busy overseeing the building of the Atlantic House, he was constantly interrupted by people asking where the new town was going to be built. Miller went to Whitney and told him he was getting no work done due to these constant interruptions. Whitney, knowing that one needs to strike while the iron is hot, immediately took action. He had two furrows, 100 feet apart, plowed from the Miller House to the railroad grading. Lots sold quickly and the new city of Atlantic was effectively launched.

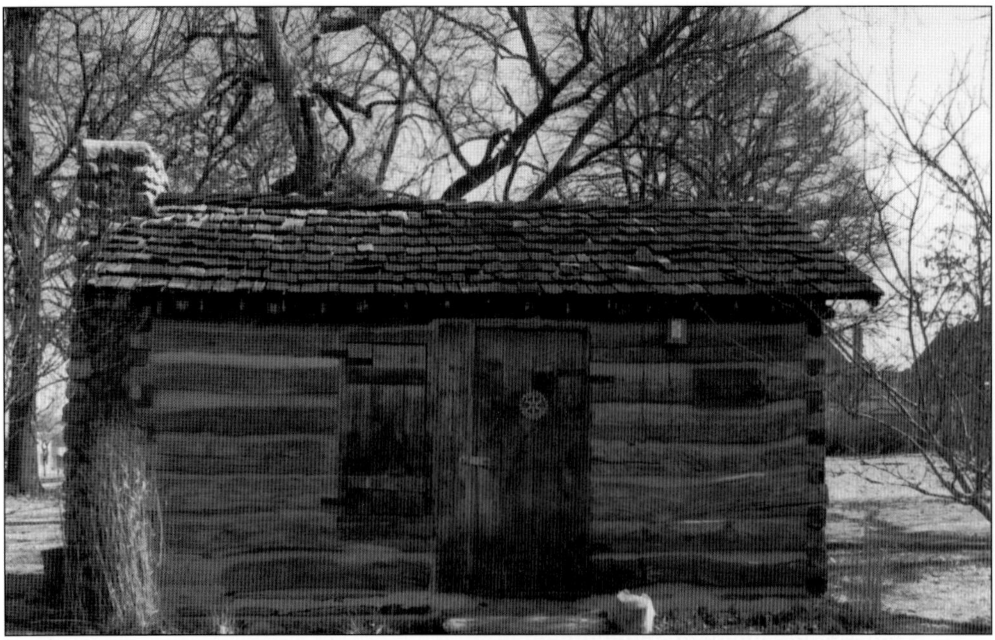

In 1863, twenty-six-year-old John Gingery built this log cabin in the Atlantic area. Nine of the ten children born to Gingery and his wife, Mary, were born here. As a bicentennial project in 1976, the Atlantic Rotarians and Boy Scout Troop 60 restored the cabin. It was dismantled and each log numbered for rebuilding. Today the cabin can be seen in the Atlantic City Park.

In the spring of 1854, John R. Kirk and his wife, Millicent Hoblitt Kirk, settled in Atlantic Township, which was later named Grove Township. They joined about 15 other families as pioneer settlers in what is now Cass County. When the Civil War broke out in 1861, Kirk left his home to serve in the Fourth Iowa Infantry under the command of Col. Grenville Dodge. The Fourth Infantry fought courageously and won distinction at the Battle of Pea Ridge, Arkansas, in March 1862. The original Kirk home, a modest log cabin, was the site for the first school in Atlantic Township. Mary Curry served as the first teacher.

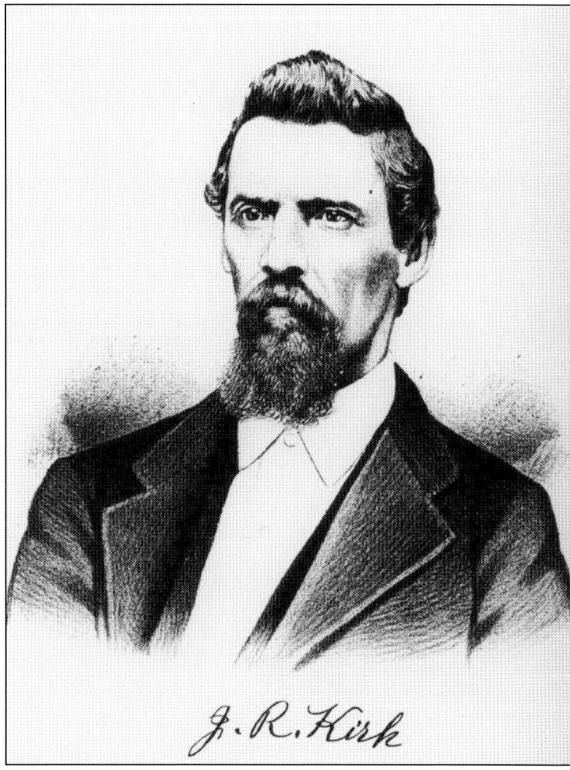

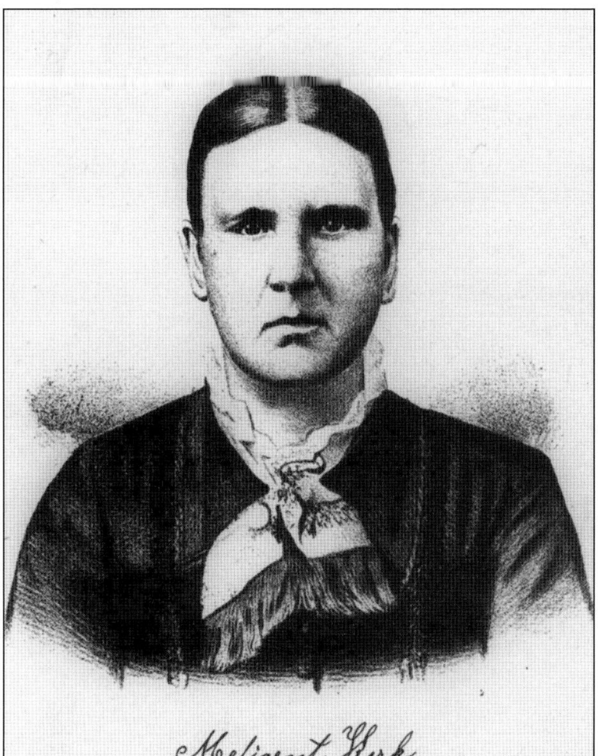

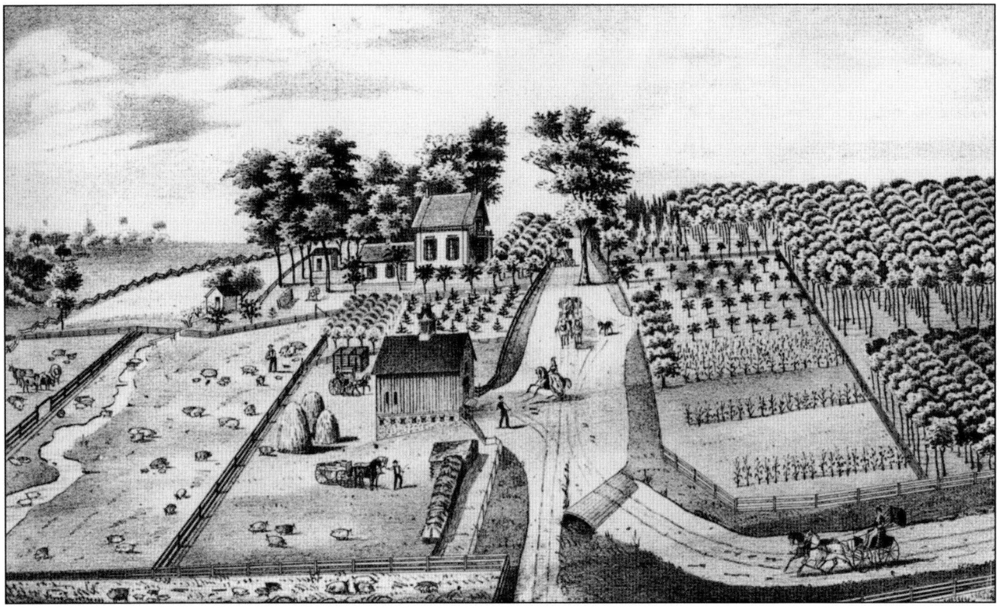

Kirk had a sterling reputation and, by dint of hard work, was soon able to build a substantial home and increase his holdings to 550 acres, as seen in this *1875 Andreas' Historical Atlas of the State of Iowa* etching. As well as developing cropland and raising stock, he planted extensive vineyards and orchards. After being ordained a deacon by Bishop Andrews at Red Oak in September 1884, Kirk held the position of preacher for the Methodist Episcopal Church, where he also led the Sabbath school for 20 years.

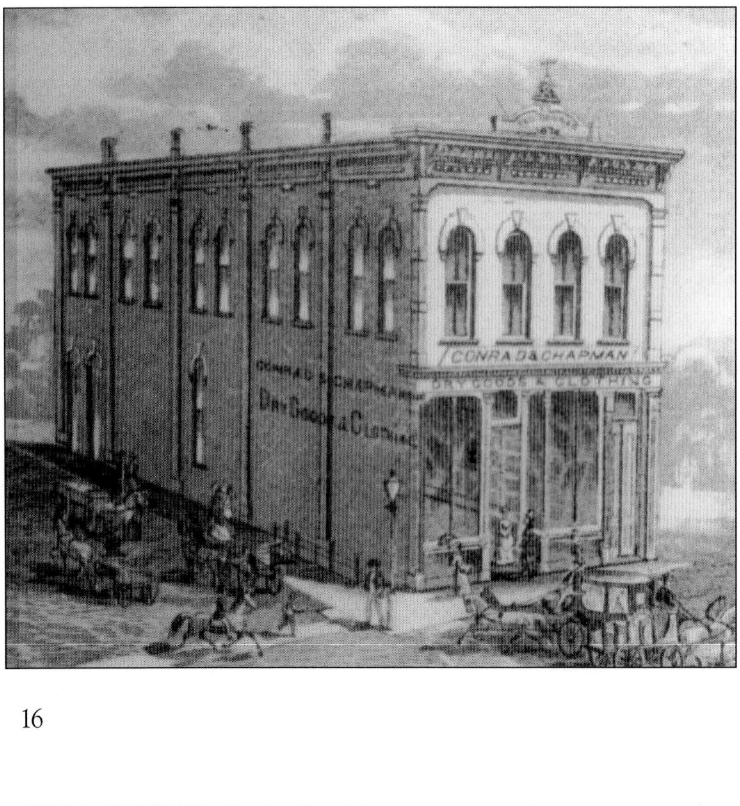

Arriving in 1854, George Conrad was one of the earliest white settlers in Cass County. In 1860, he established a dry goods and clothing store in Grove City. Once Atlantic was established in 1869, Conrad moved his business there. The business at Fifth and Chestnut Street was very successful, but he soon retired to look after his substantial property interests.

The Honorable Isaac Dickerson first arrived in Cass County in 1856. Starting in 1857, he served as the county treasurer and recorder for nine years. The 1862–1863 Iowa General Assembly passed an act separating the two branches of this office. Dickerson chose to remain as treasurer. When the town of Atlantic was laid out, he was one of the property owners of that site and very instrumental in the growth of the new town.

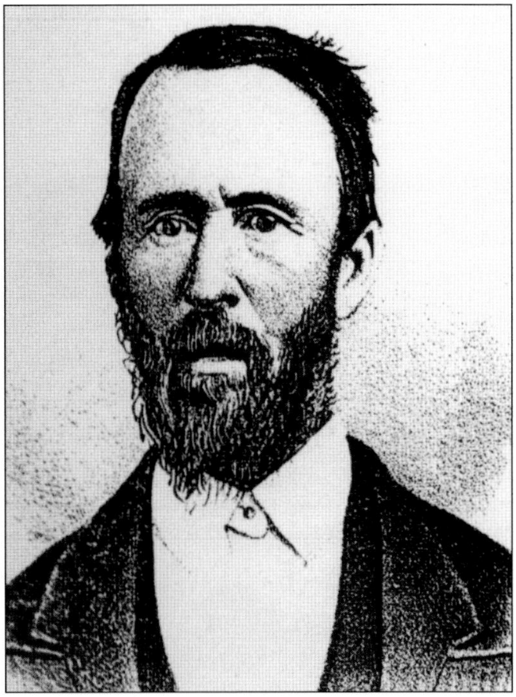

This etching in the *1875 Andreas' Historical Atlas of the State of Iowa* shows the home of the Honorable Isaac Dickerson. He served as mayor of Atlantic for three terms, spent two terms on the city council, and was involved in the Dickerson and Wood real estate business, the Cass County Bank, and several other enterprises.

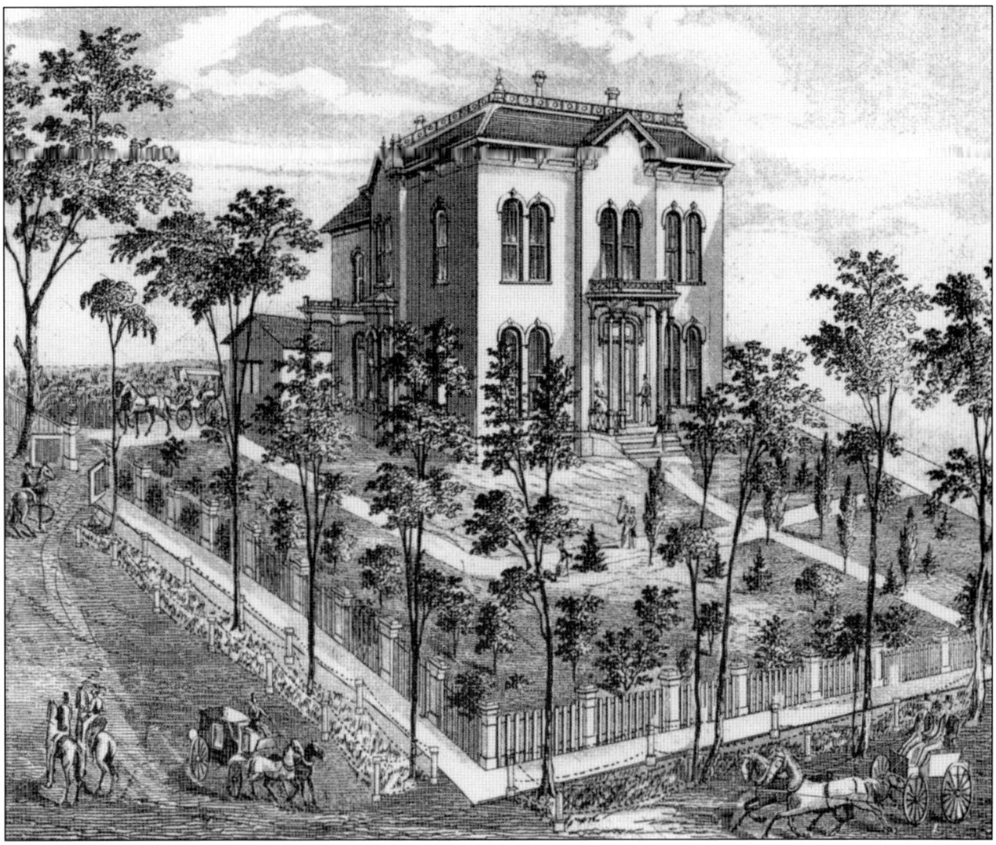

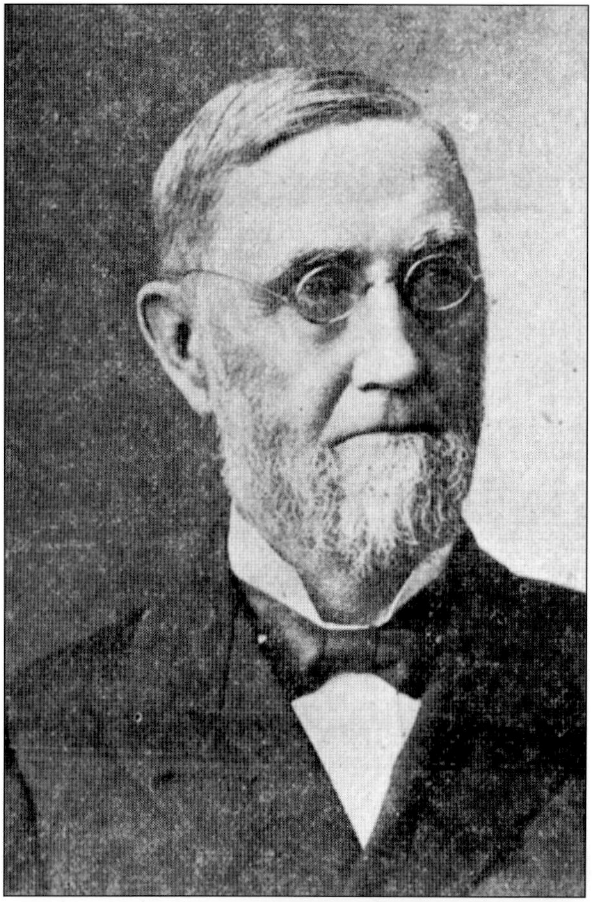

Dr. David Findley was Atlantic's pioneer physician and surgeon. After graduating from college in 1853, he set out for the goldfields of California. He took the long route around South America and was shipwrecked off the coast of California. Clinging for hours to a small chicken coop, Findley and seven others were rescued and put ashore on a small, barren island. They spent three days without food or water until a whaler rescued them and took them to San Francisco. Over 250 persons, including two of Findley's personal friends, lost their lives in that wreck.

Typical of those used by early professionals in Atlantic, this horse and buggy belonged to a Mr. Dimig, a local druggist. Dr. Findley made his rounds in such a conveyance. Findley arrived in Atlantic during a raging scarlet fever epidemic, and his heroic efforts in administering to patients in the area earned him a special place in the hearts of the people.

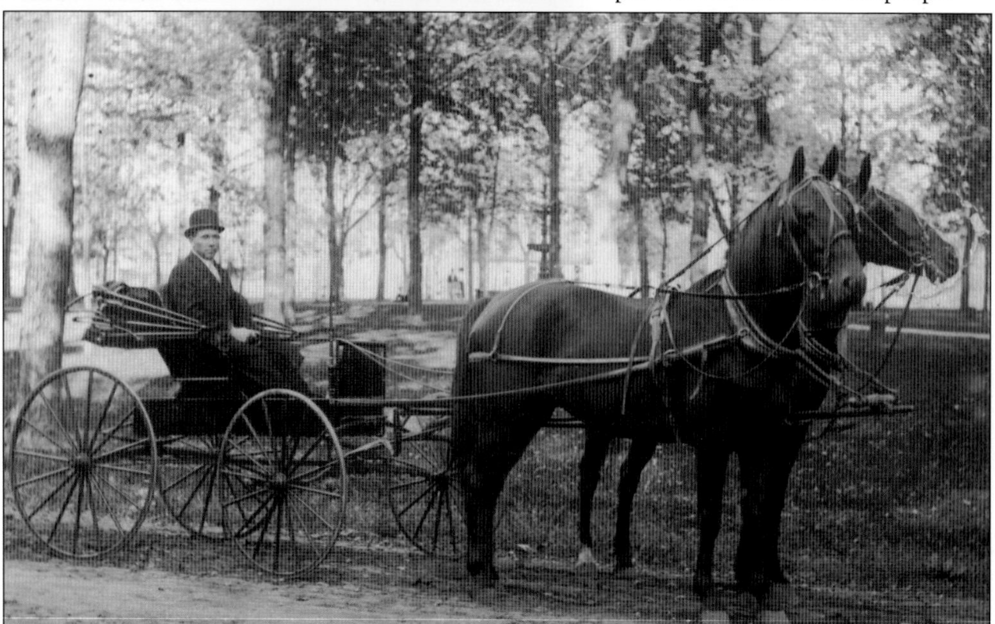

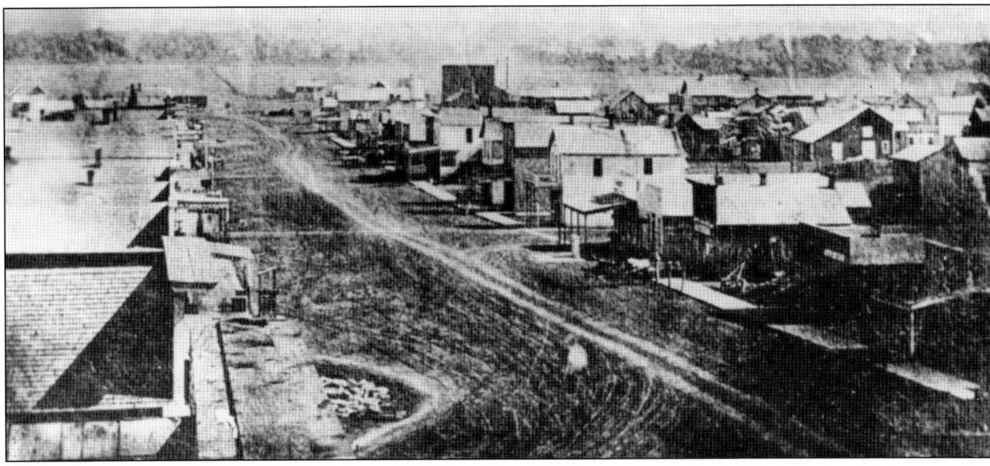

The first business in the new city of Atlantic was Eggleston's, which opened in October 1868. When the railroad bypassed Grove City, wise business owners realized that their future rested in the developing railroad center of Atlantic. Eggleston's store was torn down in Grove City on Saturday, moved, and set up in Atlantic in time to open on Monday morning. A drugstore, McFadden and France, was the second store to open, followed by Southwicks, a dry goods establishment.

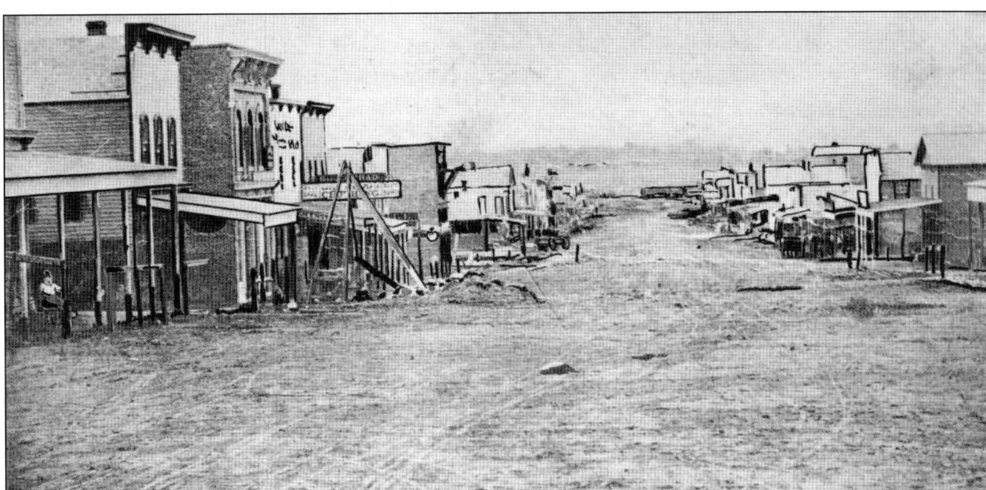

There were lots of complaints about the condition of Chestnut Street, which could be impassable at times. When it was dry, the street was engulfed in dust, and when it rained, the roadbed turned to bottomless mud. An early newspaper reported that a local minister complained, "Atlantic has ten saloons but not one yard of paved streets."

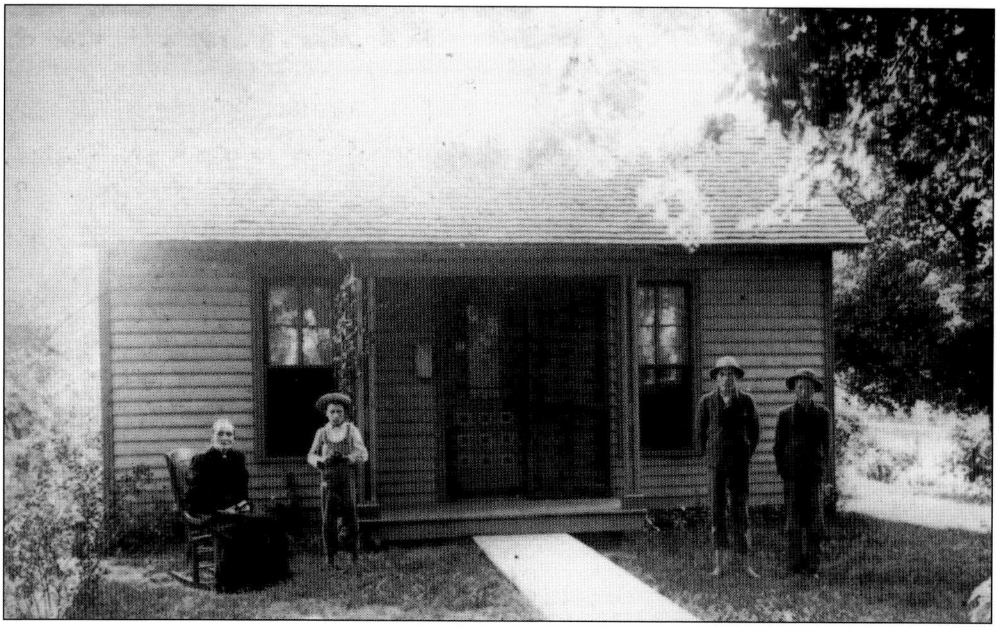

This 1890 photograph above shows the home of the Leo Beener family at 507 Spruce Street in Atlantic. Mrs. Beener is shown with three young lads. It is known that two of the three are her sons, Nick and Bill. Later Bill Beener operated a bakery on Chestnut Street. Pictured below is the Beener Bakery on the west side of Chestnut Street. It was not only a place where bread and bakery goods could be purchased, but a place where one could get a good home-style meal. The early 1900s was a profitable time to be in business in Atlantic, as the population was growing rapidly. One local newspaper reported at the time that it was almost impossible to find a house to rent in town.

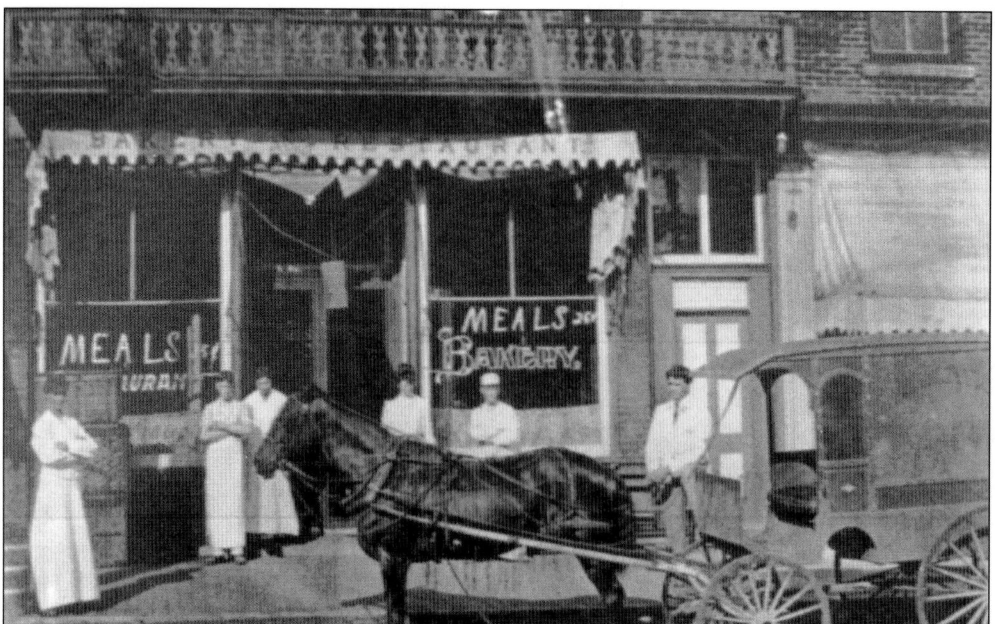

Two

ESTABLISHING A SETTLEMENT

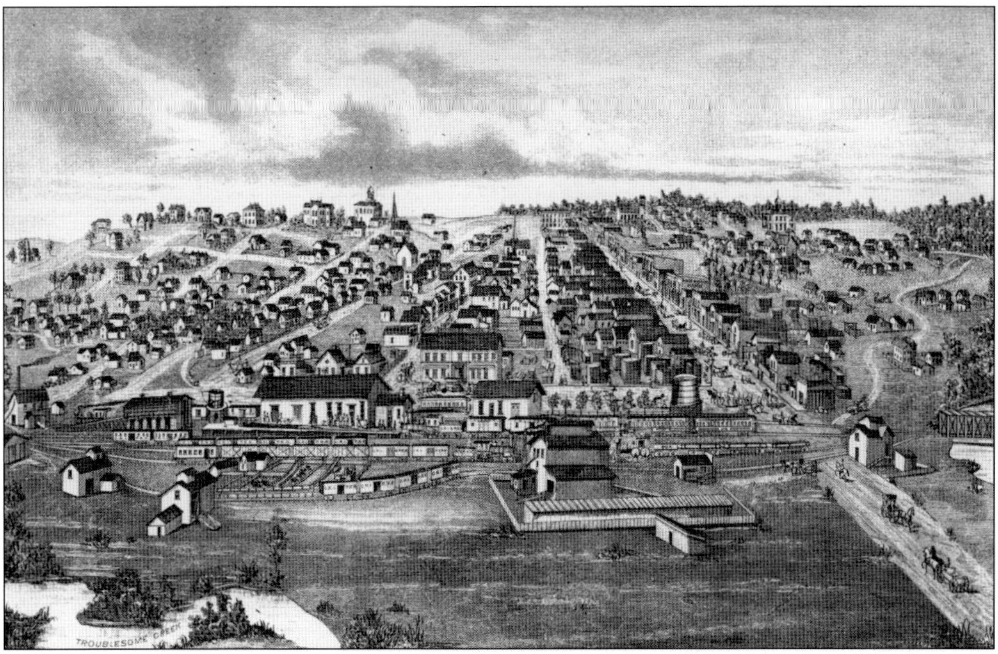

In an 1869 *Des Moines Register* article, Atlantic is described as the "fair, young queen of the Botna valley. . . . There are three valleys converging at this point, and from this circumstance, the location is embellished by nature with a variety of scenery which must commend it to all admirers of the beautiful." Atlantic is located 82 miles west of Des Moines and 56 miles east of Council Bluffs. The plat of the town covers about 640 acres.

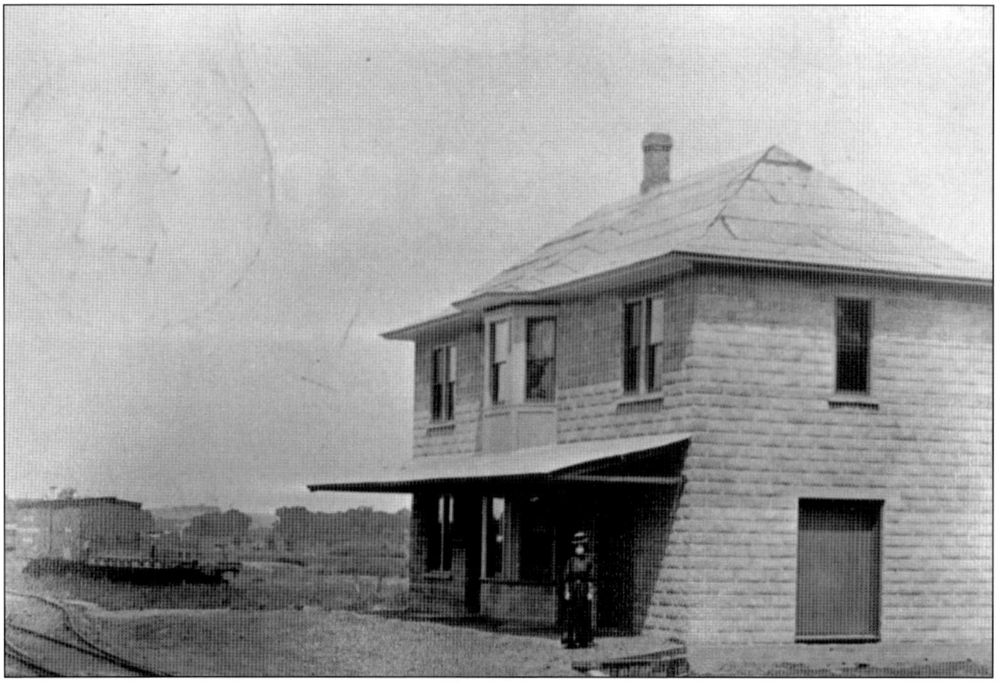

The above photograph shows the original Atlantic Northern and Southern depot in Atlantic. The rails of the Atlantic Northern and Southern Railroad extended from Atlantic to Elkhorn by Christmas Day, 1907. Local women fixed Christmas dinner and all the trimmings for the railroad workers. There was a deadline to meet; the rails were to reach the town of Kimballton, three miles away, by New Year's Day. When it became evident that the deadline could not be met, the clever city fathers of Kimballton met in a quick session. They extended the city limits of Kimballton by one mile to meet the rails, thus satisfying the legal technicality of the contract. In the photograph below, Atlantic and Northern cars are loaded at the depot.

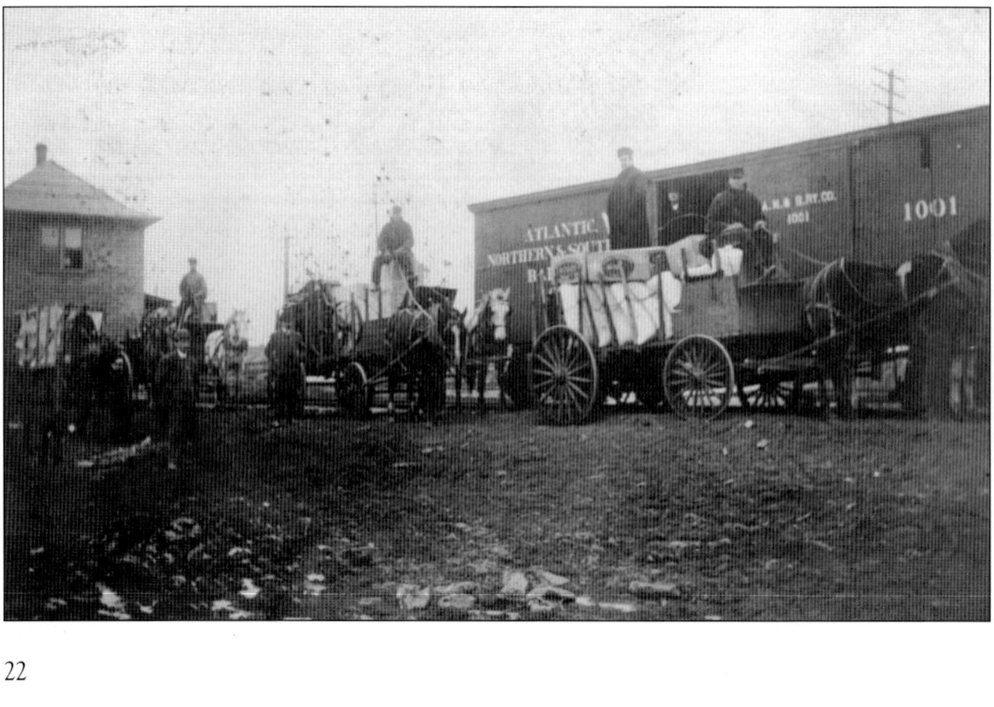

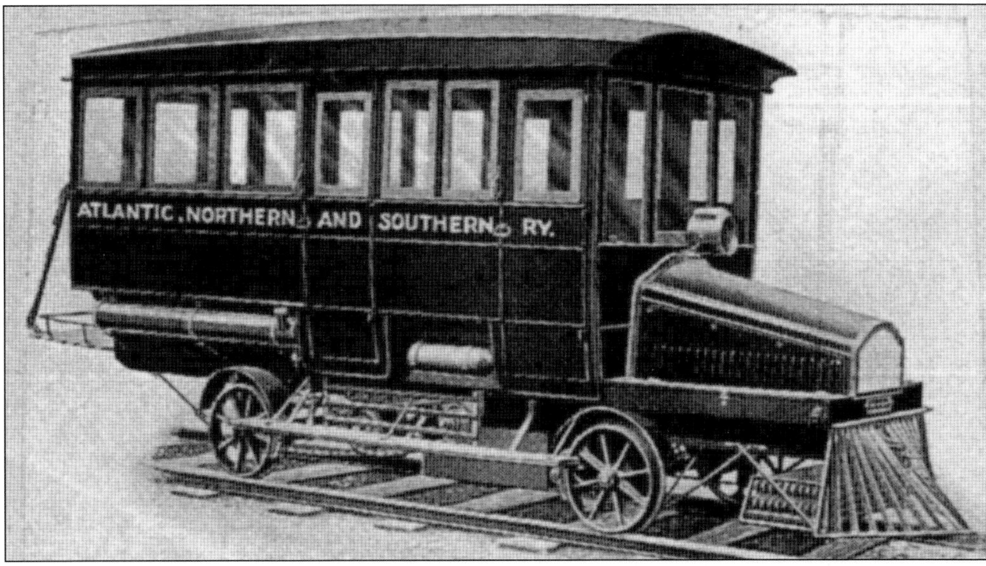

In the early 1900s, the Atlantic Northern and Southern Rail Company was the only farm-owned rail company in America. H. S. Rattenborg was the main promoter and general manager. This trolley (above) ran from Atlantic to Elkhorn and Kimballton, stopping along the way at Harrisdale, Smith Lake, Gates, Hansen Heights, and anywhere in between (see tickets below). The rail line was started for the purpose of moving livestock and grain as well as passengers. An extra car would be added on weekends to take people to Smith Lake, a very popular recreation spot at that time with swimming and boating available. The trolley carried schoolteachers to their jobs and many a young lady to meet her beau. This route was discontinued in the late 1930s.

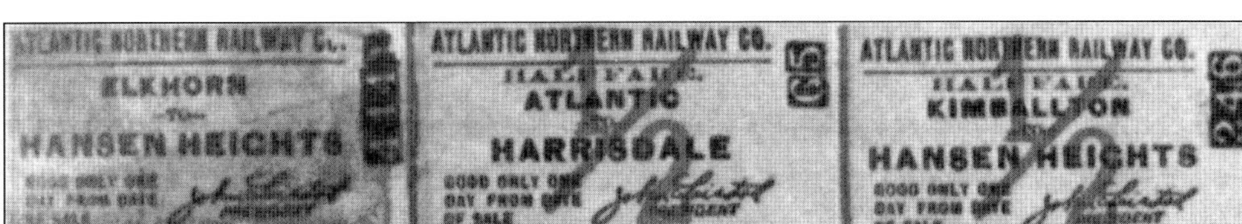

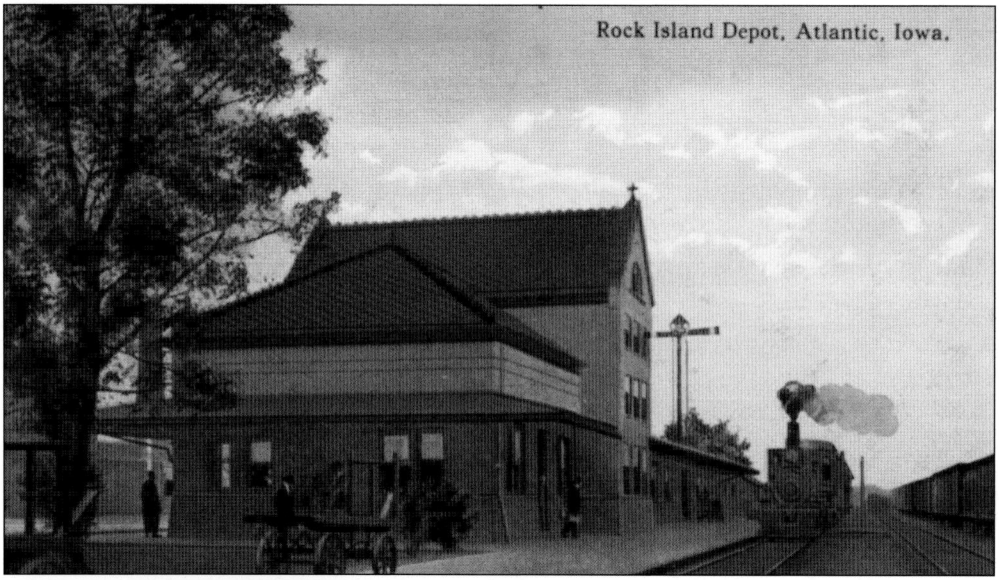

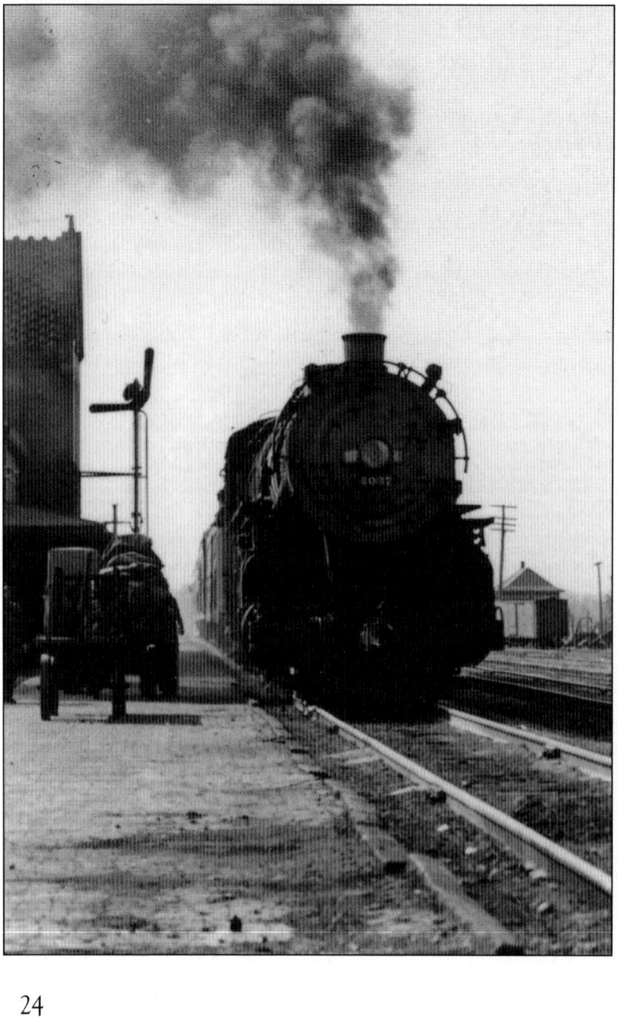

The prime factor in the early development of Atlantic, as it was for many other towns, was the coming of the railroad. The Rock Island Line reached Atlantic in 1868 and expanded its service to Lewis and Griswold in 1880. This redbrick depot has long been the symbol of Atlantic. Atlantic was served by two other lines, the Atlantic Northern and Atlantic Southern. The Southern branch of this line extended to Villisca, where it met the Burlington Line.

Engine Number 4037 pulls into the Rock Island depot. Franklin H. Whitney insured that the town of Atlantic would profit from the railroad when he negotiated a clause in the original Rock Island Railroad contract that required every train using the line to make a stop in Atlantic. Later, when speedy Zephyr trains wanted to eliminate the Atlantic stop, the old contract was brought out and the conditions honored; every train made a stop in Atlantic.

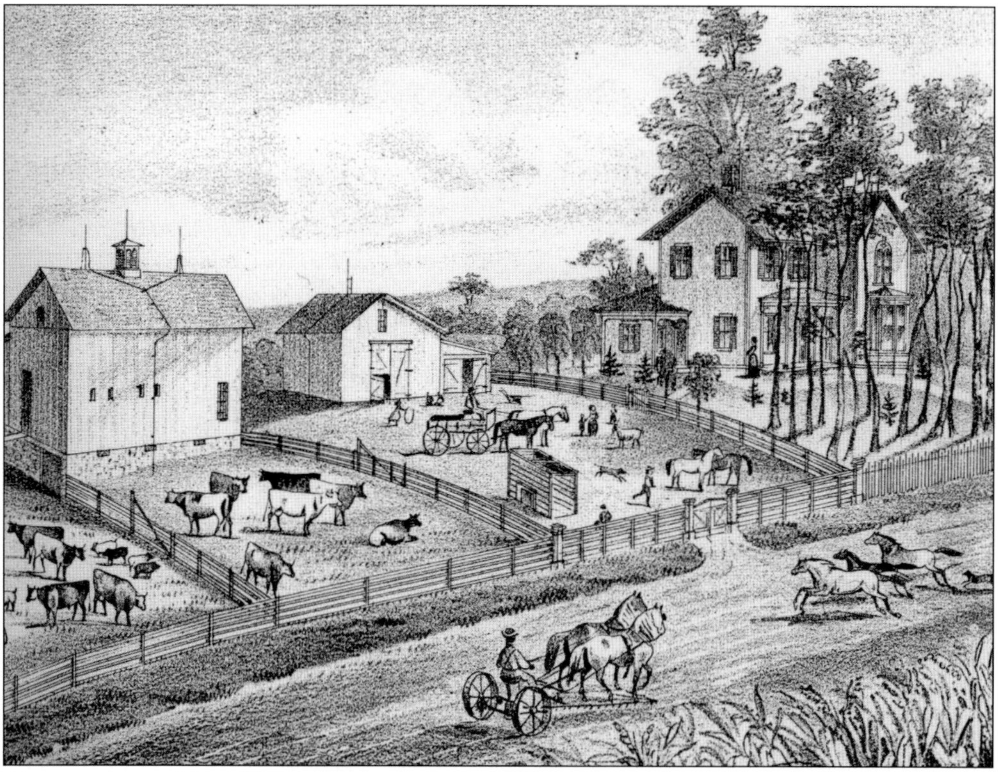

The engraving of the William Hopley farm, from the *1875 Andreas' Historical Atlas of the State of Iowa*, illustrates how substantial buildings were on early farms in Cass County. William Hopley was born in England, but in 1853, he tied up all his worldly possessions in a red handkerchief and set sail for America. He came to Cass County in June 1858. By 1865, he was able to purchase a farm of 120 acres, which he soon enlarged to 700 acres. Hopley developed a prosperous stock business, introduced Clydesdale workhorses from Scotland, raised thoroughbred horses, and dealt in cattle and hogs.

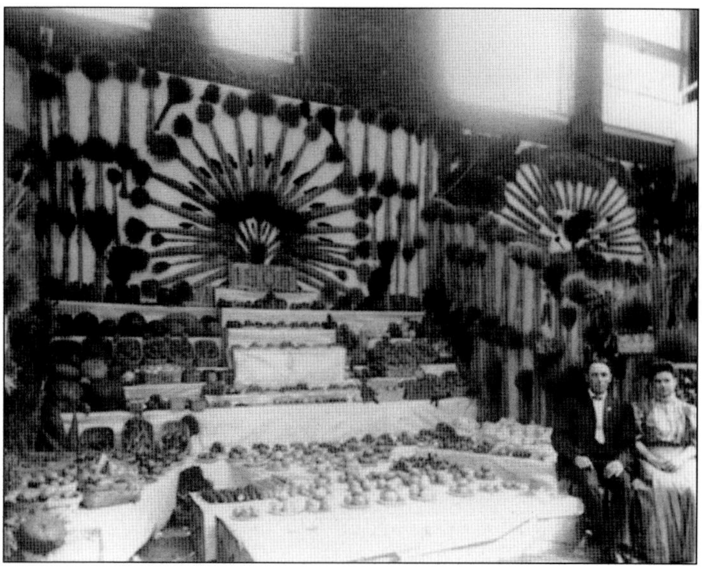

Charles E. Malone operated a seed company and retail store at 305 Chestnut Street. Malone also owned several seed growing farms and a corn drying plant on Olive Street. The company grew rapidly and specialized in a variety of seeds and nursery plants. In this 1908 photograph, the Malones are seated in front of their exhibit at the Iowa State Fair.

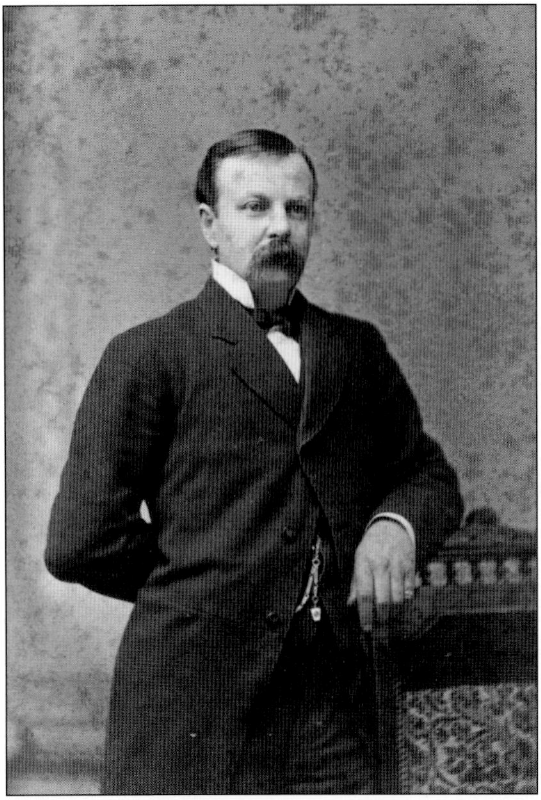

Cyrus B. Osborne was a pioneer and a civic-minded citizen of Atlantic. He served in the army during the Civil War and came to Cass County in 1866. In 1868, he moved to Atlantic. He was a charter member of the Atlantic GAR (Grand Army of the Republic.) In 1872, Osborne married Belle Tiffany, the local schoolmarm. The wedding took place in Chicago. The Osbornes were business and social leaders in the community.

This photograph of the Cyrus B. Osborne home at 709 Locust shows, from left to right, Corrie Osborne Herbert, Tom Brown, and Belle Tiffany Osborne seated on the front porch. Corrie was the Osbornes' daughter. Zeta, another daughter, married Hugh M. Reinig, a prominent Cass County banker. Her wedding dress can be seen in the Cass County Historical Museum in Griswold.

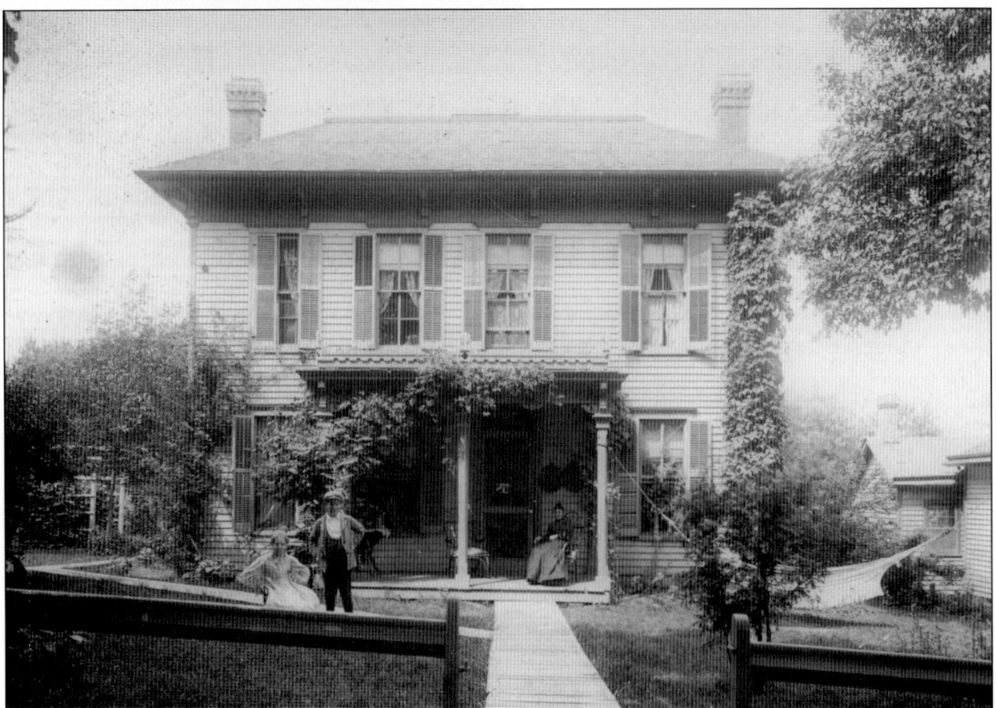

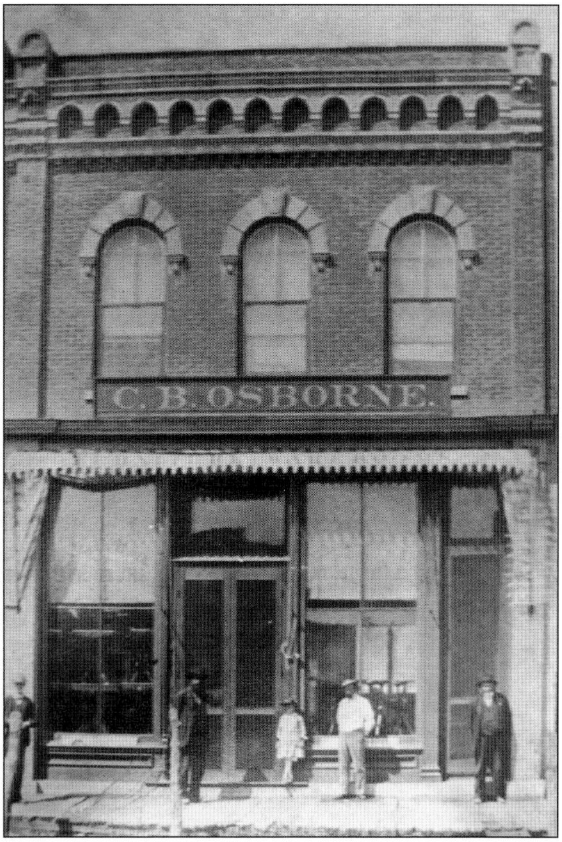

Cyrus B. Osborne was more than just an outstanding Atlantic businessman. He was known as one of Atlantic's most enterprising men and was always ready to support anything that contributed to the advancement of the city's interests. These exterior and interior photographs are of his furniture store on Chestnut Street. According to an early history, the salesroom, reputed to be one of the most pleasant in town, was 100 feet long by 24 feet wide. He carried a large stock of both fine and common furniture that invoiced upwards of $8,000. The first floor held the salesroom and a work area, while the second story was designated for storage.

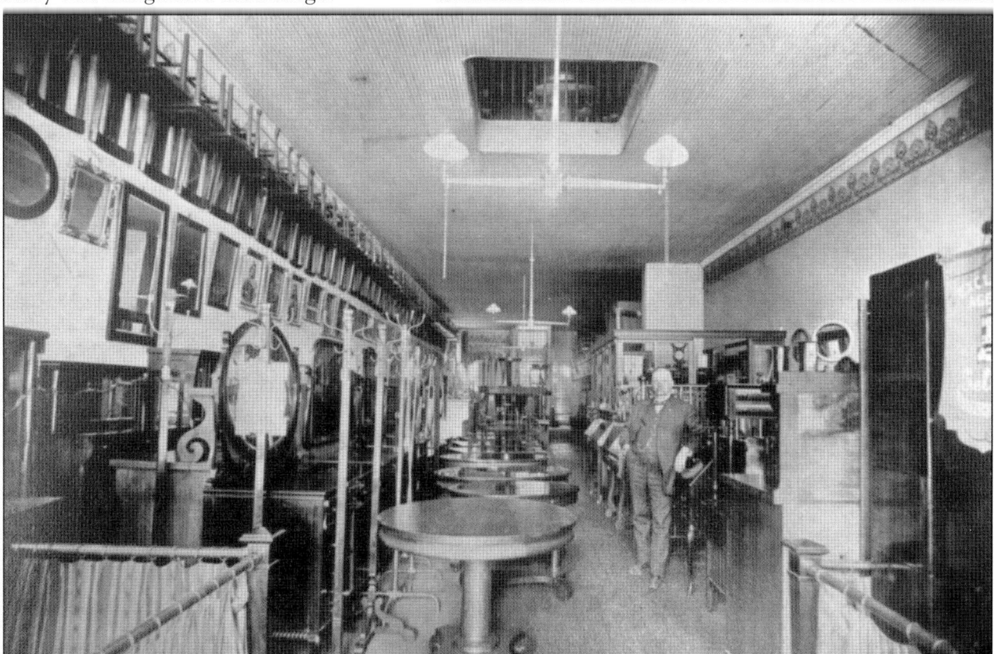

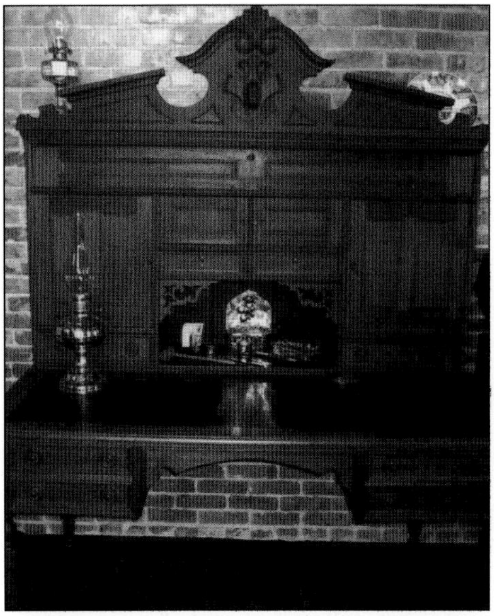

Cyrus B. Osborne built this beautifully crafted desk, which was commissioned by Franklin H. Whitney for his office in the bank known as F. H. Whitney and Company. The desk was built in 1871 at a cost of $30. The original bill of sale is displayed inside the top left-hand door. The desk remains in excellent condition and can be seen in the Cass County Historical Museum in Griswold, Iowa.

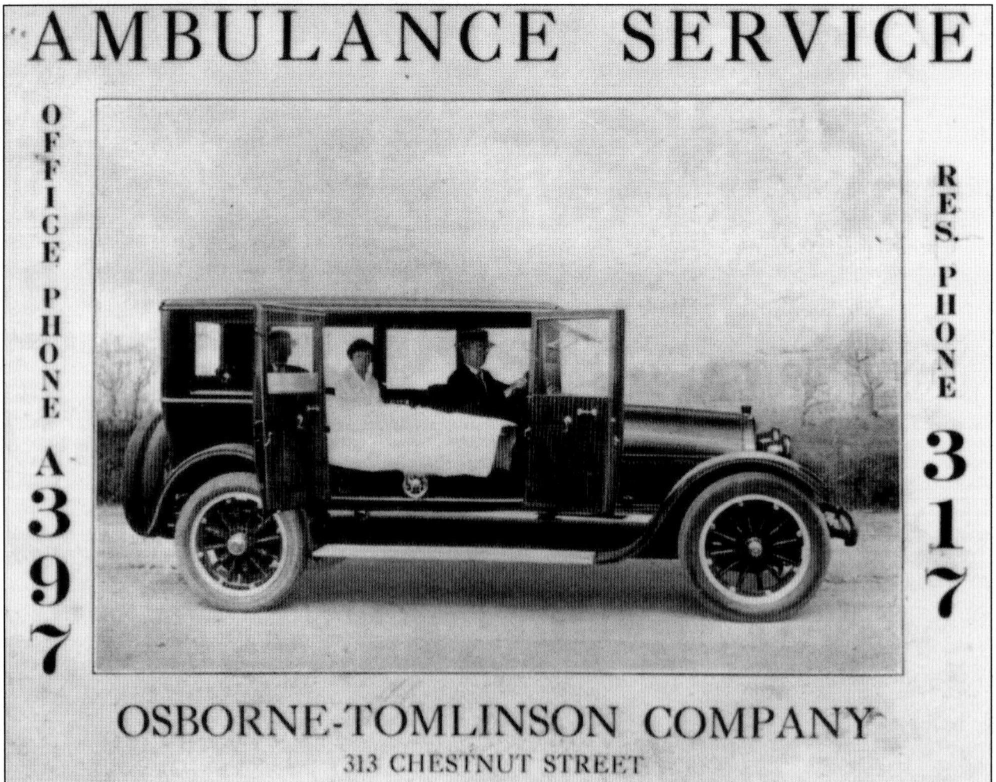

Osborne had a prosperous undertaking business and owned a handsome hearse that boasted a fine red leather interior. This photograph shows an advertisement for another of his businesses, the ambulance service he operated with his partner, Malcolm Tomlinson. The vehicle was made by the Peerless Motor Car Company. Peerless was one of the three "Ps"—Peerless, Packard, and Pierce Arrow. In the photograph, Tomlinson is the driver. He also served as the embalmer.

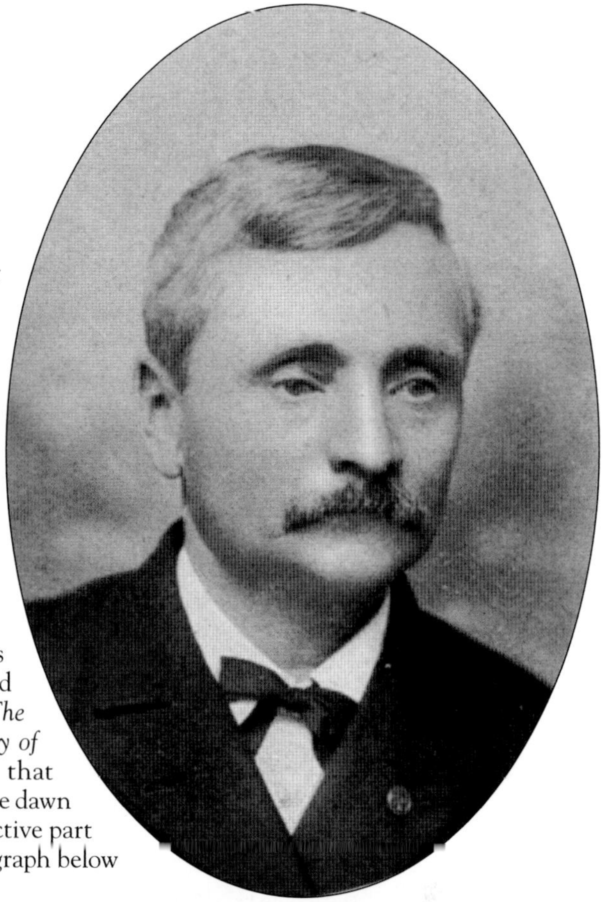

The Hon. Julian Phelps, a pioneer attorney of Cass County, arrived in Atlantic in 1867. He was a lawyer of general practice and in great demand as counsel and advocate. He was called to the service of one side or the other in every important case. While serving in the Iowa State Senate, Phelps authored the "anticigarette bill." In the autumn 1897, President McKinley appointed him U.S. consul in Crefeld, Germany. This position, which he accepted, kept him abroad for four years. In 1871, he married Persis Case in Atlantic, and the couple adopted two children. An early account from *The Compendium of History and Biography of Cass County, Iowa (1906)* explains that Phelps "has been a Republican since the dawn of his manhood and always took an active part in the affairs of his party." The photograph below shows the Phelps home, the Oaks.

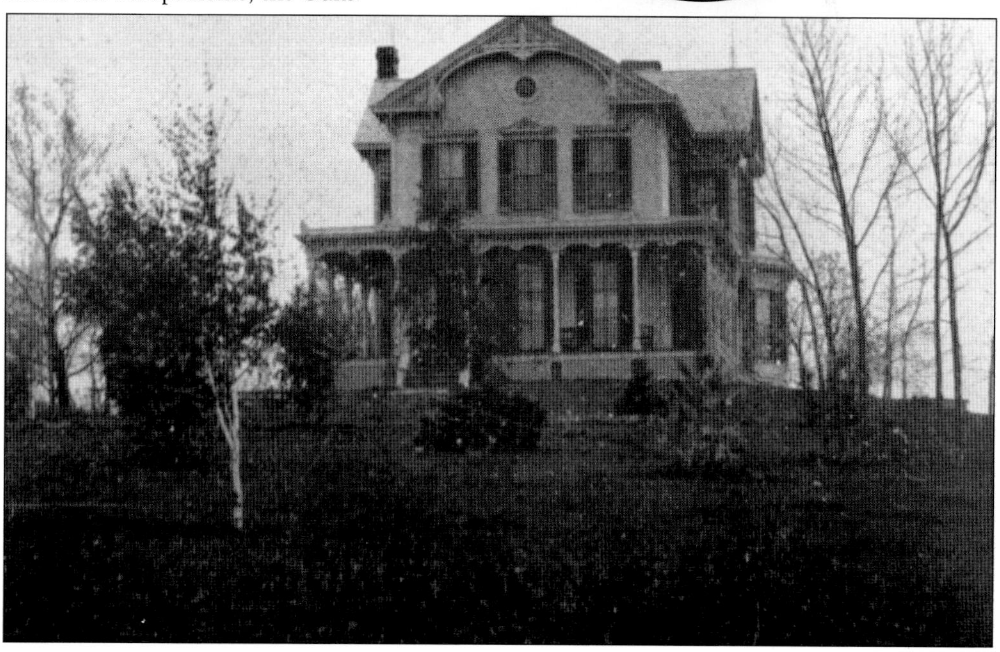

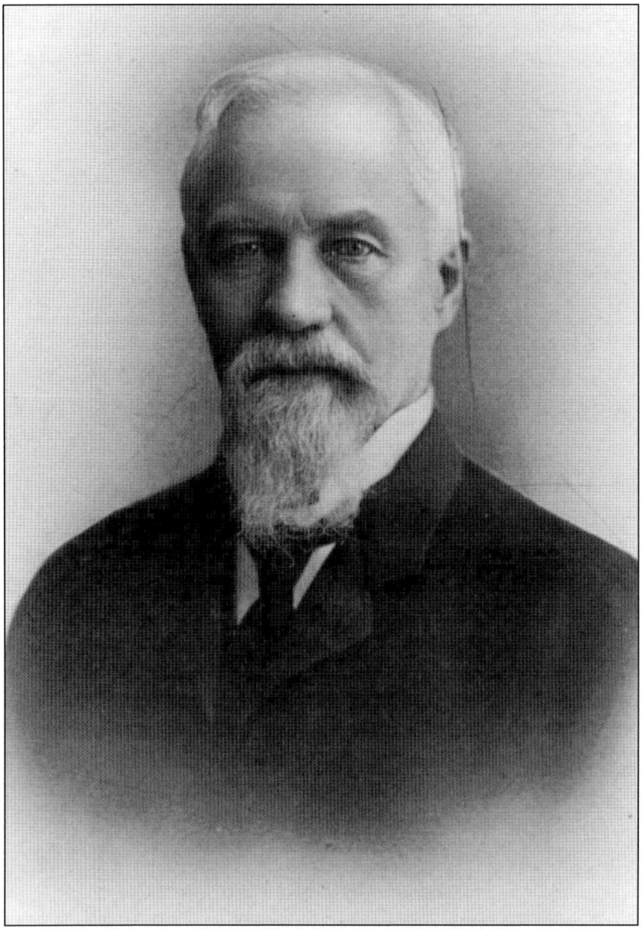

J. A. McWaid came to Atlantic in 1869 and was involved in wagon making and blacksmithing. In 1882, this inspired man saw the need for a canning plant and, along with S. F. Martin and Dr. R. W. Wilkins, built the Atlantic Canning Company, of which he became the sole owner. The company was eventually sold to his son William and J. W. Cuykendall. A tireless worker for the good of Atlantic, McWaid was instrumental in organizing the Atlantic Packing House Company, served as president of the Atlantic National Bank, and was the first chairman of the board of directors for the Carnegie Library. He also served three terms on the city council and spent four years as mayor. McWaid was described as a man of abounding energy, executive ability, and remarkable foresight. Pictured below is the McWaid home.

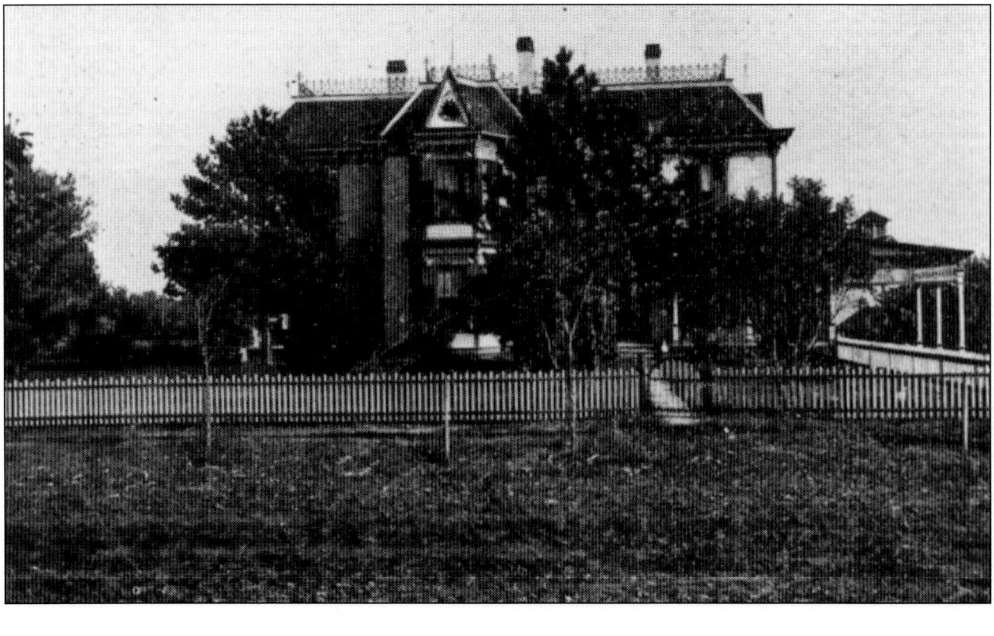

This is a photograph of Johnson H. Needles, a carriage manufacturer. In 1869, at the corner of Third and Walnut Streets, Needles and J. A. McWaid established the first blacksmith and wagon shop in the city. This business also sold farm implements. McWaid left the business in January 1879, and Johnson's son Charles became a partner.

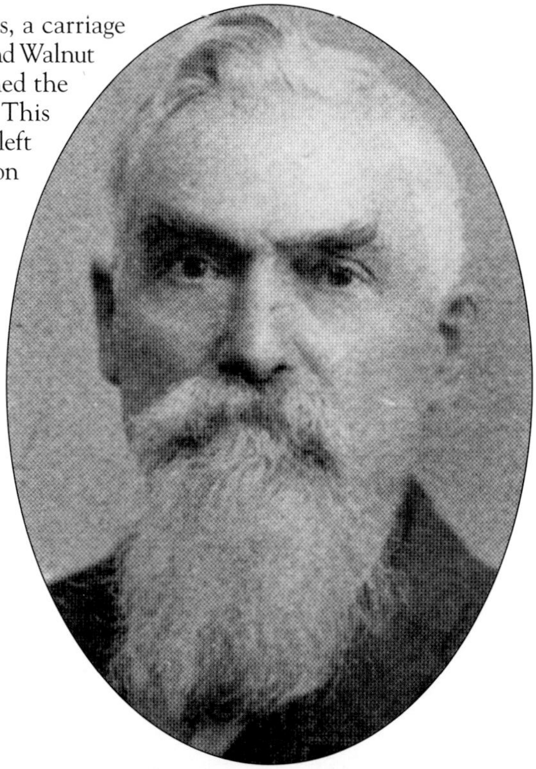

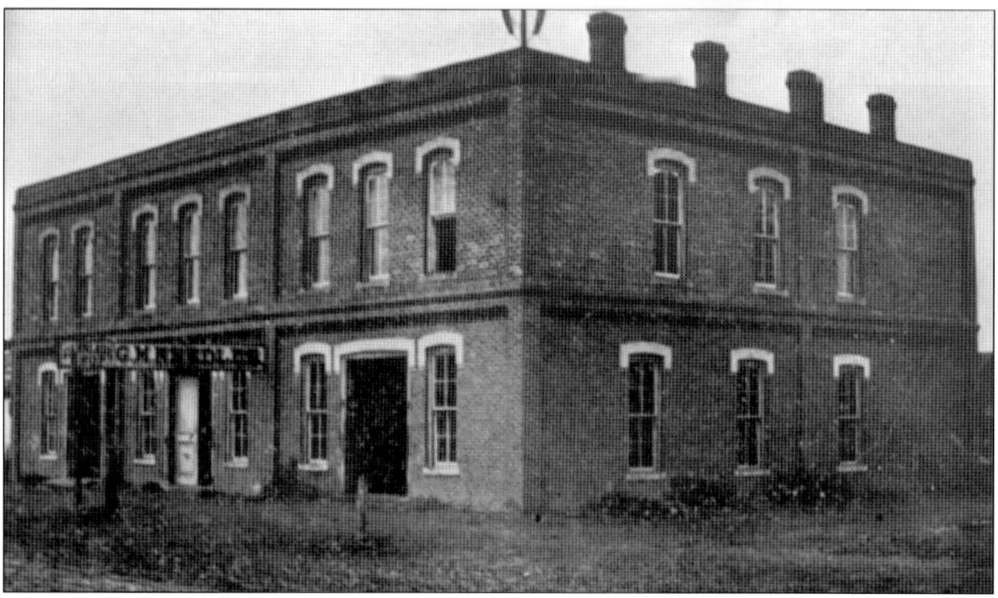

With demand high, The Needles Company outgrew the small shop and erected a large brick structure at Third and Chestnut Streets. One advertisement stated that the enterprise built buggies, carriages, road carts, and spring wagons to meet the specific needs of customers. The new plant featured the blacksmith and woodworking shop on the first floor and the paint and varnish room on the second floor. An elevator took the buggies and carriages from floor to floor as required in the manufacturing process.

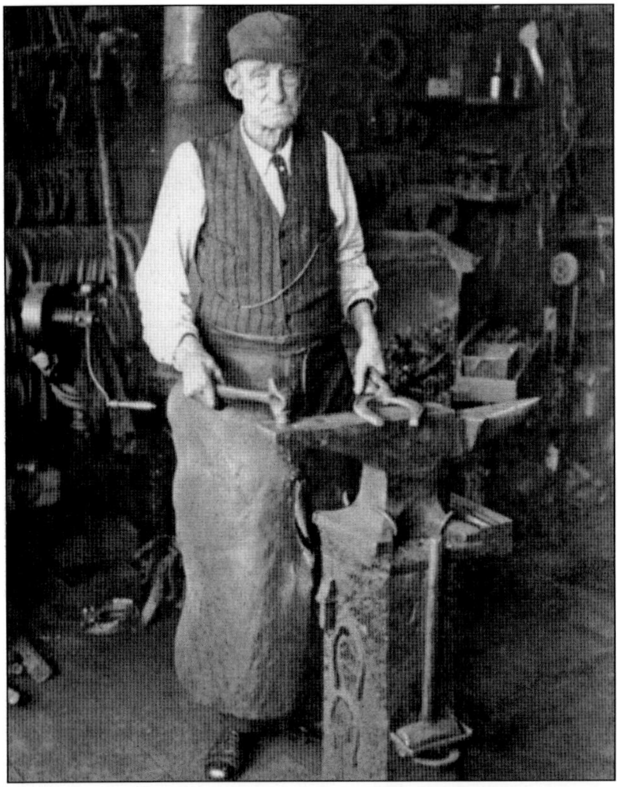

Frank Snouffer, an early Atlantic blacksmith, works in his shop. The profession derived its name from the color of the iron with which the smiths traditionally worked. Blacksmithing was a necessary business in the early days, when horses supplied most of the power and stores were not always available for the purchase of new tools. Shoeing the horses was only a small part of the blacksmith's work. He also worked at a forge to shape iron into whatever items customers required.

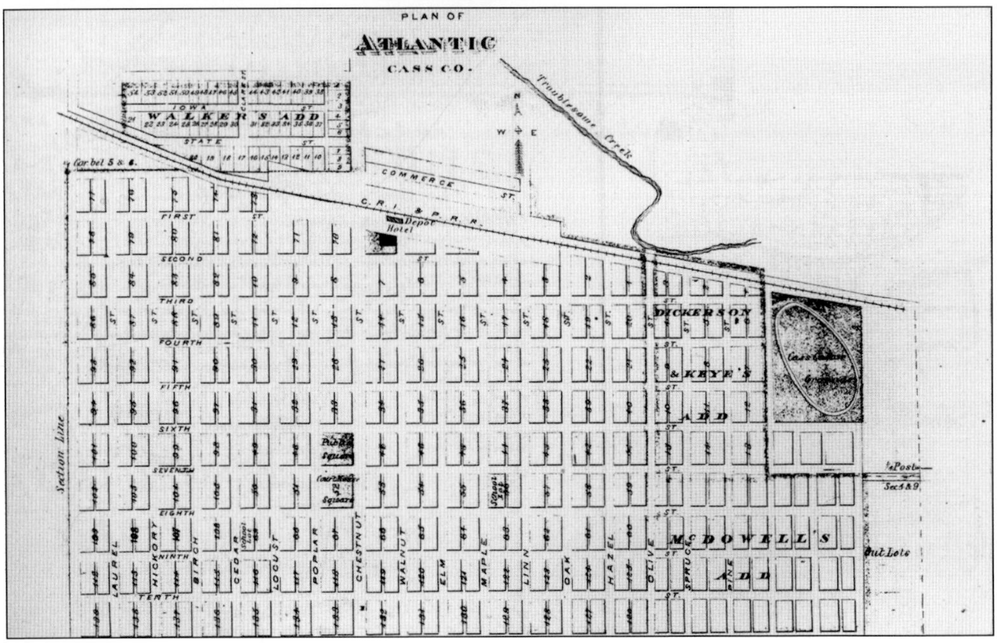

This plat map from the *1875 Andreas' Historical Atlas of the State of Iowa* shows the Chicago, Rock Island, and Pacific Railroad tracks with the depot and hotel. The public and courthouse squares can be seen as well as the East Side School. This plat map shows Atlantic about seven years after the railroad reached the area and the city of Atlantic was incorporated.

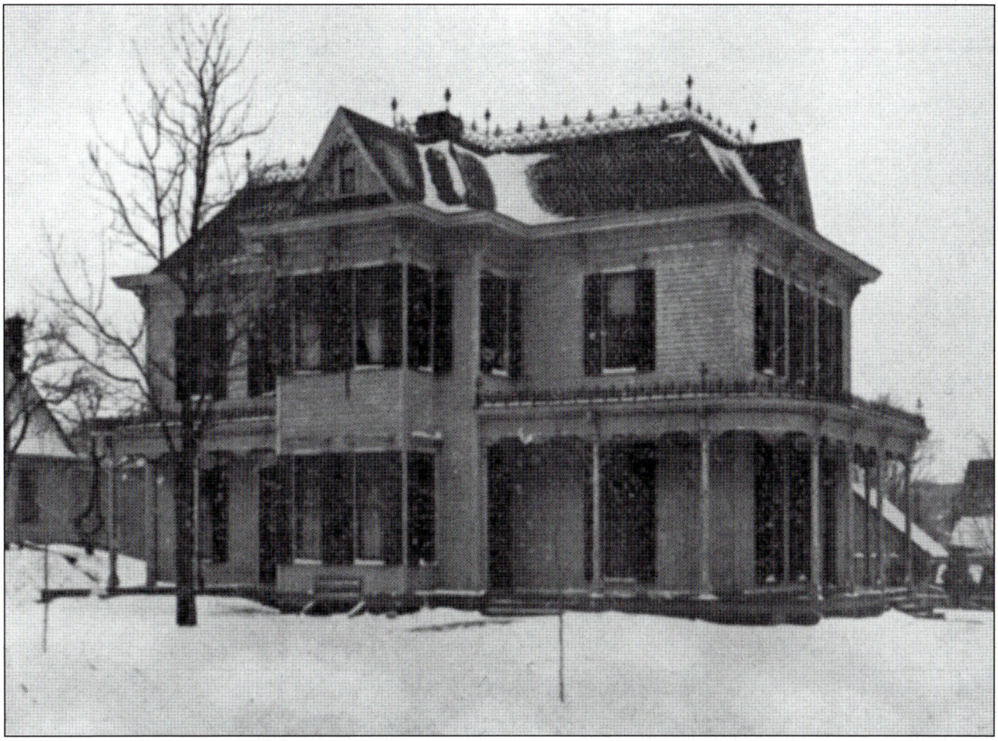

Nurseryman and state representative the Honorable Silas Wilson lived in this imposing home in Atlantic. In 1877, he established what was then the largest nursery in the country. It was located between Grove City and Atlantic. Wilson was elected president of the Iowa State Horticultural Society in the 1880s. Wilson also served as the area's state representative for many years. He was one of the founding elders of the United Presbyterian Church of Atlantic.

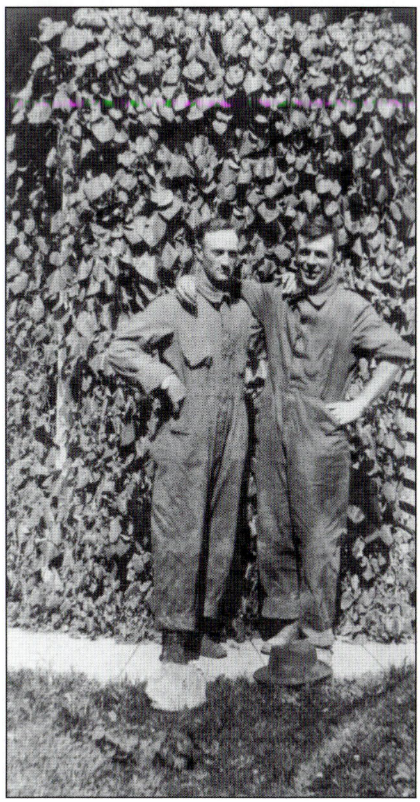

Wilson owned 120 acres of trees and 70 acres of grapes. By 1883, he had 800,000 grapevines. His specialties were grapevines and apple seedlings. The apple seedlings he sold were a hardy variety that could withstand harsh temperatures. His trade extended into every state and territory in the Union.

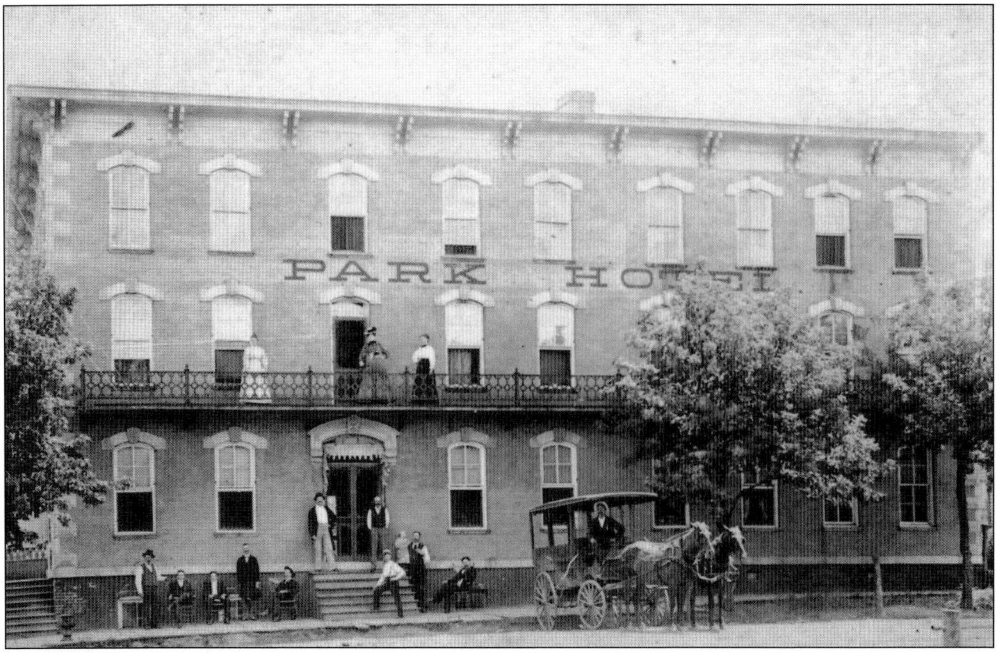

Atlantic had a number of fine hotels, such as the Park Hotel located at Sixth and Chestnut Streets. The building was started in 1871 and was first used as offices for the county at a rental of $1,200 per year. When the Cass County Courthouse was completed in 1882, improvements were made on the structure, and it was operated as a hotel. The hotel hack would go down Chestnut Street to the railroad station to pick up passengers. In rainy weather, complaints were frequent, as the hacks could become mired in the mud on Chestnut Street. Signatures in the Park Hotel register from the year 1900 (below) show that Atlantic had visitors from all parts of the country. The register can be seen at the Cass County Historical Museum in Griswold, Iowa.

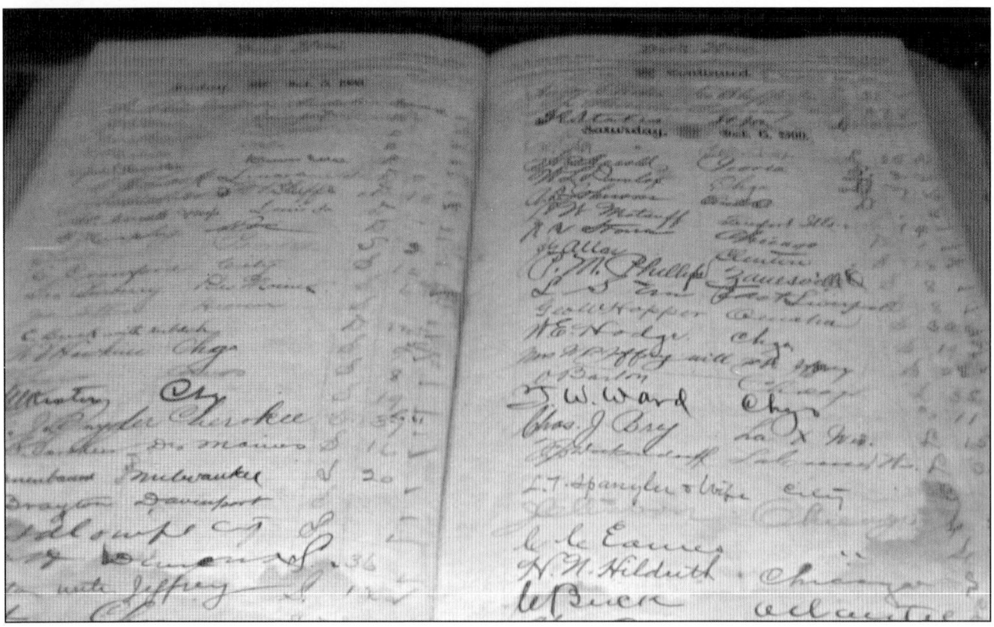

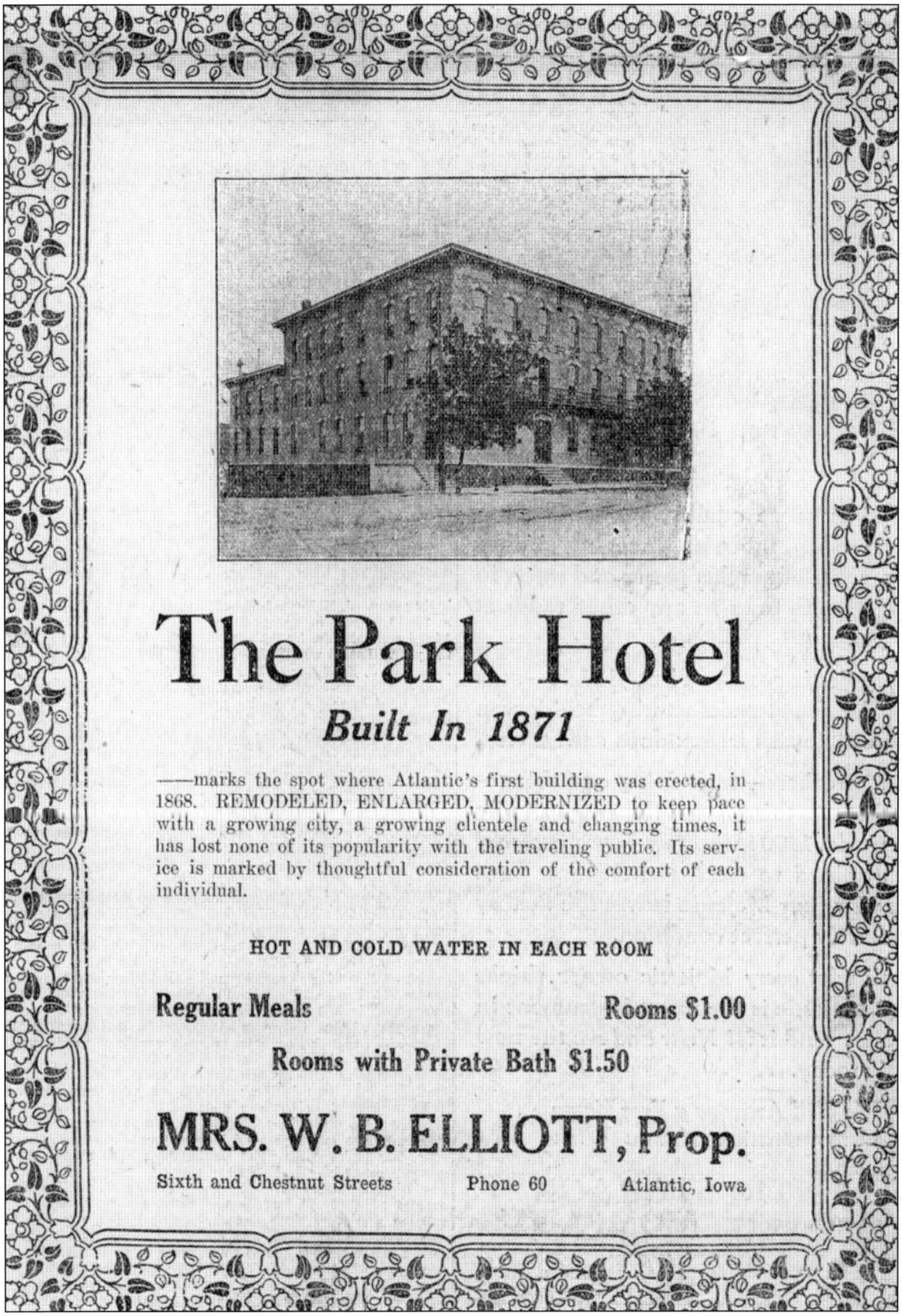

Warden B. Elliott came to Atlantic in 1893 and took possession of the Occidental Hotel. In 1897, he purchased the Park Hotel, which he successfully operated for several years. Elliott was married to the daughter of Joseph Burnea, whose brick company had made the bricks not only for the construction of the Park Hotel but for many of the other early brick buildings in Atlantic. As seen in this advertisement, Mrs. Elliott took over the running of the hotel upon the death of her husband.

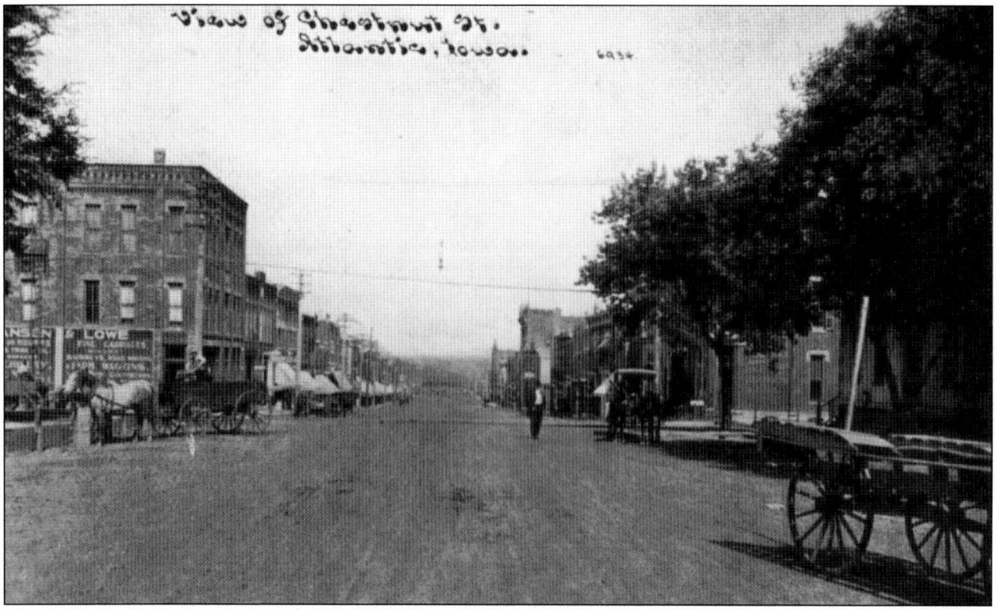

Atlantic was rapidly improving its image as more and more individuals arrived to set up businesses in the new rail center. This photograph was taken looking north on Chestnut Street toward the depot. It shows some of the businesses like Hansen and Lowe, which advertises the making of fine carriages and farm wagons.

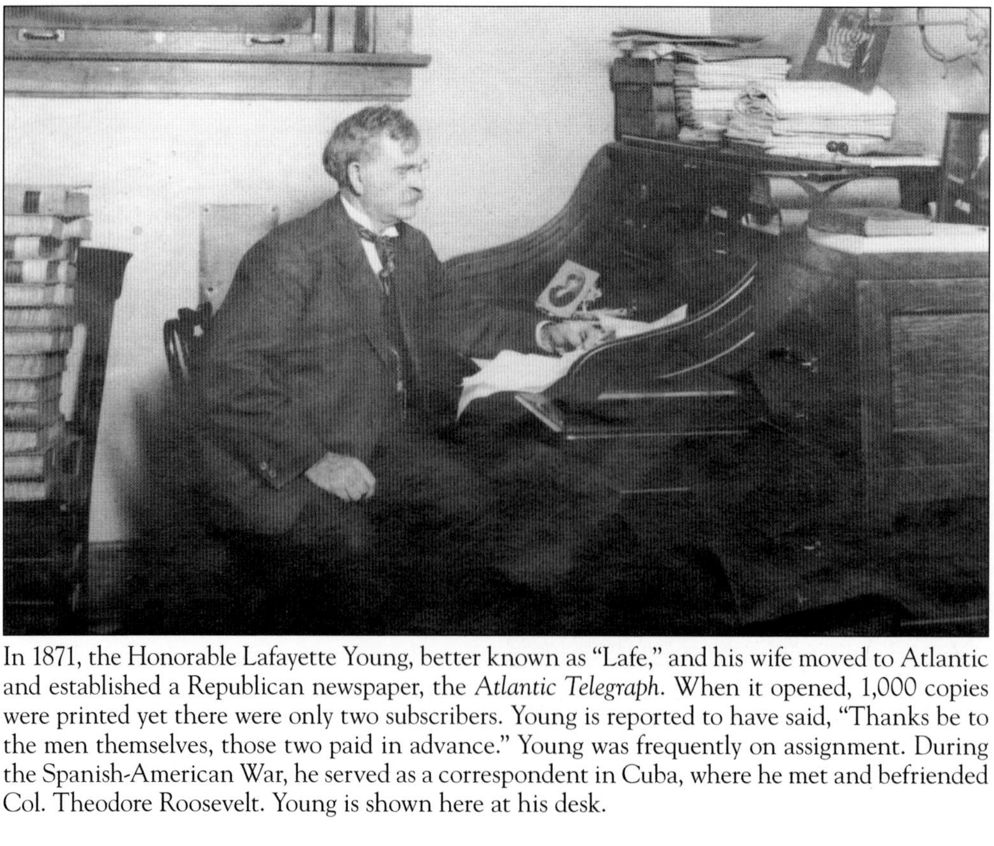

In 1871, the Honorable Lafayette Young, better known as "Lafe," and his wife moved to Atlantic and established a Republican newspaper, the *Atlantic Telegraph*. When it opened, 1,000 copies were printed yet there were only two subscribers. Young is reported to have said, "Thanks be to the men themselves, those two paid in advance." Young was frequently on assignment. During the Spanish-American War, he served as a correspondent in Cuba, where he met and befriended Col. Theodore Roosevelt. Young is shown here at his desk.

This solid brick building was the home of the *Atlantic Telegraph*. The structure stands on East Fourth Street, and the word *telegraph* is still clearly visible to the naked eye. In 1905, Lafayette Young and his wife were guests of Secretary of War William Howard Taft during a state visit to the Philippines. Continuing his dashing life, Young served as a correspondent in the Balkan States and, in 1915, was charged with spying and imprisoned for a time by the Austrian government.

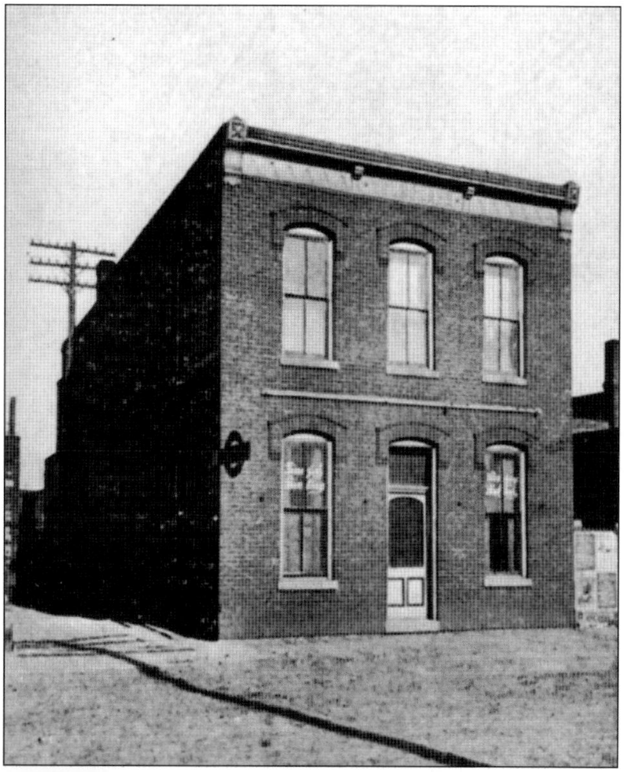

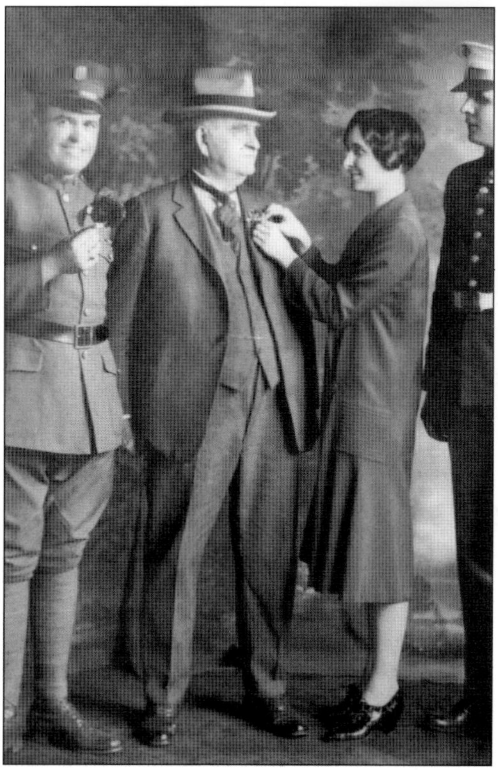

The Honorable Lafayette Young is shown here receiving a red poppy from members of the Military Veterans' Association in Des Moines, Iowa. Young, among all his other activities, served several terms as an Iowa state senator. He also served as chairman of the Iowa State Council of Defense in 1917. During his later years, Young moved to Des Moines and purchased the *Des Moines Capital*, which he edited until his death in 1926.

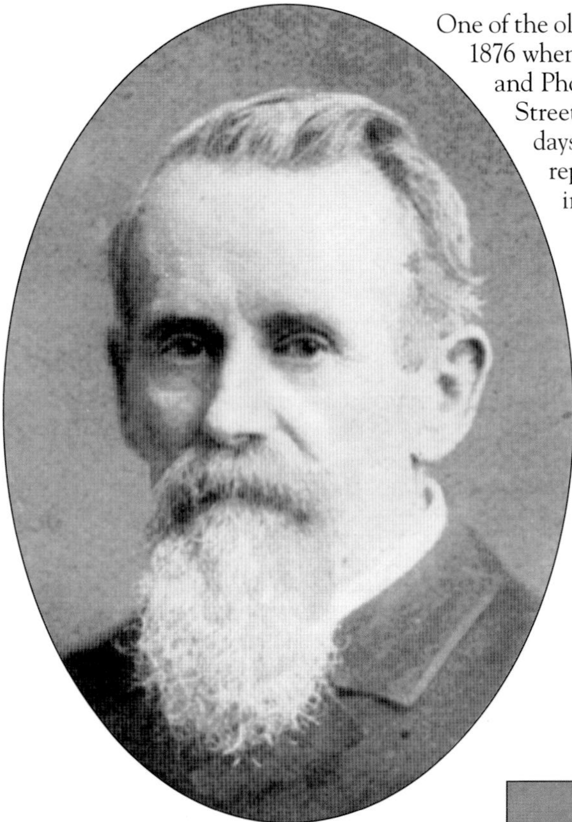

One of the oldest businesses in Atlantic was started in 1876 when W. P. Egbert opened the Egbert Gallery and Photographic Studio at Fifth and Chestnut Streets. A pioneer in his profession since the days of the daguerreotype, Egbert earned the reputation as one of the best photographers in the United States, if not the world.

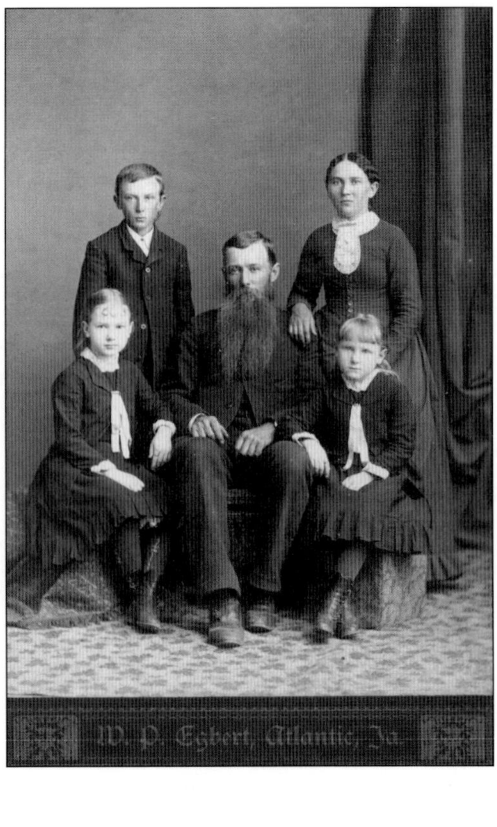

This family photograph is the work of W. P. Egbert. In the late 1800s, many families had their pictures taken as new and better methods of photography were developed. Most of Egbert's photographs must have been produced using the difficult wet plate method, because the easier dry plate technology was not available until George Eastman began manufacturing it in 1880.

In his youth, Hal H. Egbert, son of W. P. Egbert, spent all of his spare time in his father's studio, learning the trade and developing a talent for it. In 1890, he became associated with his father in the business. Upon his father's death in 1903, Hal became sole owner of the business and maintained the high standards with which the Egbert name was always associated.

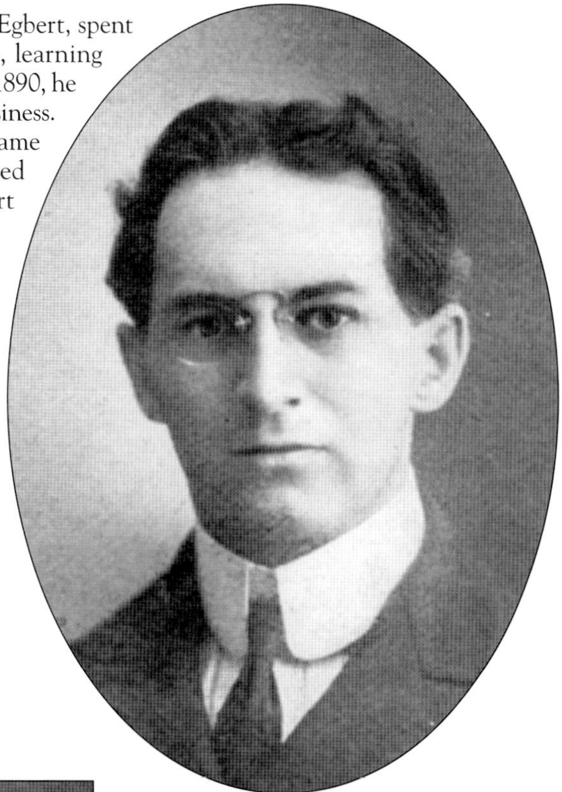

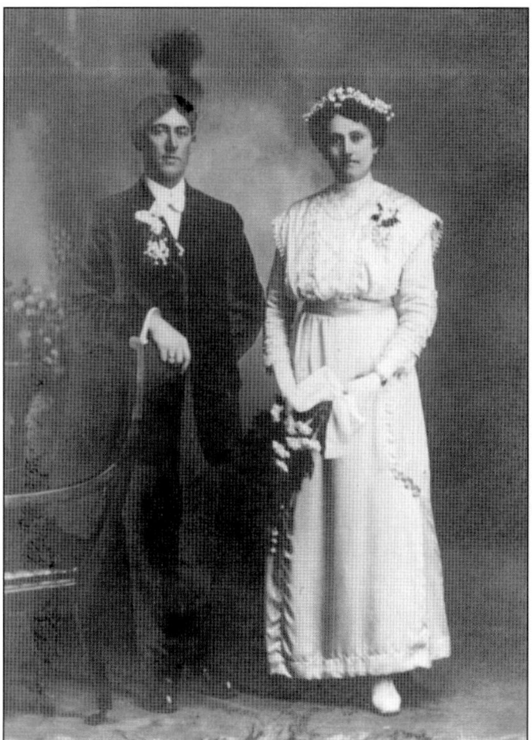

This Hal H. Egbert wedding picture is that of Henry Brix and Grace Walter. They were married on January 14, 1914, at Zion Lutheran Church in Atlantic. Grace was born on July 10, 1884, and Henry was born in Germany on May 12, 1883. They resided in Atlantic. This is one of many vintage photographs in this book that are identified as coming from the Egbert Gallery and Photographic Studio.

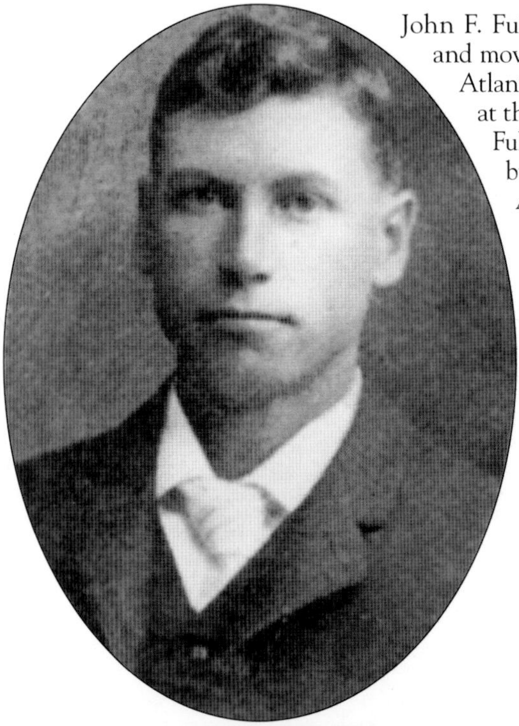

John F. Fuhlendorf was born in Scott County, Iowa, and moved with his parents to Atlantic in 1882. The Atlantic Bottling Works had been established in 1877 at the north end of Chestnut Street, and, in 1906, Fuhlendorf bought the business and erected a new building to house his expanding business. In the *Atlantic News-Telegraph*, this early company advertised Royal Palm, Golden Spike, and Canadian Club ginger ales.

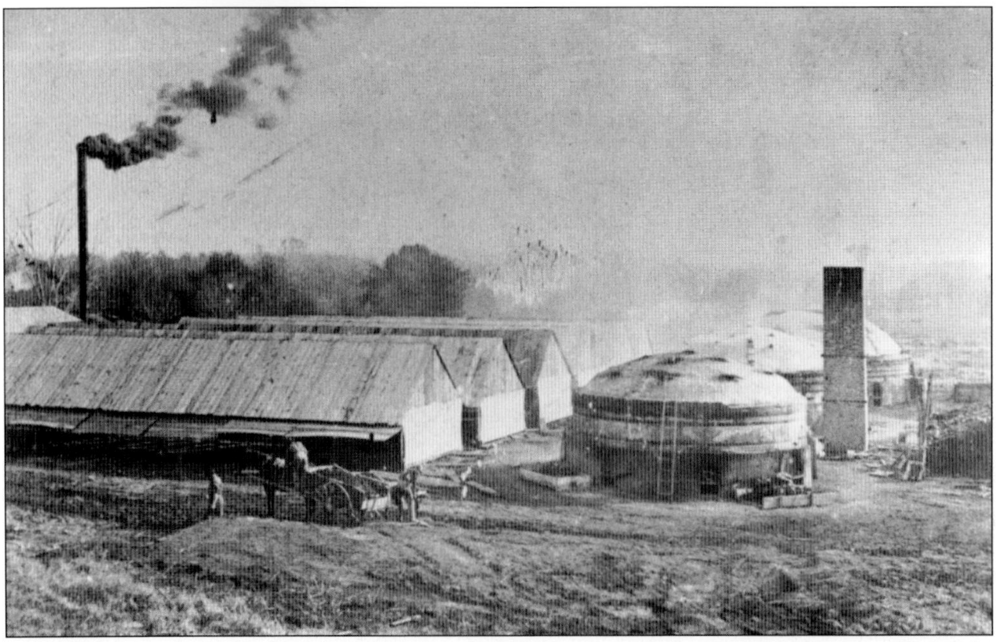

Bricks for many of the early Atlantic businesses and homes came from this brickyard. The bricks were made in molds, turned out onto the ground to harden, and then transferred to kilns for firing. In 1903, owner Robert Taylor installed tile-making machinery. The tile operation was a crude one: clay was mixed in a pit with horses supplying the power needed for the mixing. The business was then known as the Atlantic Brick and Tile Company. This 1907 photograph was taken by Taylor.

J. W. Cuykendall came to Atlantic in 1889 and became sole owner of the Atlantic Canning Factory. An early description of Cuykendall in *The Compendium of History and Biography of Cass County, Iowa (1906)* states, "He who makes two blades of grass grow on a spot of ground upon which but one grew before, is to be regarded as a benefactor to mankind, how much more of public esteem and grateful recollection does he deserve who introduces, or amplifies, a new industry, whereby increased employment is given to the toilers in the community and the comforts of life are multiplied and improved for all its people."

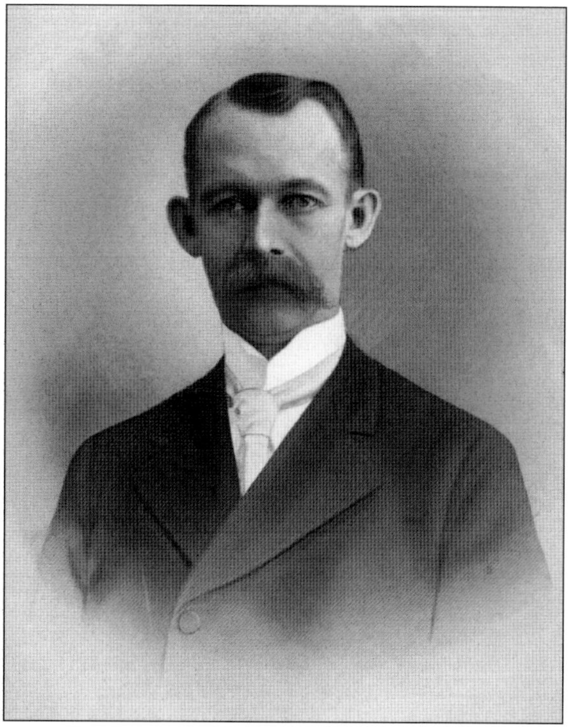

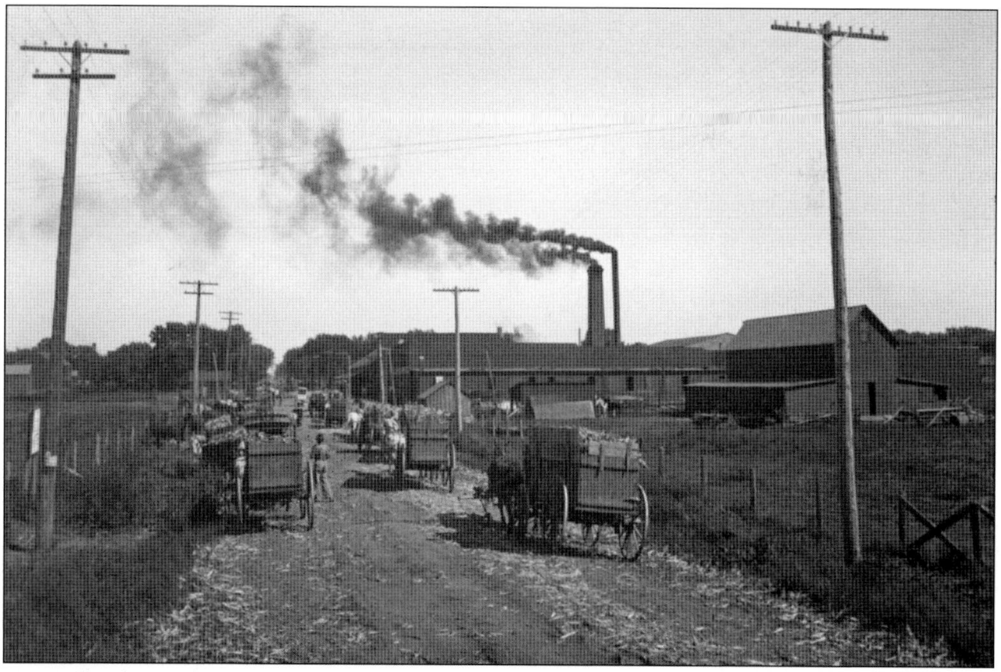

Naturally the work at the factory was largely seasonal. Cuykendall liked to use local products if possible. Farmers were willing to grow the crops of corn, peas, and pumpkins to supply the factory, but they disliked waiting to unload at the plant. Sometimes there would be 25 to 30 teams waiting in line. This photograph shows the factory in the background with impatient farmers in the foreground. (Courtesy of the State Historical Society of Iowa.)

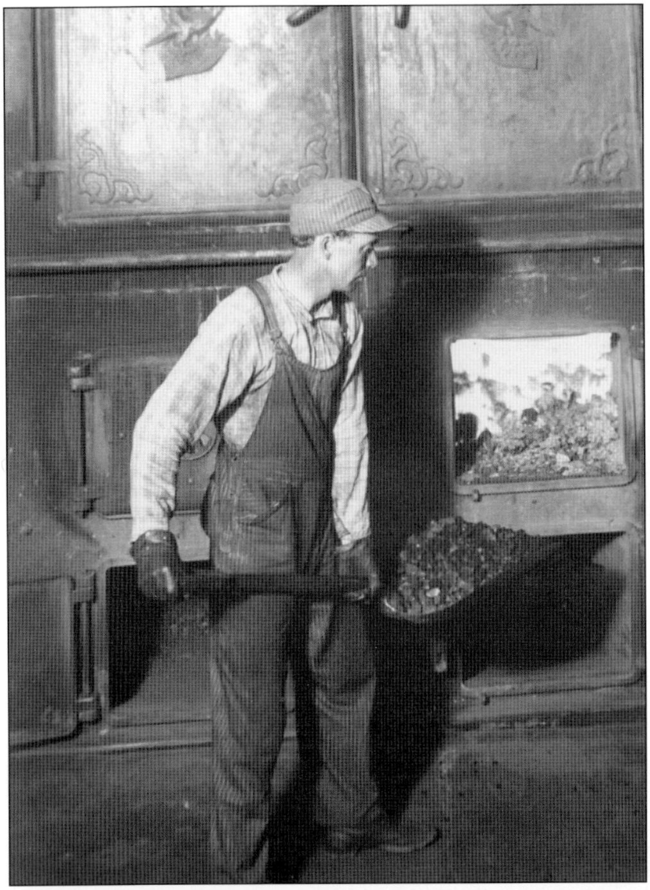

An itinerant photographer is thought to have taken these 1902 images of the Atlantic Canning Factory. They were developed from glass-plate negatives found in the early 1980s and given to local historian Philip Chintz. In 1993, Chintz donated the Cuykendall photograph collection to the State Historical Society of Iowa. They are now stored at the society's archives in Des Moines. The photograph to the left shows a factory worker stoking a fire. In the image below, workers take a break from stoking the hot furnaces with coal in what is thought to be the brick boiler room. It was hard, hot, dirty work. (Courtesy of the State Historical Society of Iowa.)

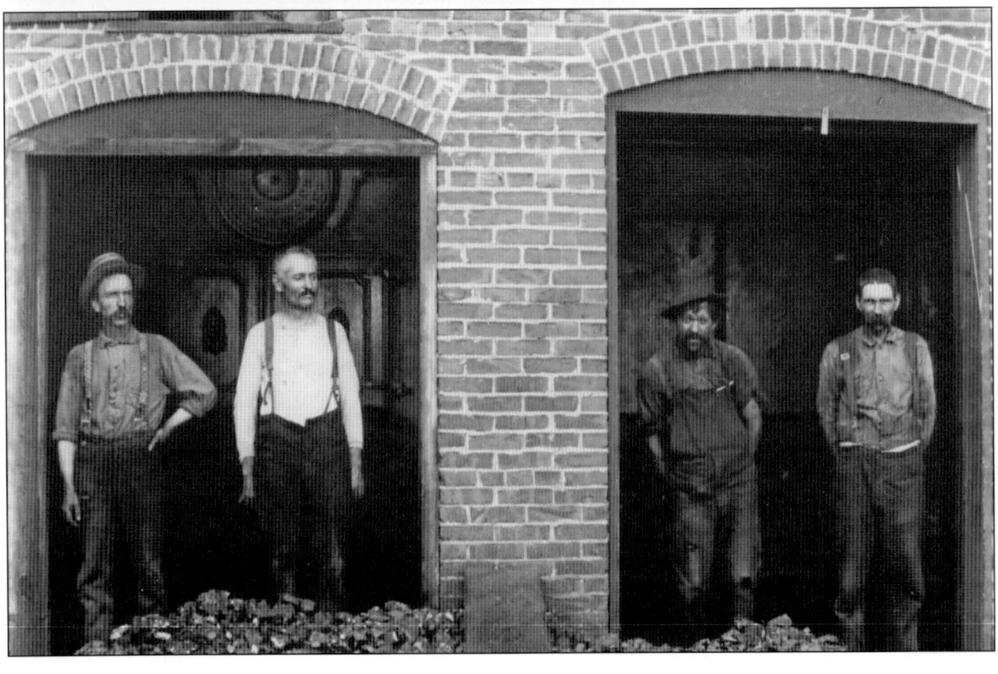

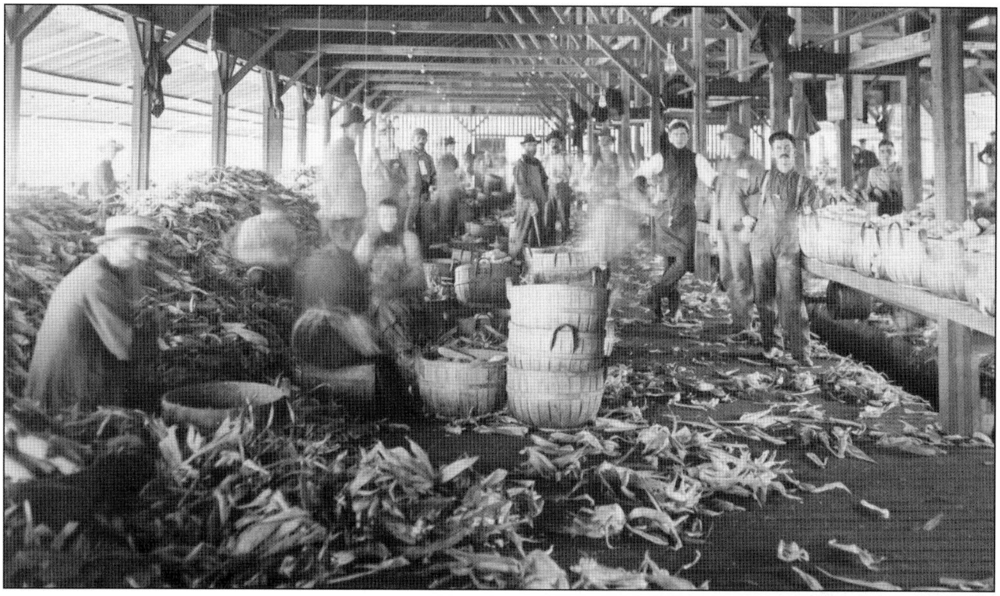

When Cuykendall took sole ownership of the factory, he replaced many of the old wooden buildings with brick. However, the husking shed was made of wood and was open-sided to allow for good ventilation. Workers were able to sit on wooden boxes as they husked corn from the bushel baskets that were lined up on a conveyor belt. (Courtesy of the State Historical Society of Iowa.)

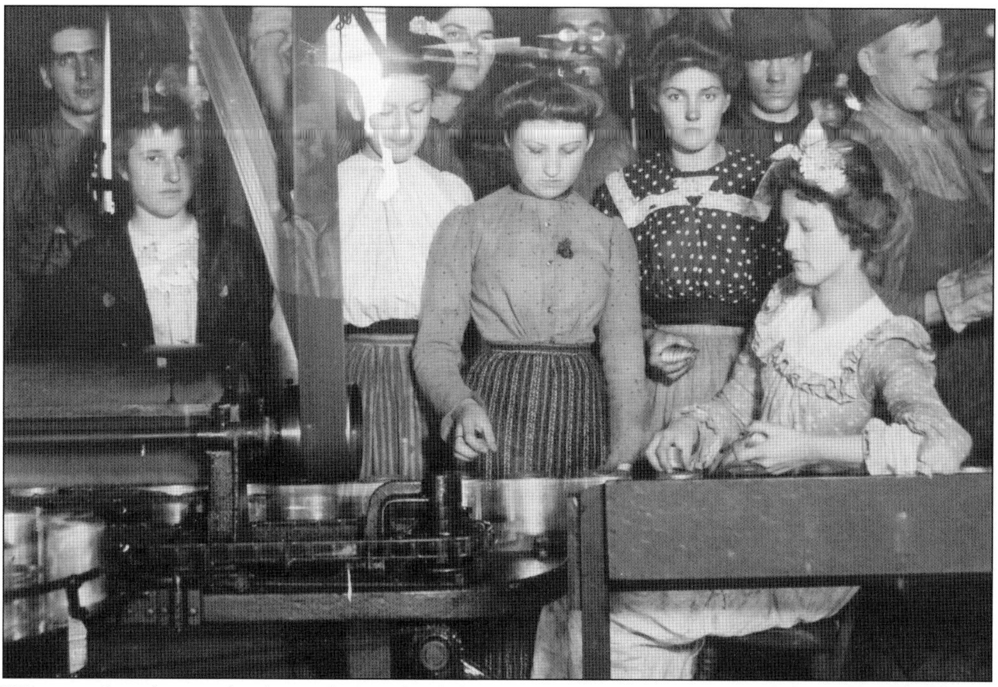

Women played a vital role in the work of the canning factory. Their small, quick hands were needed for some of the more delicate jobs. Here a young woman demonstrates the positioning of metal lids on cans of peas, which reach her by means of a conveyor belt. One wonders if the young women always dressed so fashionably, or if they had advance warning that a photographer would be visiting the factory that day. (Courtesy of the State Historical Society of Iowa.)

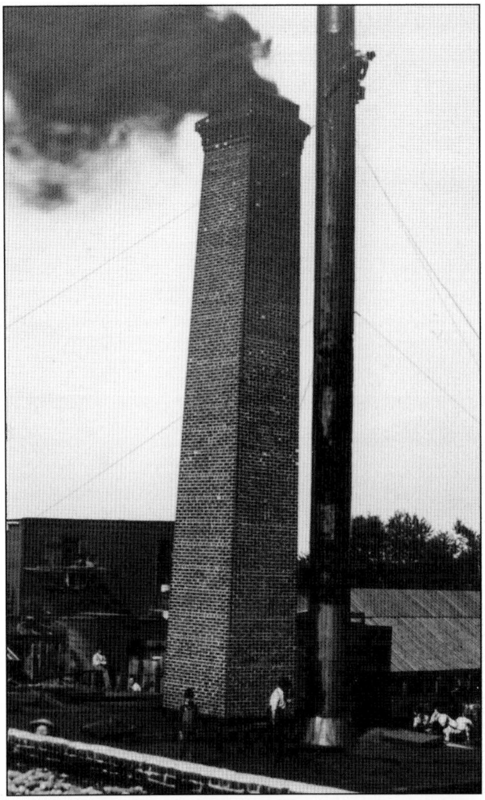

The impressive stacks at the canning factory poured black smoke into the atmosphere during the busy canning season. The produce had to be canned while in peak condition, so there were days when shifts worked around the clock. The cannery was a good source of employment for many young people in the region. A man with a paint can works near the top of the second stack. (Courtesy of the State Historical Society of Iowa.)

The Atlantic Canning Factory was built in 1882 by three local men and sold to J. W. Cuykendall in 1889. The company would contract for sweet corn, and production of canned corn and pumpkin ran into the hundreds of thousands of cans each season. About 60 railroad carloads of canned corn would be shipped at one time. It was claimed that this factory was the largest of its kind in the world. With the advent of frozen foods, the canning industry declined, and the plant was eventually purchased by Walnut Grove Products.

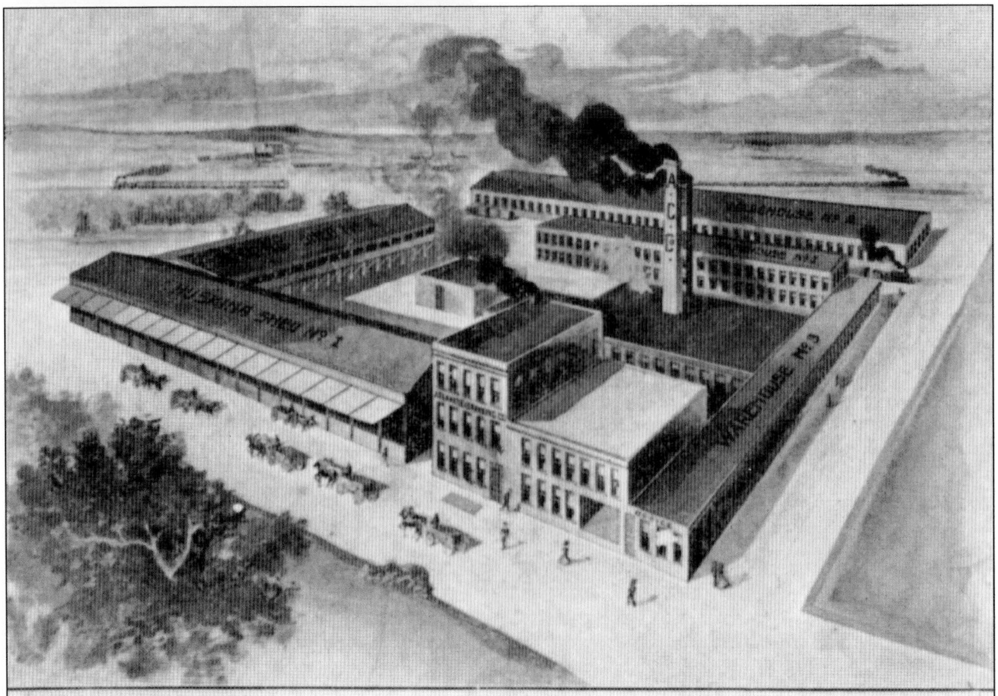

CANNING FACTORY, ATLANTIC, IOWA

Levi Downs was born in the state of New York but traveled extensively before settling in Atlantic in 1881. He opened a general merchandise business and was later able to purchase the building that housed his store. In a 1904 book, Downs was characterized as being public spirited and always in the first ranks of those who were striving for a bigger and better Atlantic.

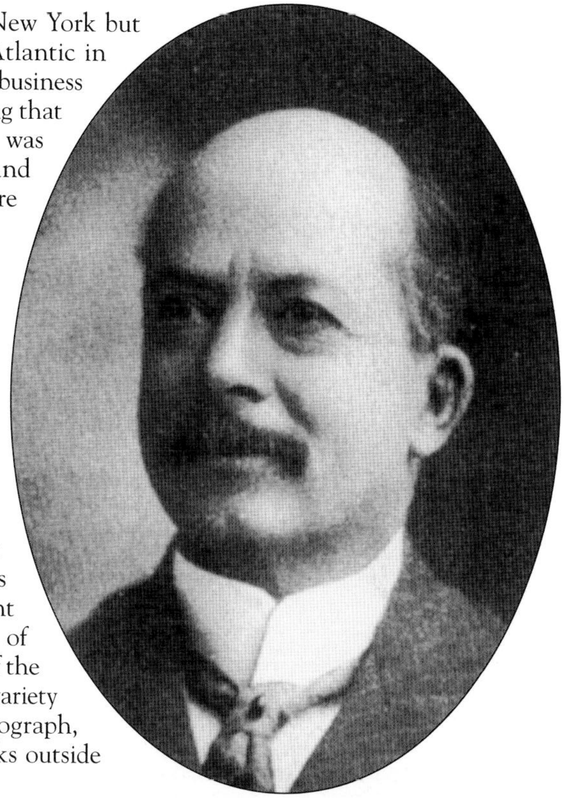

The Levi Downs Store on the northwest corner of Sixth and Chestnut Streets enjoyed what was described as a magnificent business. The general merchandise store of the late 19th century was the equivalent of the modern department store. It carried a wide variety of goods and merchandise. In this photograph, customers stand on the wooden sidewalks outside the Downs store.

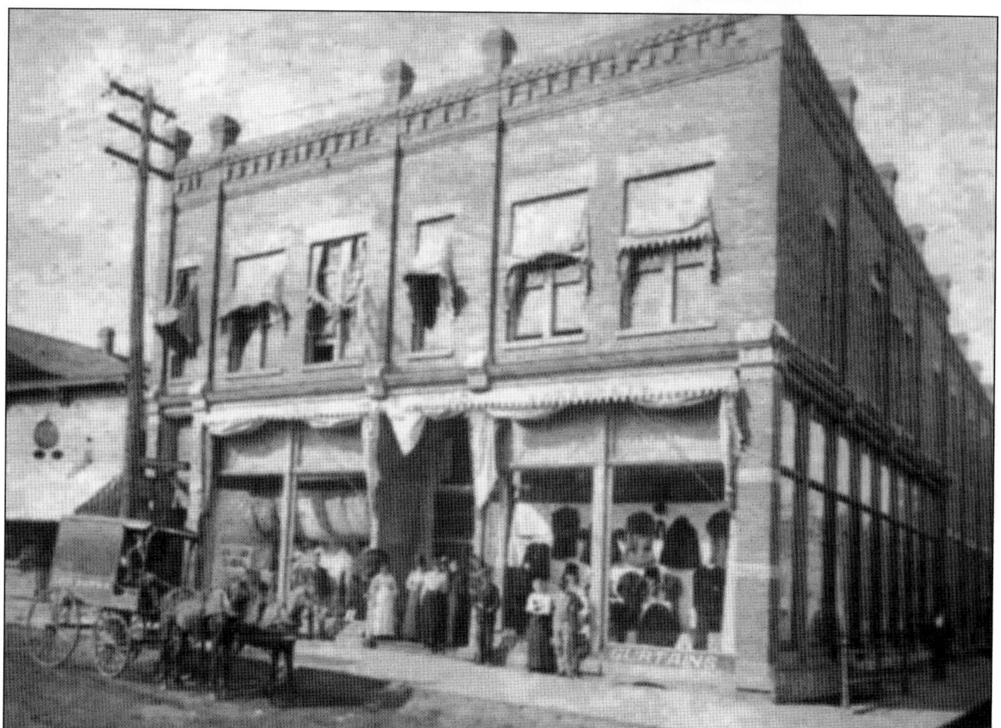

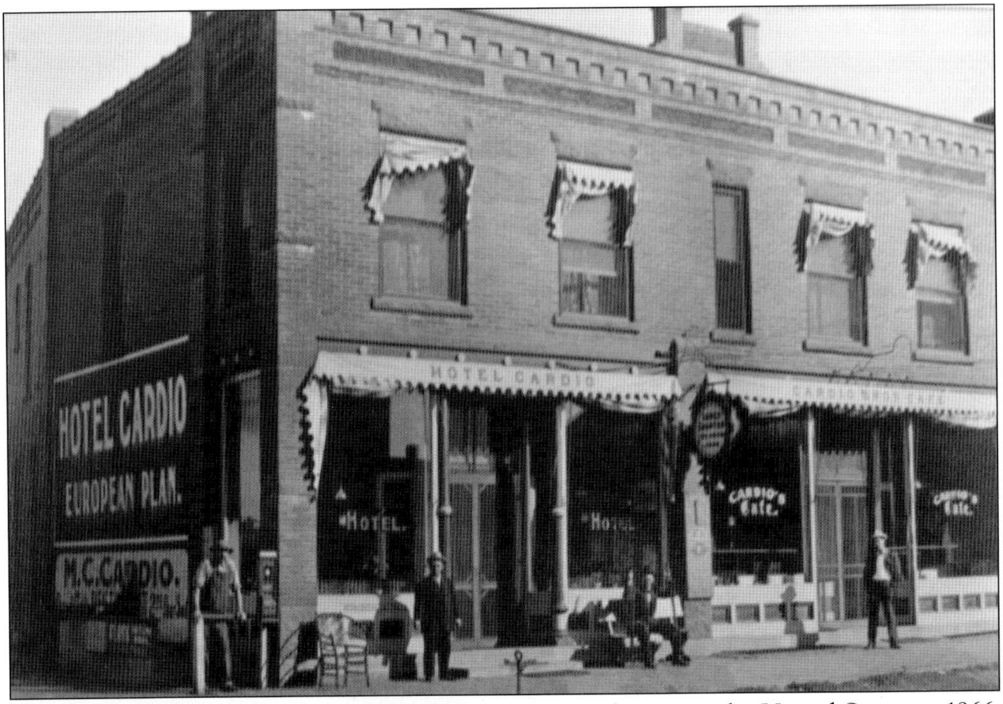

Charles M. Cardio was born in Naples, Italy, in 1864 and came to the United States in 1866. He settled in several other places around the country before landing in Atlantic with a troop barnstorming under the auspices of the Ray-Hayden Novelty Company. While doing a show in Atlantic, the company went broke, and Cardio had to find work so he could pay his hotel bill and reclaim his personal belongings. After trying several occupations, he settled into the restaurant business in Atlantic. He married Christina Fuhlendorf in 1885, and their reception was held at the German Hall on Elm Street. Eventually the couple built the Cardio Hotel at First and Chestnut Streets, seen in these images.

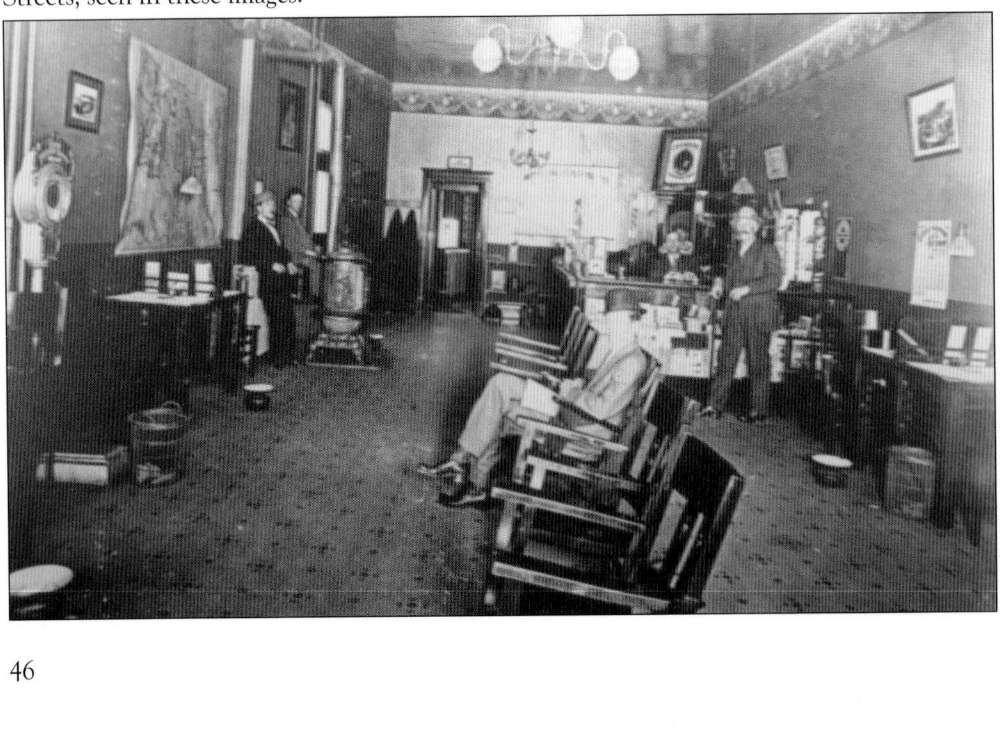

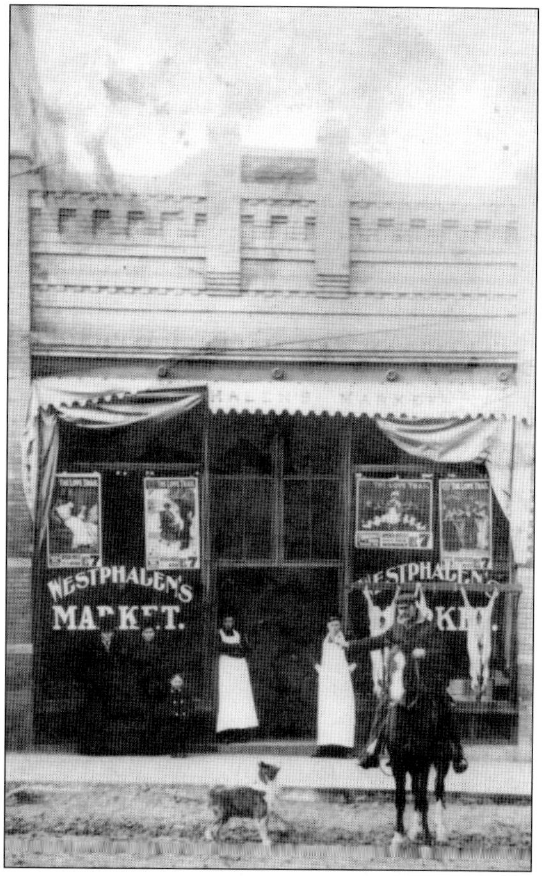

In the late 1890s, Rudolph Westphalen owned and operated the Westphalen Meat Market, located at 405 Chestnut Street. In 1884, Westphalen and his brothers came to the United States from Schleswig-Holstein, Germany. While his brothers went into farming, Rudolph chose to enter the meat business. The man on the horse outside the store is Fred Long, a local cattle buyer. Advertisements posted on the windows announce *Love Trail* coming to the Bacon Opera House.

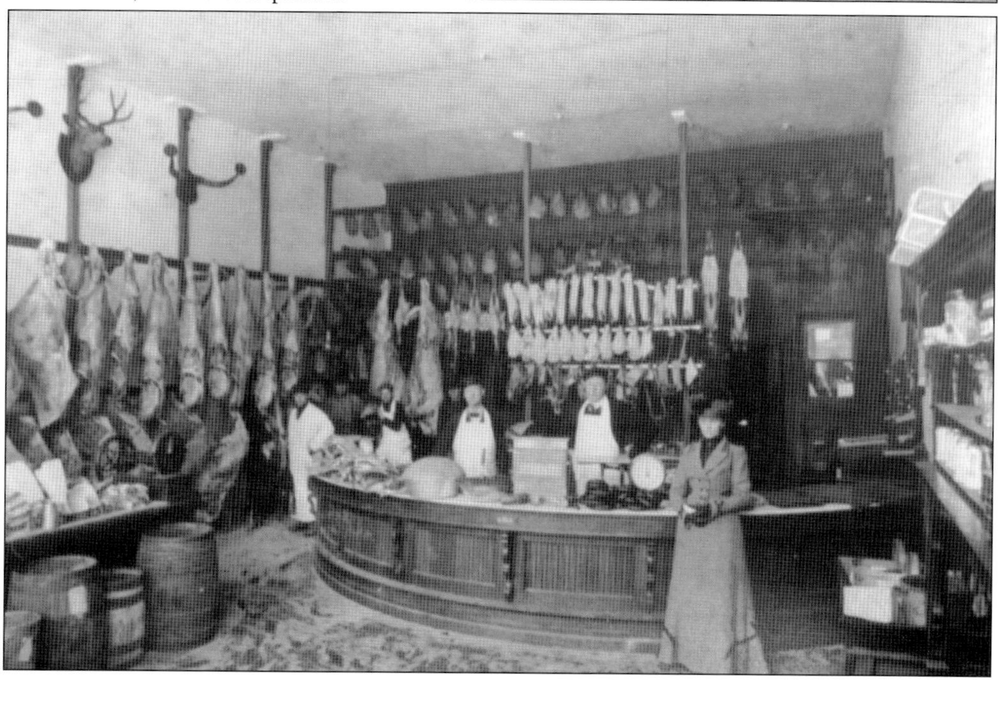

The interior of the Westphalen Meat Market, known as one of the best in the state, shows the remarkably large supply of meat that the store provided for its customers. Owner Rudolph Westphalen (far right, behind the counter) was reputedly never known to tell a customer he was "out of meat." The woman in front of the counter is Rudolph's well-dressed wife, Annie Westphalen.

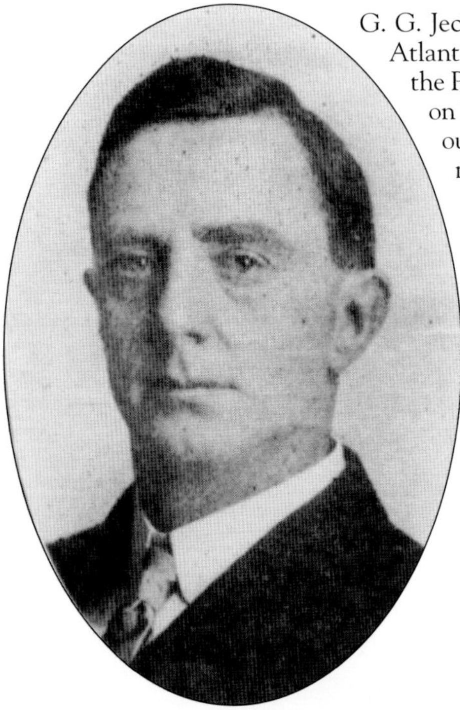

G. G. Jeck, better known to his friends as Bert, arrived in Atlantic in 1899. He was hired by W. F. Priebe to operate the Priebe-Simater Poultry Company, which was located on lower Locust Street. When the company was bought out by Swift and Company in 1905, Jeck continued as manager. In a 1904 booklet, he is described as being "a hustler and a royal good fellow."

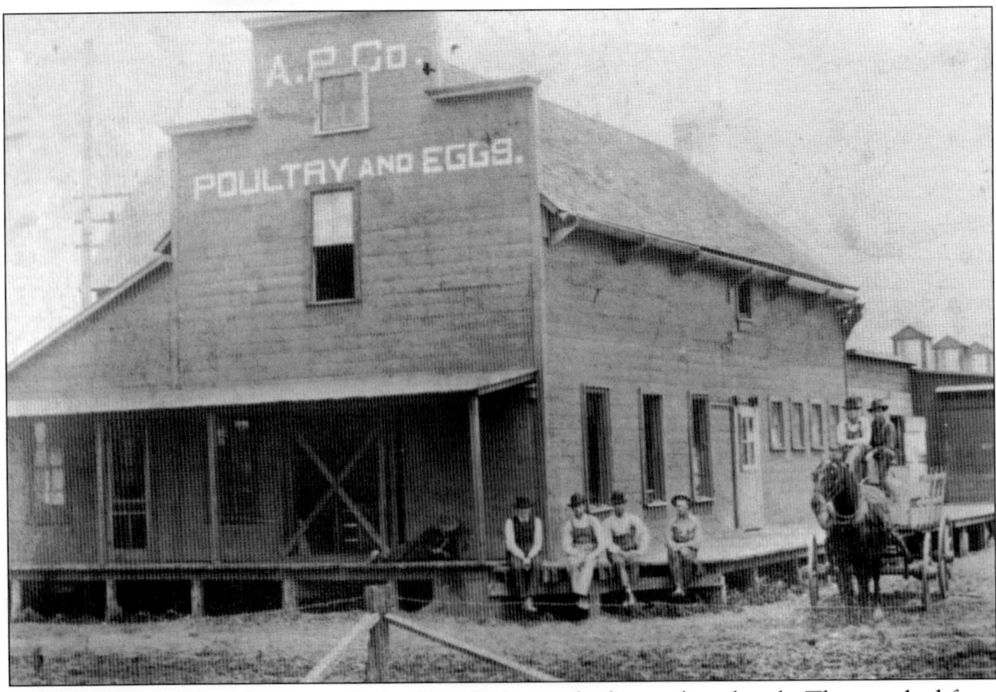

These poultry workers have a wide loading dock on which to take a break. They worked for a company that had a good reputation. An early description states that the company "does not do a great deal of cackling, but it lays many a golden egg for Atlantic and the people whose poultry and eggs it buys." The business did change names several times over the years, once being called the Atlantic Poultry Company.

Workers at the two Atlantic poultry companies produced not only poultry and eggs but butter as well. They later expanded their product lines to include ice cream and ice. Both businesses contributed greatly to the Atlantic economy. At one time, over $1.5 million per year was paid out for poultry and labor by the two Atlantic companies.

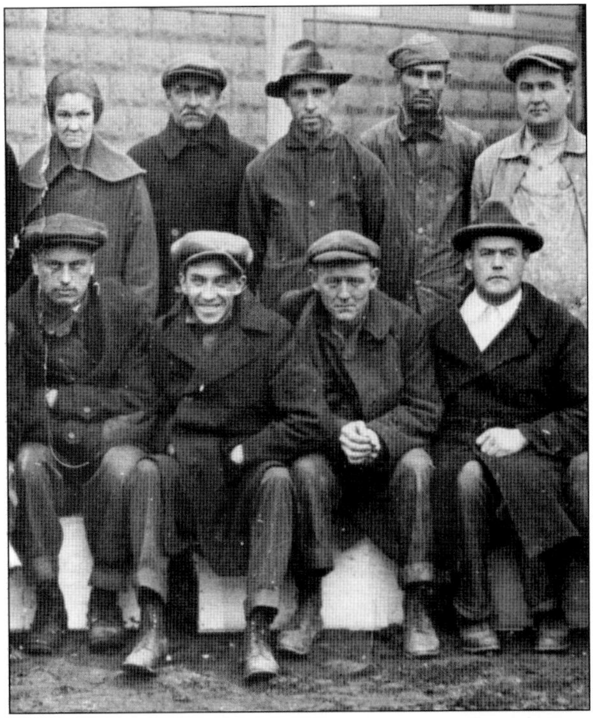

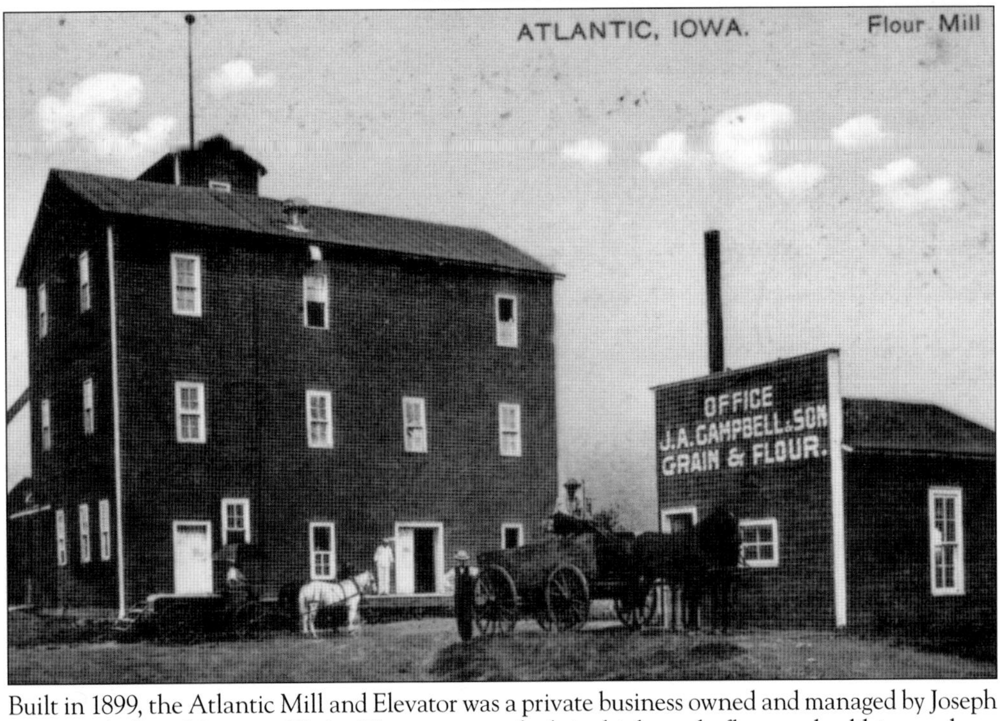

Built in 1899, the Atlantic Mill and Elevator was a private business owned and managed by Joseph A. Campbell and his son Clyde. The company dealt in high-grade flour and sold its products nationally. The Campbells were committed to using local products insofar as they were able and provided a reliable market for the grain grown in the area. The grain elevator could store up to 20,000 bushels, and the plant was capable of producing 150 barrels of flour per day.

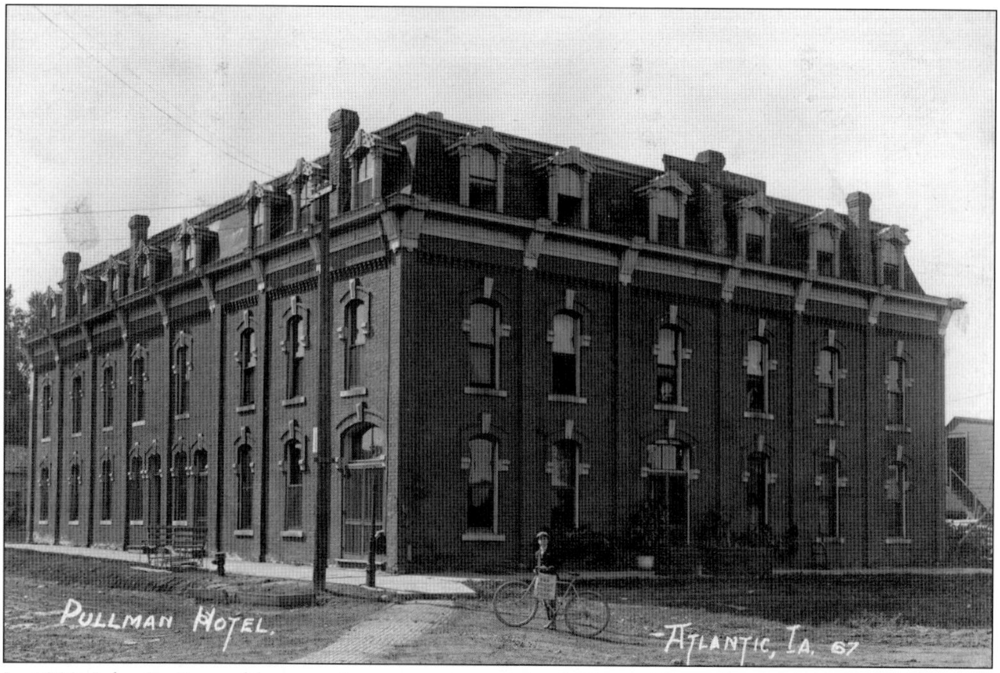

In 1882, John R. Reynolds started construction of the Pullman Hotel, located on Walnut Street. It was a solid brick building and featured a dining room that resembled the interior of a Pullman railcar. An unusual feature was that diners could watch scenery pictures revolving on an endless loop that gave them the feeling of being on a moving train.

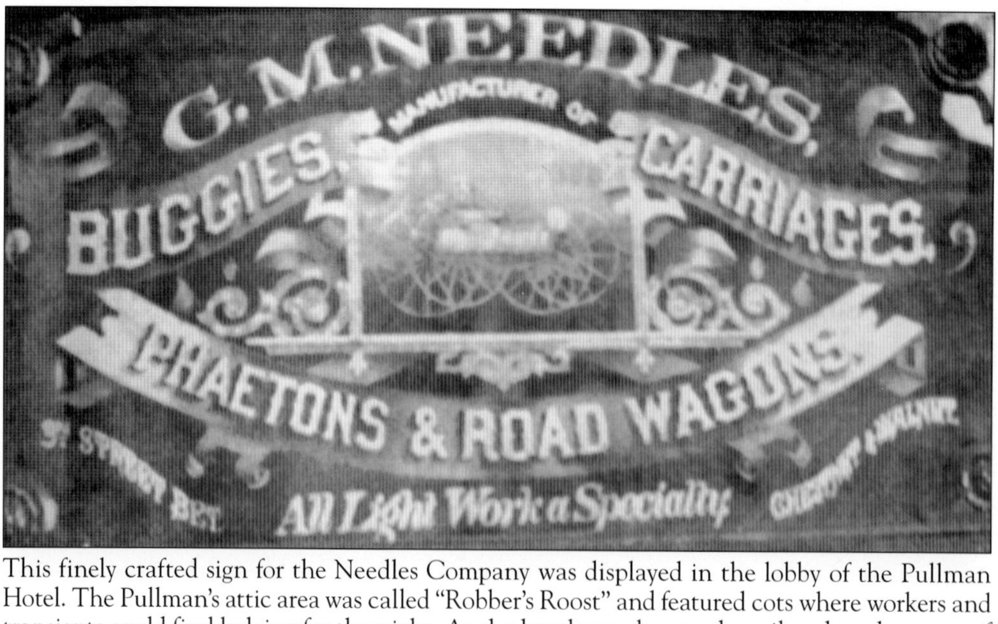

This finely crafted sign for the Needles Company was displayed in the lobby of the Pullman Hotel. The Pullman's attic area was called "Robber's Roost" and featured cots where workers and transients could find lodging for the night. As the hotel was close to the railroad tracks, some of the transients gave the hotel a rather unsavory reputation. Mrs. George B. Holland leased the hotel in the early 1900s and restored its reputation by maintaining a fine restaurant and keeping the hotel a model of neatness.

Three

Investing in a Town

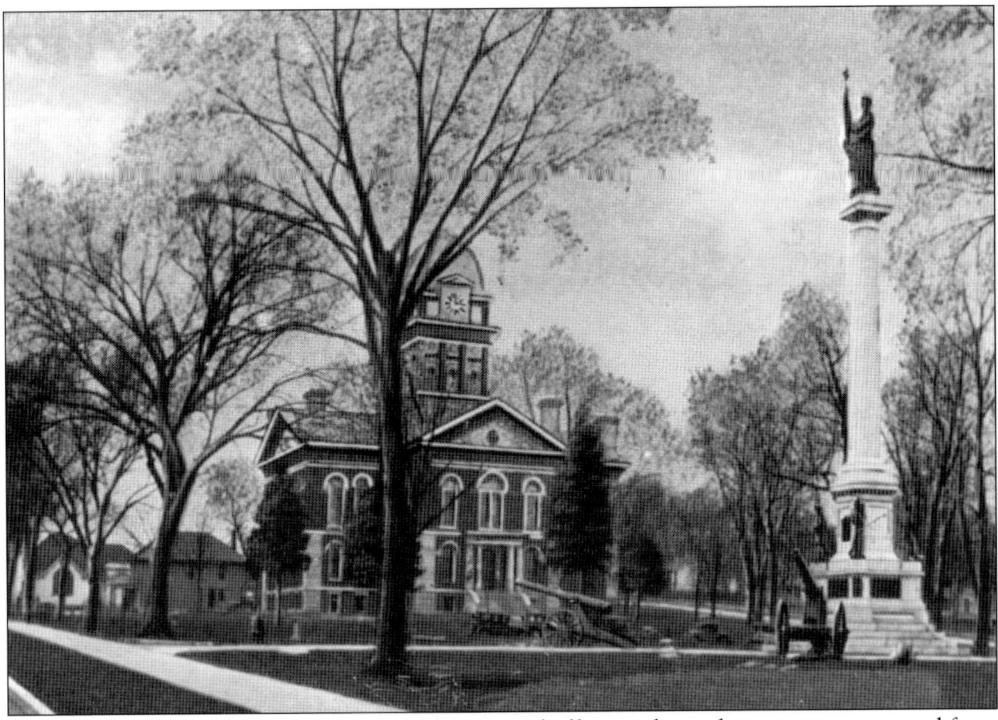

Twice the residents of Grove City made determined efforts to have the county seat moved from Lewis to Grove City; both attempts failed. By 1869, most of Grove City had relocated to Atlantic, and a vote was taken to determine if the county seat should be moved there. In the 1869 general election, Atlantic won by a 343-vote advantage. The Cass County Courthouse in Atlantic was built in 1882. The small brick building to the left in the photograph was the city jail.

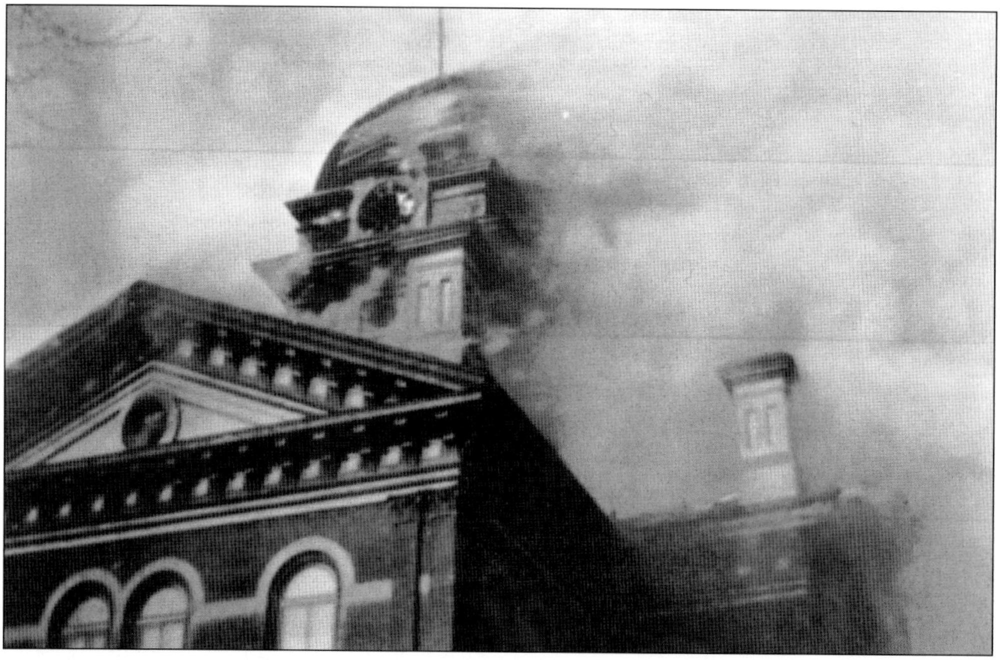

The Atlantic Town Company, under the leadership of Franklin H. Whitney, issued a warranty deed for the land upon which to build the new courthouse in Atlantic. The agreement was that the new county building would be completed in 60 days, and all the county offices would be required to move to Atlantic at that time. A small courthouse was duly erected, but it soon proved to be inadequate for the volume of business in the rapidly growing county. A larger courthouse was completed in 1882 and served until fire consumed it in March 1932. The county used the Herring Automobile Company building as offices until a new courthouse was erected.

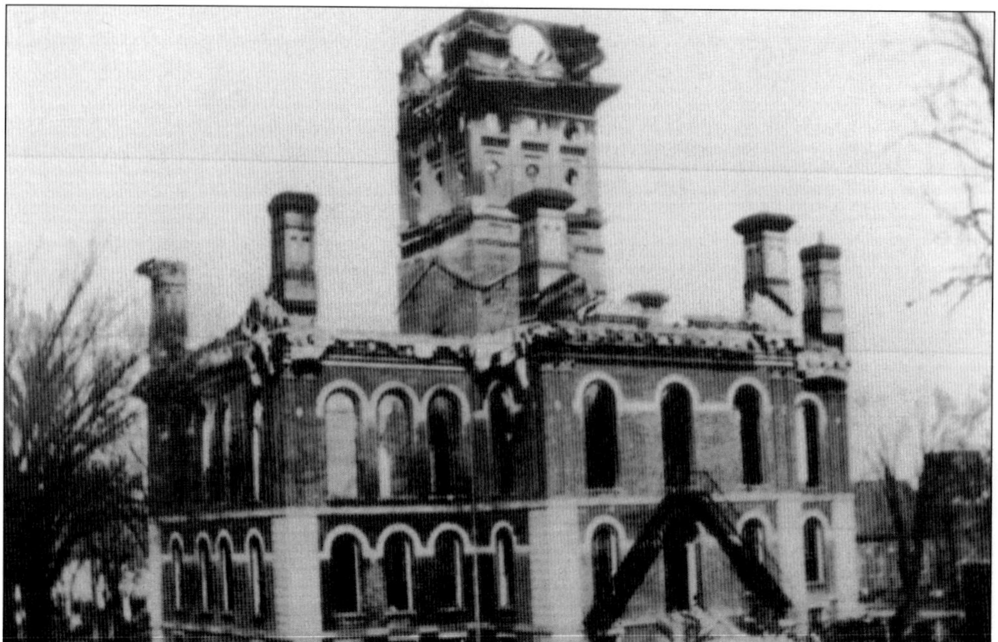

The cornerstone of the new Cass County Courthouse was laid on March 23, 1934. After the 1932 fire in the old courthouse, the citizens of the county had voted a bond issue of $65,000 for the building of a new one. Insurance money and a designation as a federal Public Works Administration project increased funds to $120,000. Gov. Clyde Herring, a longtime Atlantic businessman, laid the cornerstone and was the featured speaker at the dedication.

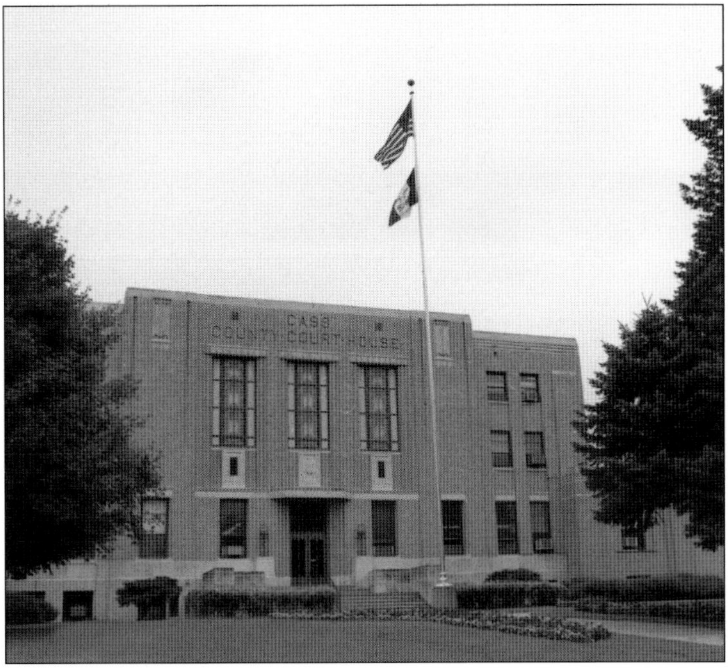

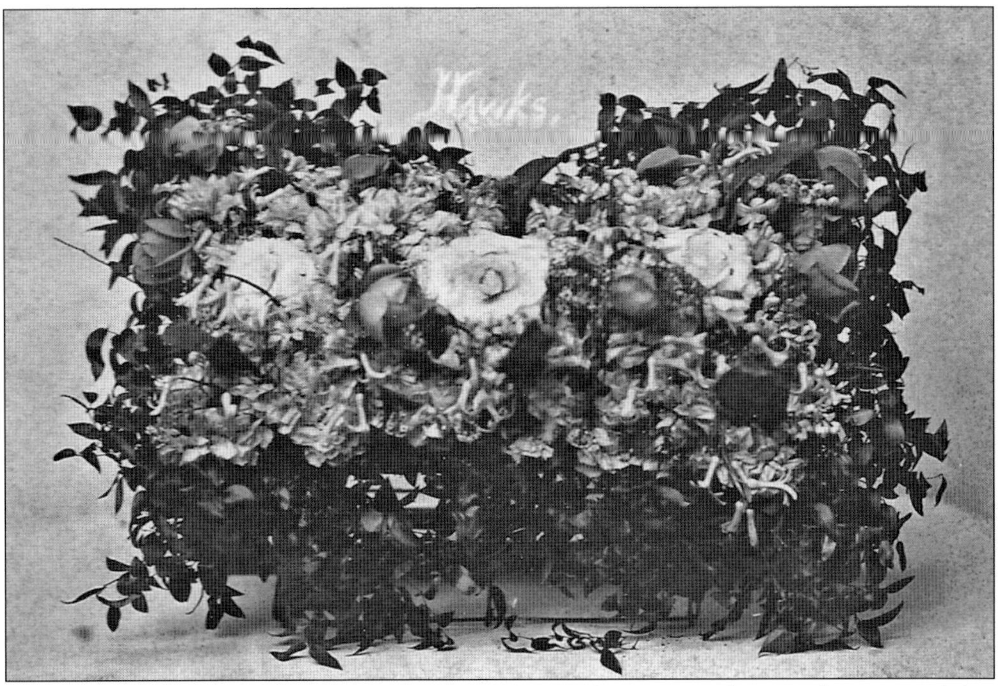

Dexter F. Hawks was an early businessman and Atlantic's first mayor, taking on that responsibility when the city was incorporated in 1870. He was in the dry goods business with D. H. Stafford. They operated under the firm name Stafford and Hawks. Hawks's wife was the sister of Belle Tiffany Osborne. This is the elaborately adorned casket of Hawks. Note his name printed on the photograph.

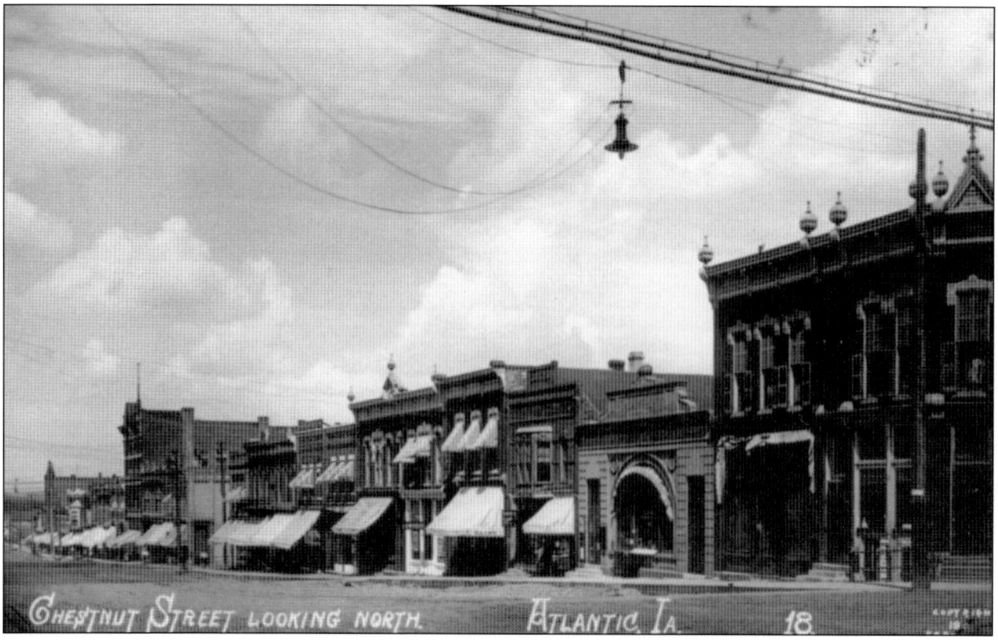

For years, up until the late 1890s, when lamplighter Ed Johnson made his rounds to light the street lamps each evening, he carried a small ladder to be able to reach the lamps. These scenes of Chestnut Street were taken when the first electric lights, called electroliers (a blend of *electric* and *chandelier*), were installed. An electrolier is actually the branching frame or assembly that holds the light. In November 1911, electroliers were installed on Chestnut Street and turned on briefly. The load was too much for the electric plant, so they had to be turned off until heavier machinery could be installed. Between 1910 and 1920, the city council passed an ordinance prohibiting hitching horses to the electroliers.

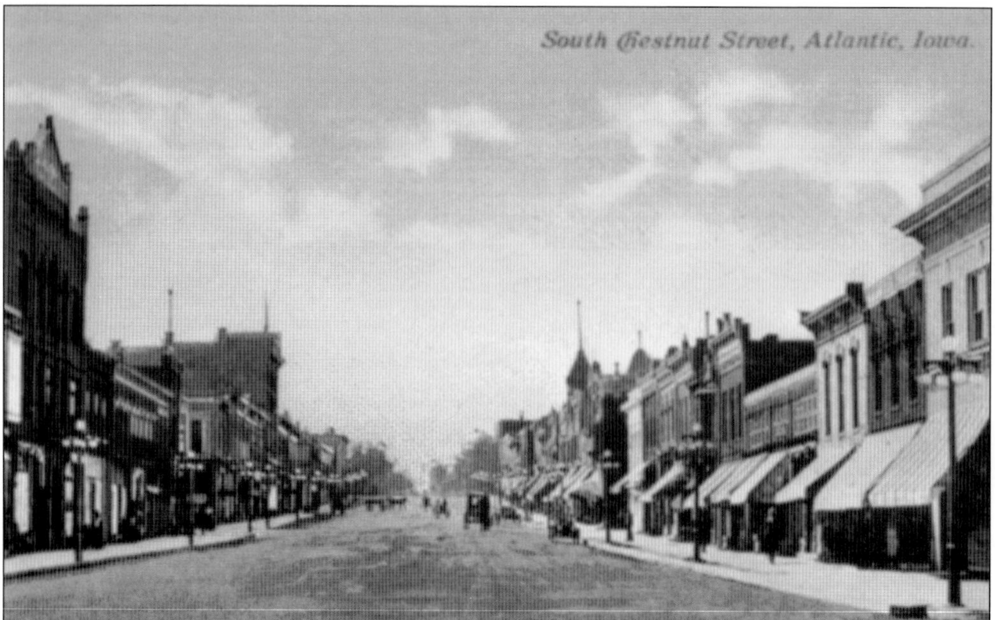

On October 17, 1882, J. D. Patton and C. D. Jones opened the Atlantic Gaslight Company. This franchise furnished gas for illuminating purposes only. Using gas for heating or cooking was unknown at the time. After changing owners several times, the company was purchased by the Iowa Electric Company on April 3, 1925. The new owners erected a modern factory, which opened on May 3, 1928. Award-winning photographer Harley Johnson took this photograph of the plant.

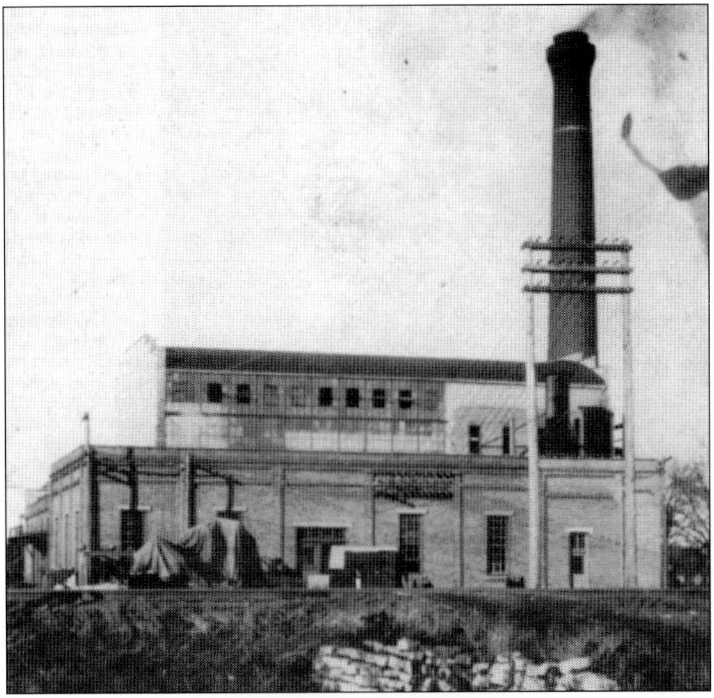

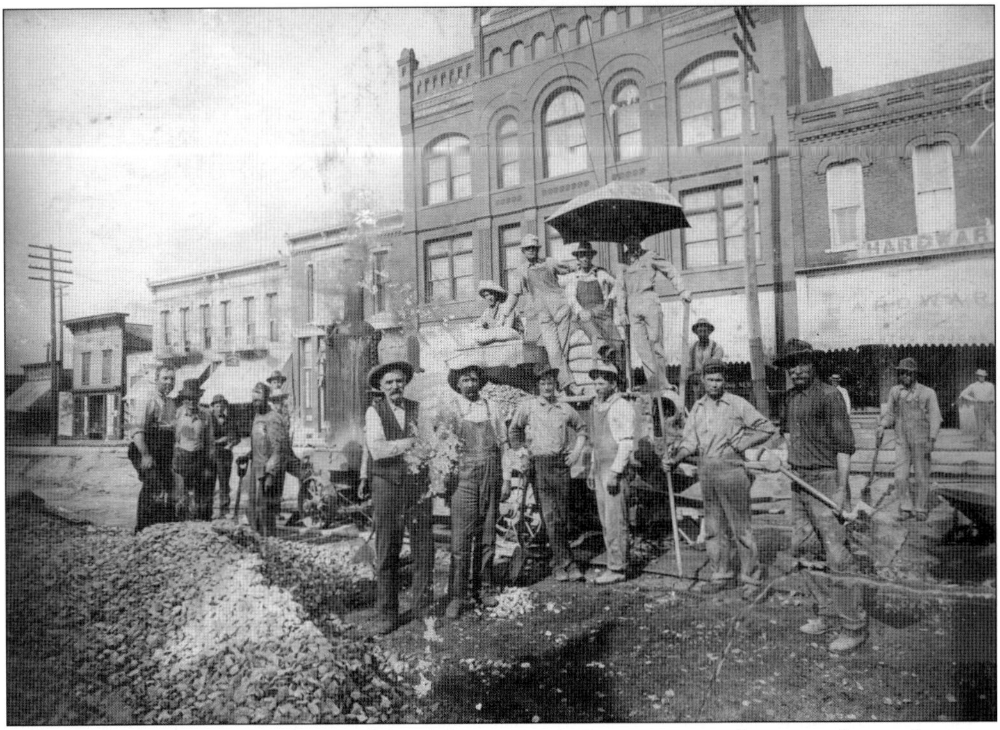

R. C. Taylor, owner and operator of the Atlantic Brick Company, was foreman of several paving crews, including this one shown working on Chestnut Street. Hansen and Son of Sioux City had the contract for most of the first paving projects in Atlantic, including 58 blocks in the residential area.

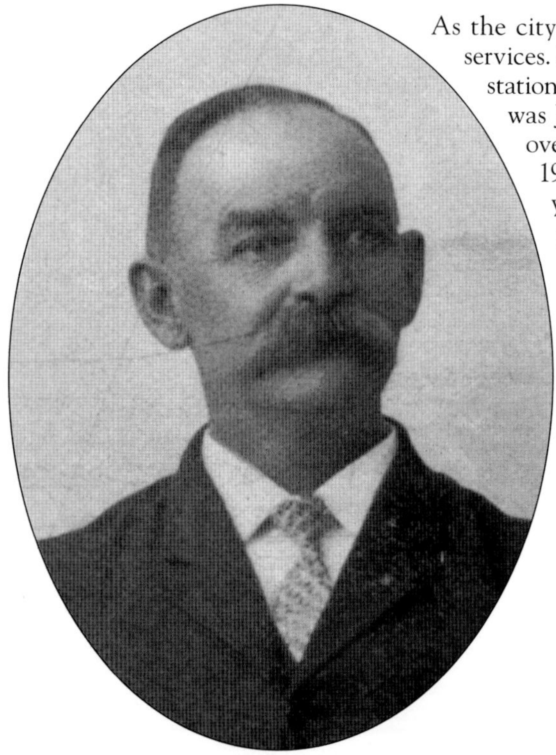

As the city grew, so did the demand for municipal services. In 1882, the Atlantic waterworks pumping station was built. The engineer for this operation was James W. Love, who came to Atlantic to oversee construction of this new facility. In 1905, the plant was electrified. For over 25 years, Love served as head engineer and provided a safe and reliable source of water for the citizens of Atlantic. In his spare time, he enjoyed serving as the leader of the Atlantic city band.

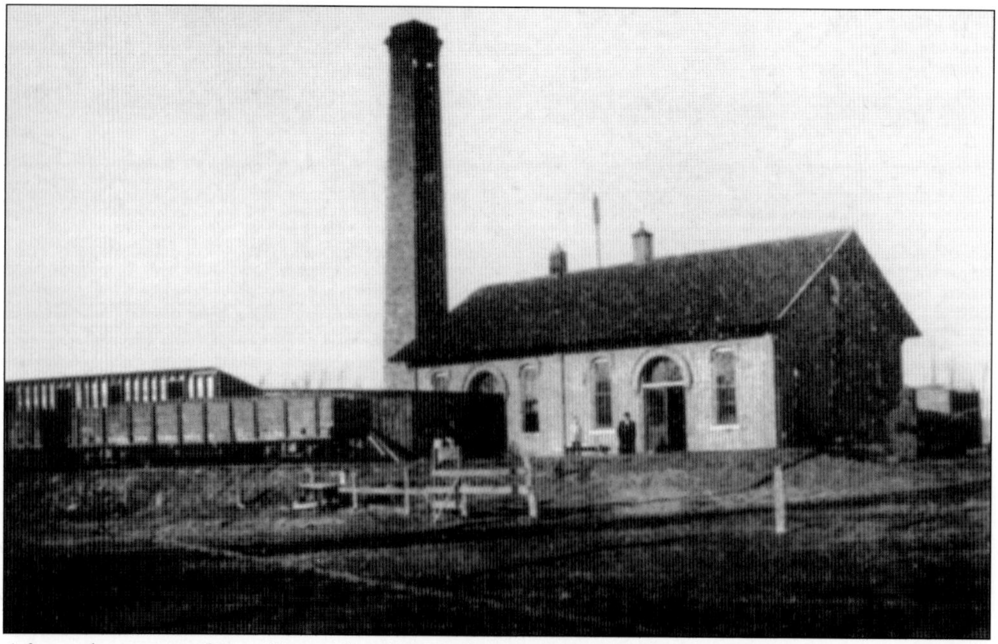

After a destructive fire in December 1880, it became evident that a reliable source of water was needed to supply the demands of a growing city. In 1882, a corporation with a stock value of $100,000 was formed to address the problem. The corporation was under the direct control of J. R. Reynolds. A station was constructed in a bend of Troublesome Creek on the east side of the city. By October 1882, it was capable of pumping two million gallons of water every 24 hours.

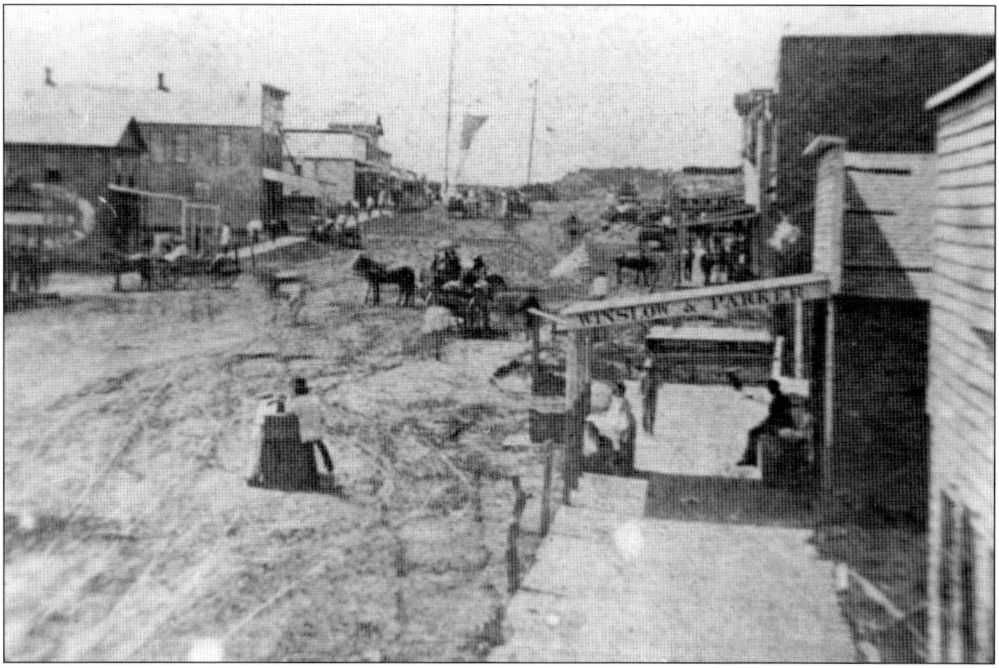

One of the most devastating fires in the history of Atlantic took place on Christmas Day, 1900. The conflagration wiped out the entire block on Chestnut Street between Fourth and Fifth Streets. Many times these early disasters were blessings in disguise as they destroyed old, hastily constructed buildings typical of boomtowns.

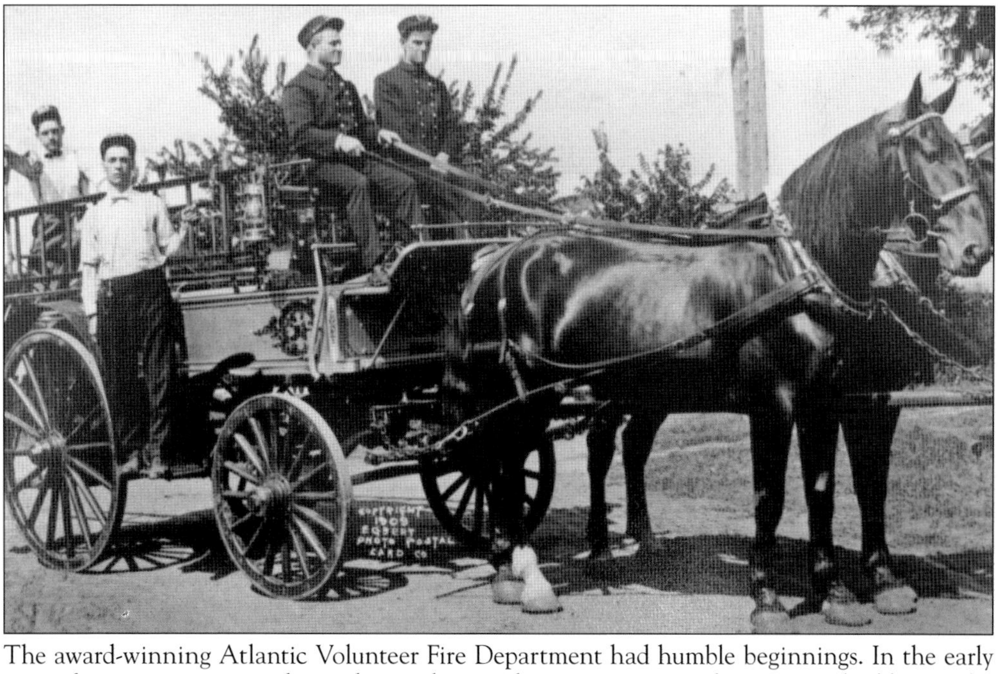

The award-winning Atlantic Volunteer Fire Department had humble beginnings. In the early years, fire was a constant threat due to the wooden construction of most town buildings. The earliest fires were fought by a bucket brigade. This photograph shows the last, and reputedly one of the best, fire department horse teams, Patch and Dan.

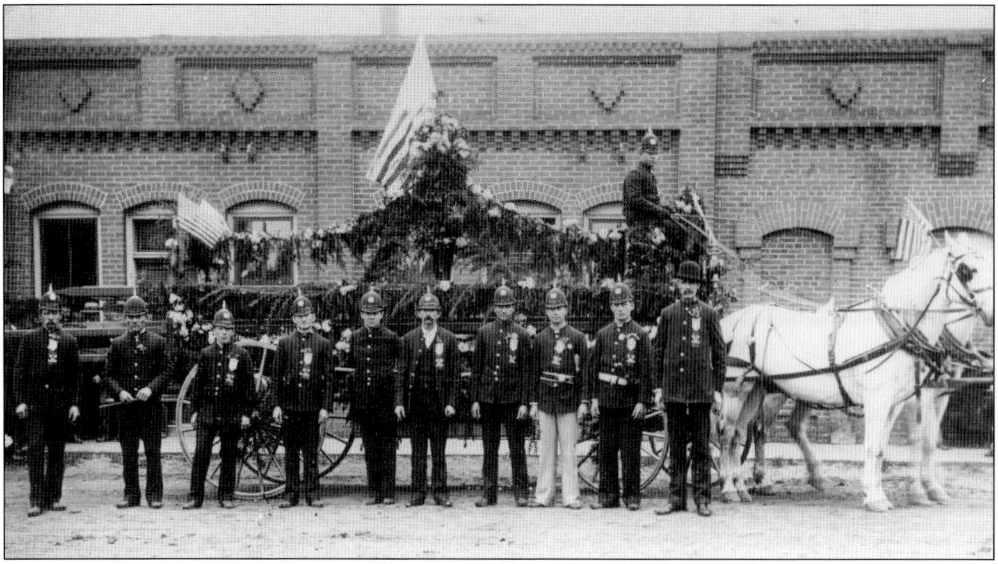

The Atlantic Fire Department was organized in 1877 with H. A. Smith as fire marshal. Two hose companies were formed in 1882, the Phoenix and the Whitney. Teams raced to see which could get to a fire first. Atlantic won the state championship in 1882, 1884, and 1893. The ladder climber, H. C. Gillett, held the world's championship for being the fastest climber of a 30-foot ladder and was idolized by Atlantic children. This 1900 photograph shows the Atlantic Phoenix Hose Company.

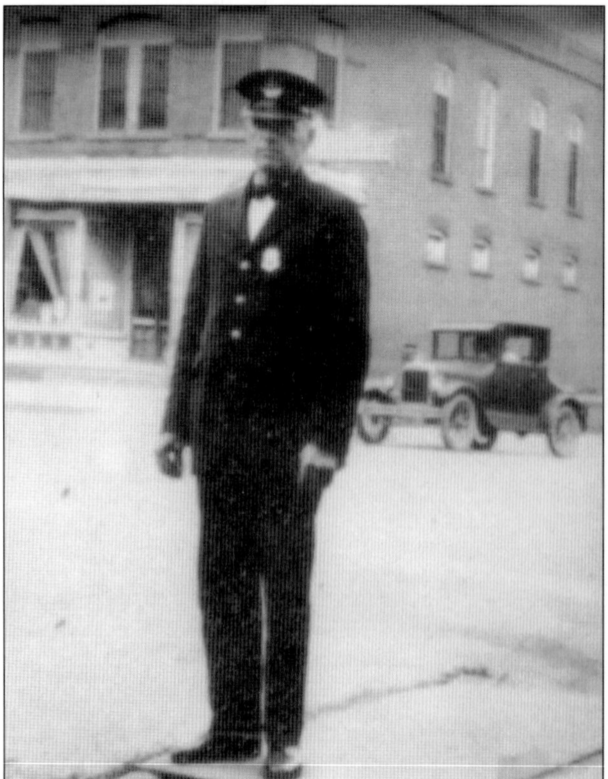

Aden Odem, better known as Dick Odem, was the Atlantic police chief in the 1920s when this photograph was taken. He served in this position for many years before being elected Cass County sheriff in 1935.

The old Atlantic Post Office was built in 1893 and was a very popular meeting spot. Posing on the plank sidewalk in front, from left to right, are Joe Frank, Mertle Frank, Charles E. Everett (postmaster from 1893 to 1897), Scott Hatton, Guy Swires, and Fred Kenrich; the three postal workers at right wear hats as part of their uniforms.

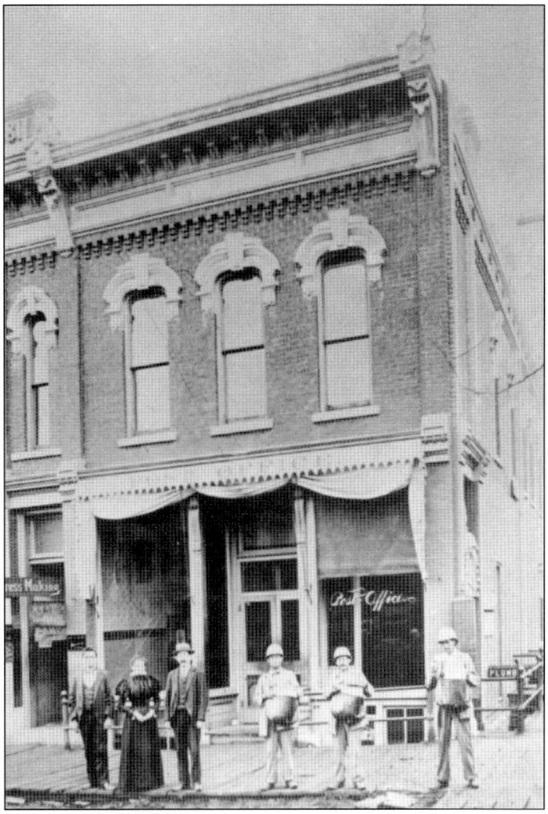

The present Atlantic Post Office, located at Fifth and Walnut Streets, was completed in 1906 at a cost of $24,380. The first postmaster at this location was S. T. McFadden. During its first year in operation, the post office did business totaling $12,000. In 1959, this building underwent a major remodeling at a cost of $189,000.

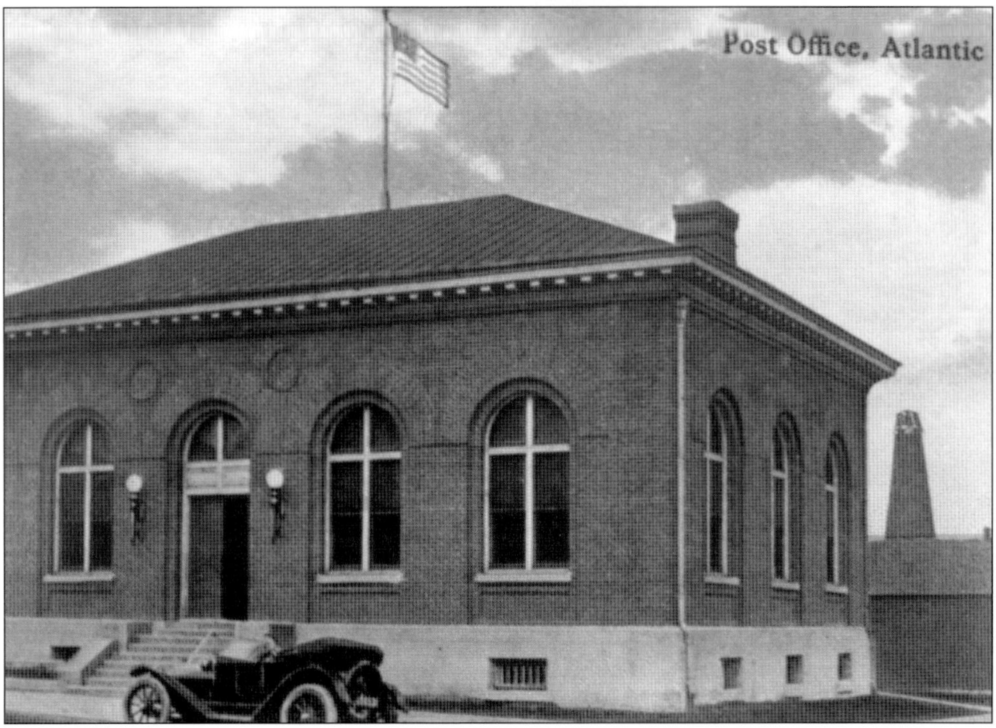

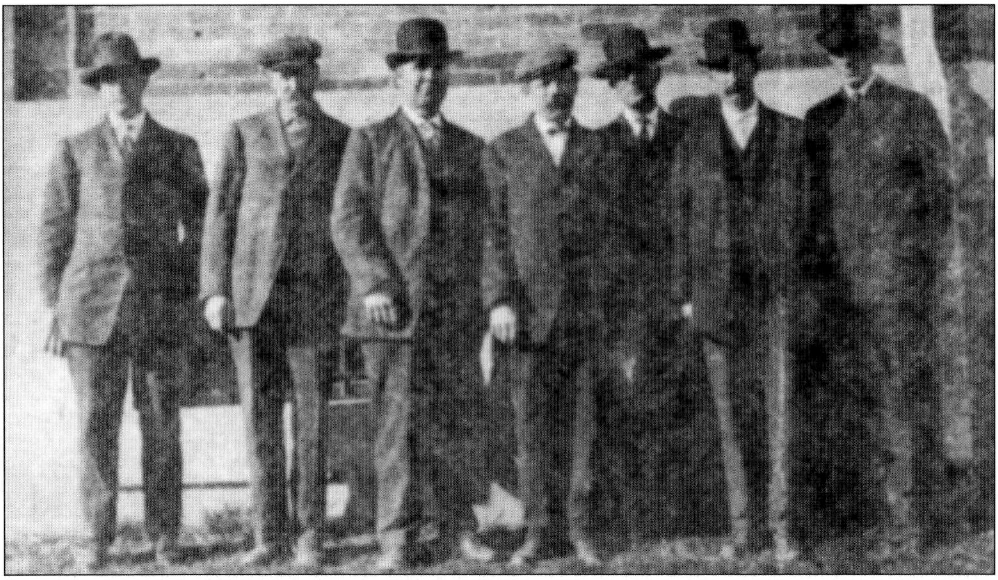

During the 1880s, the first special delivery stamp was sold at the Atlantic post office. The postmaster at that time was a Mr. Childs. In this 1908 photograph, Atlantic rural mail carriers are lined up outside the new post office. They are, from left to right, Gar Willis, Fred Stier, Al Smith, Mint Brown, Emmett Butler, Frank Perkins, and a Mr. Noon.

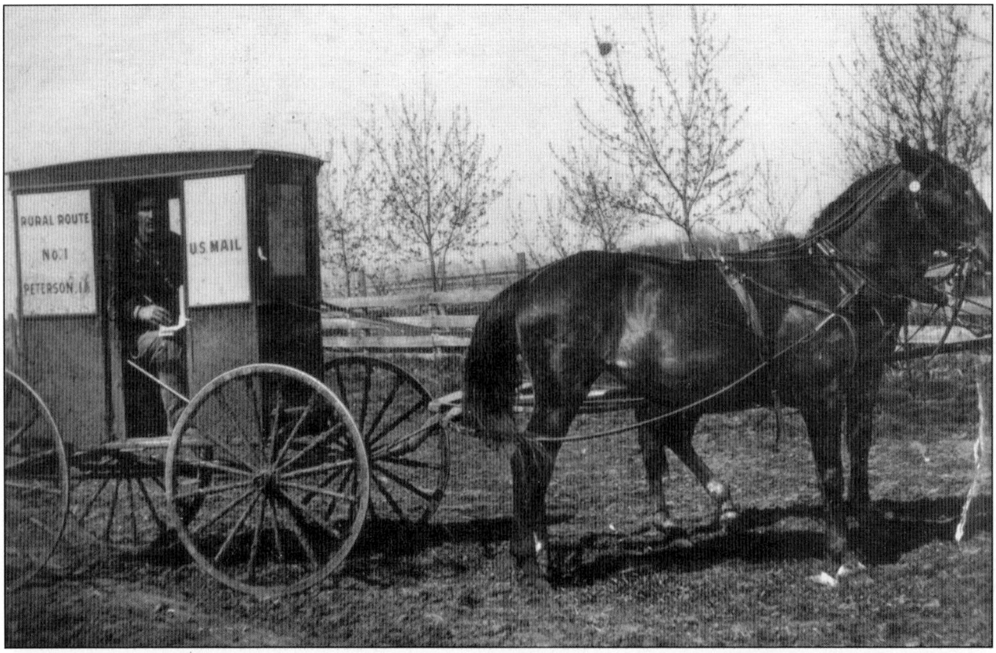

One of the most important developments in the postal service came with the inauguration of rural free delivery on October 1, 1896. Letters sent through this service were addressed "R. F. D.," followed by a route number. This 1903 photograph of an Iowa rural mail carrier shows the type of open buggy carriers used. Many a tired and cold rural carrier arrived back in town in the dark after completing his route. A carrier kept a lantern in his buggy to warm his hands.

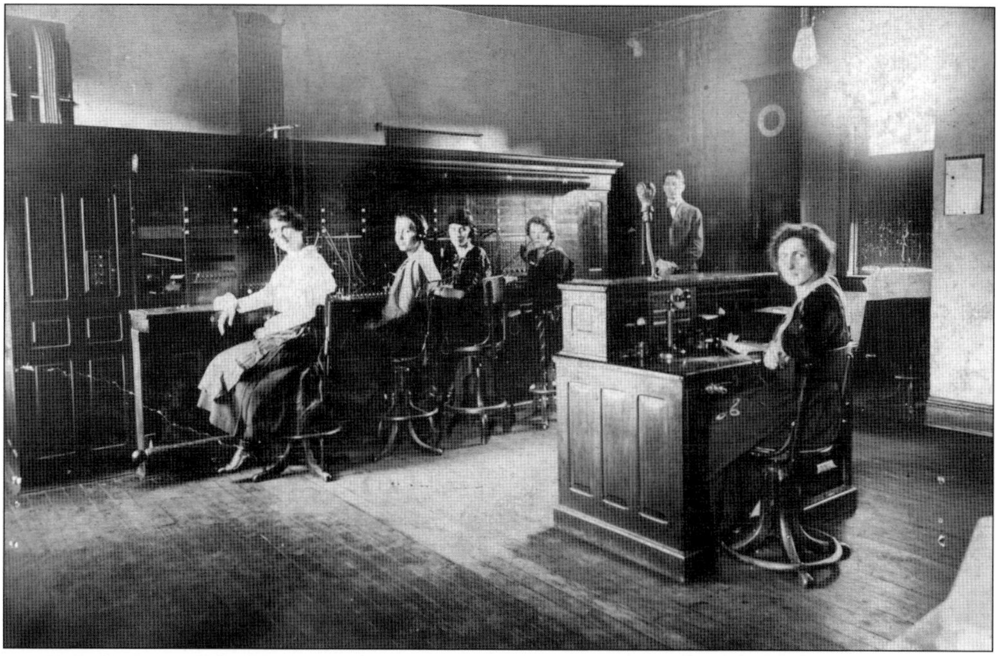

In 1882, the Iowa Telephone Company of Cedar Rapids started the first telephone exchange in Atlantic. Until 1888, the office was in the back room of the Keyes Building, and the first manager was C. B. Smith. The annual rates were $50 for a business and $30 for a residence. In the first year of operation, the company had 42 subscribers. This photograph was taken at the Atlantic office.

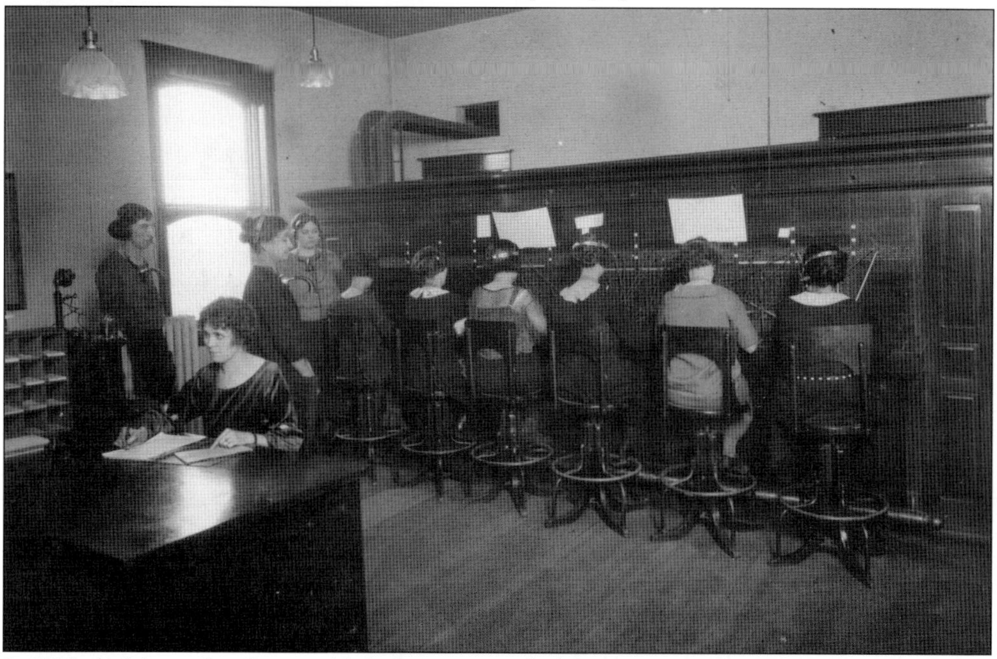

In 1900, the Musson brothers established a separate telephone company. An early newspaper reported that the Mussons purchased a railcar load of copper for the purpose of improving services. In 1913, this company merged with the Iowa Telephone Company, which in turn sold out to Northwestern Bell in 1923. In 1941, the organization moved to a new building at 614 Chestnut Street.

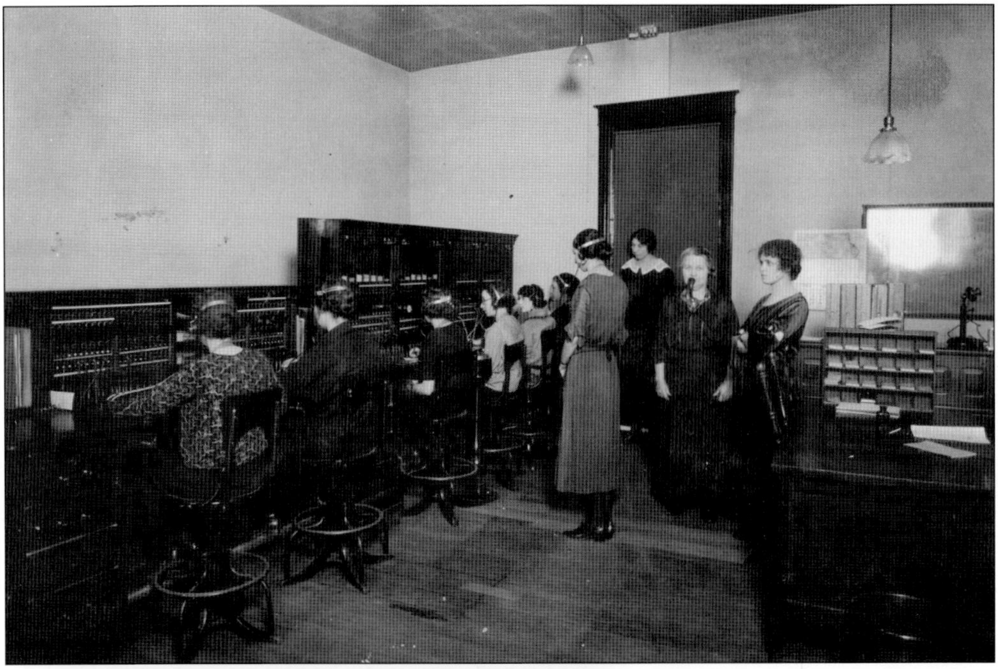

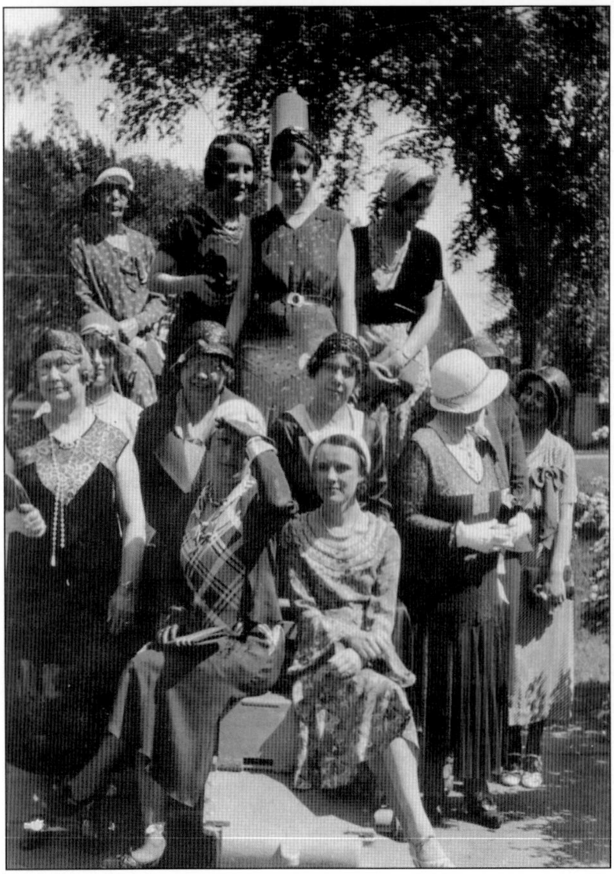

Telephone operators were usually women; the first in Atlantic was Lottie Willey. This 1924 photograph from the Atlantic office shows the operators at work and the always present supervisors looking over their shoulders. One of the rules at the time was that operators were held responsible for tolls not paid. Long-distance calls outside the state could not be made directly but had to be routed through Omaha or Des Moines.

This photograph, taken in the Atlantic City Park, shows telephone workers enjoying an afternoon outing. The women are using the Civil War cannon as a backdrop for their posed picture. Since the women were not allowed to visit while at the switchboard, these outings provided a time for social activity.

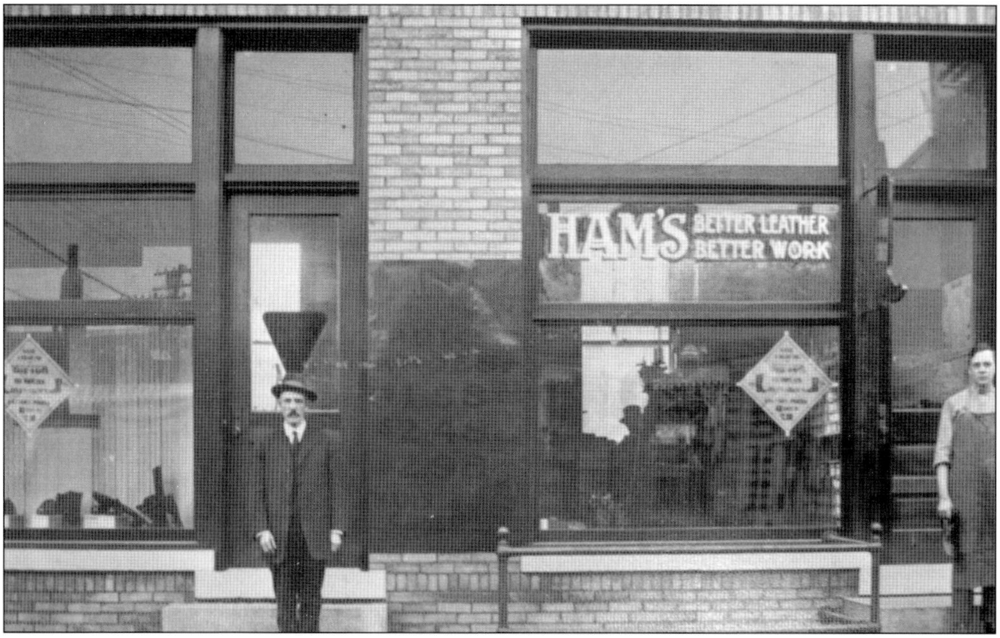

At the turn of the century, the predominant leather goods store, located on Fourth Street in Atlantic, was Ham's Leather Shop. Many stores at that time had slogans, and Ham proudly displays his in the window, "Better Leather, Better Work." The photograph shows Ham (left), dressed appropriately in a suit, and one of his shop workers, who is wearing a typical leather work apron.

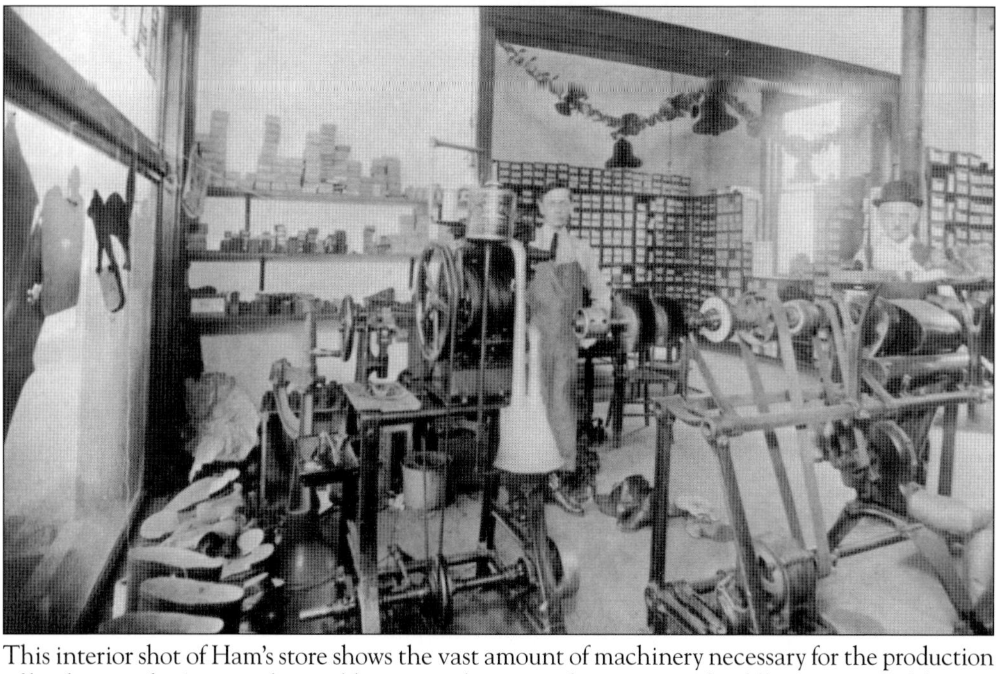

This interior shot of Ham's store shows the vast amount of machinery necessary for the production of leather goods. A man who could repair such items as harnesses and saddles was a valuable asset to early settlers who depended so much on the horse for farming, transportation, and pleasure. Only the heaviest of leathers was used for harnesses, while lighter leathers were used in making shoes, gloves, and belts.

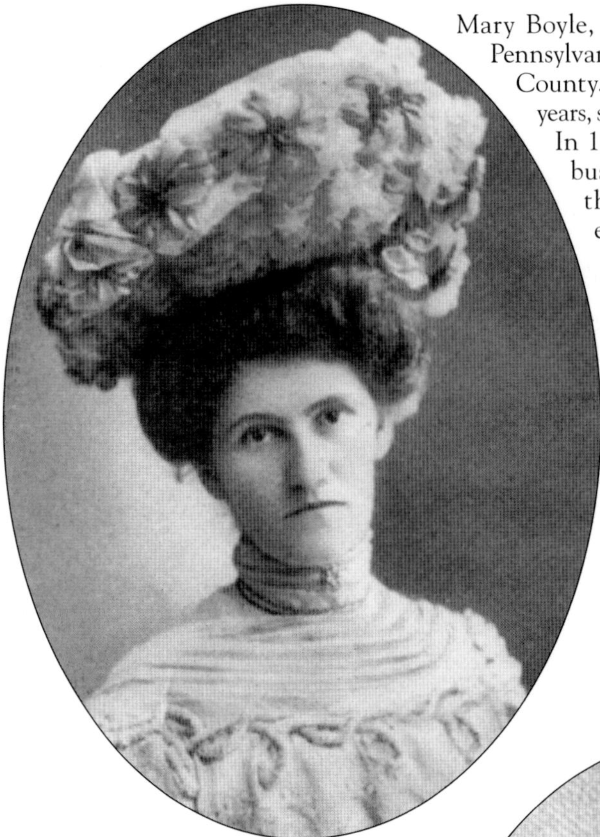

Mary Boyle, an Atlantic milliner, was born in Pennsylvania and came with her father to Cass County. After staying in Atlantic for three years, she went to New York to study millinery. In 1902, she returned and established a business. Having personal attributes that pleased customers, Boyle was exceptionally successful and known for her fine handiwork in fashioning head wear for the ladies. She carried a large and carefully selected stock of goods and was prominent in Atlantic's social scene.

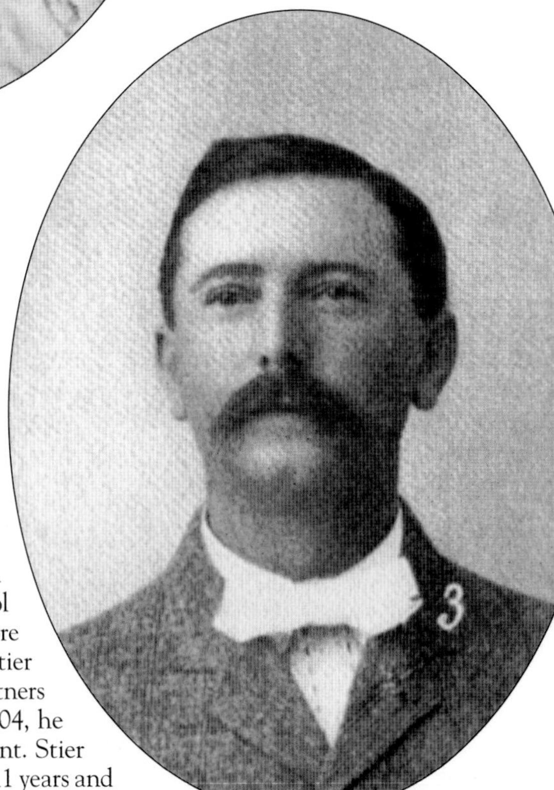

James Stier came to the Atlantic area in the spring of 1874. After attending school in Atlantic, he worked at the grocery store owned by L. H. Moeller. For a time, Stier went into the grocery business with partners W. B. Martin and A. L. Dunn. In 1904, he became sole owner of the establishment. Stier served the community as a fireman for 11 years and as a member of the city council for eight.

By the time this photograph was taken in 1911, Atlantic had several substantial brick storefronts. The Stier Grocery was located at the northeast corner of Fourth and Walnut Streets. For a time, James Stier was in partnership with his brother-in-law Al Dunn. Stier (center), Dunn (right), and Dale Morrow sit in a car in front of the Stier Grocery. The second car, festooned with advertisements, belonged to a salesman.

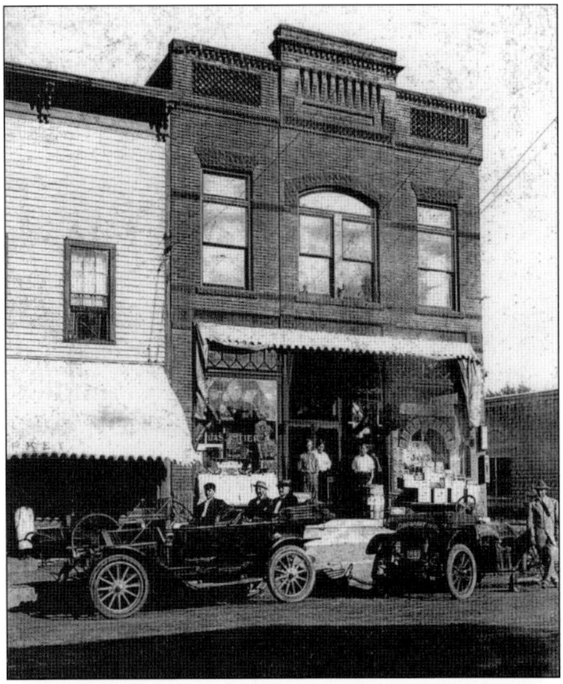

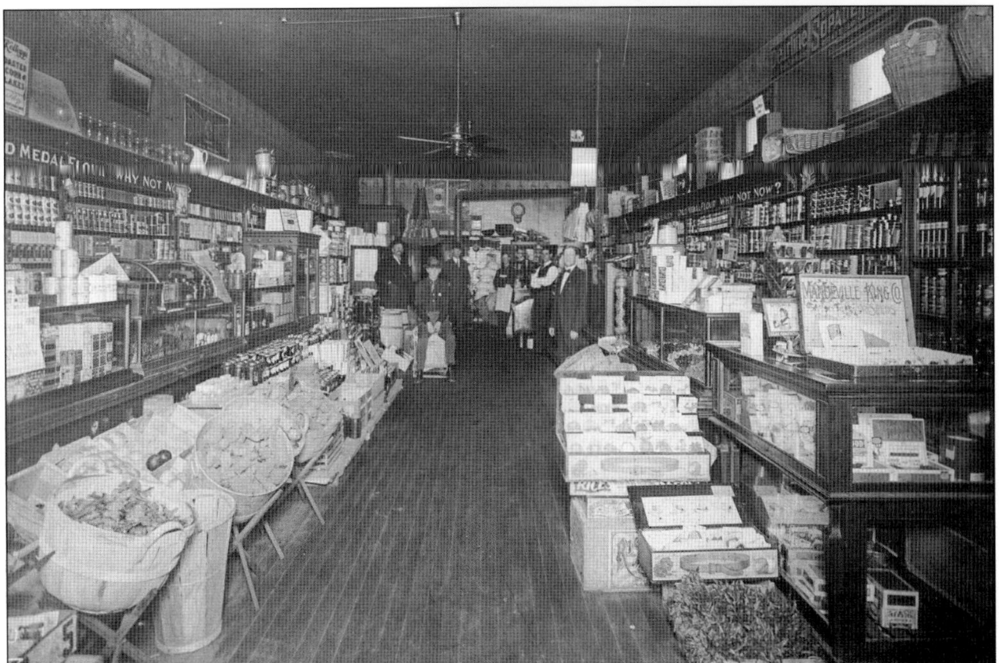

The interior of Stier Grocery shows a well-stocked establishment. James Stier was a very civic-minded individual and served on the first library board in Atlantic. His daughter Alma remembers being allowed to hold the large check the city received from Andrew Carnegie for the construction of a Carnegie library. Alma's husband, Dale Morrow, purchased the grocery store from Stier and operated it until the early 1940s.

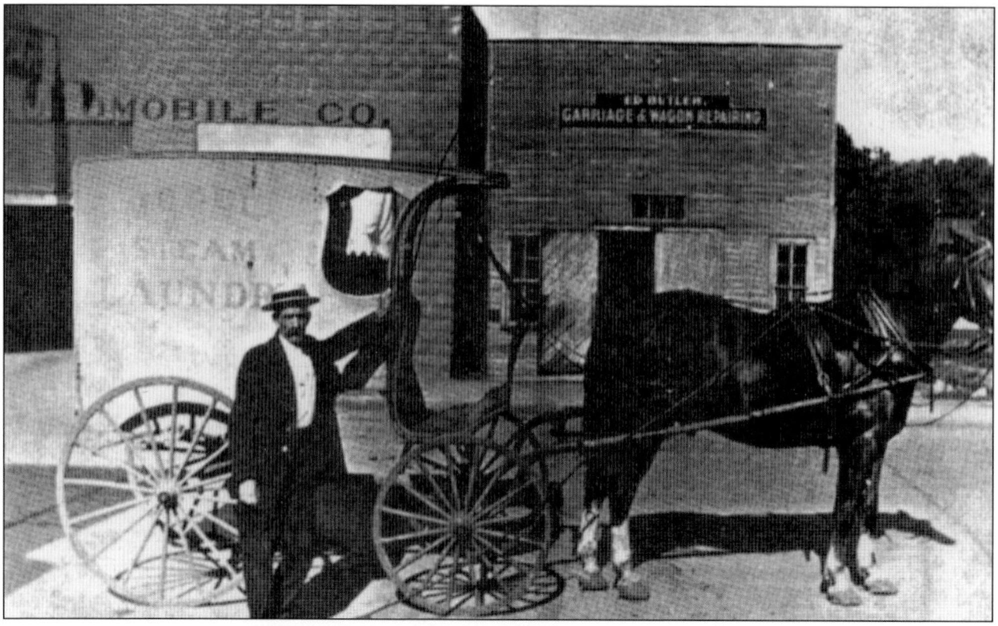

One of the services provided to early Atlantic residents was a steam laundry. The driver pictured here is J. N. "Bud" Berry. In the background is the rare combination of an automobile repair company on the right and a carriage and wagon repair company on the left. Charles Zook, who came to Atlantic in 1899, established this laundry business. The town could also boast of an authentic Chinese laundry, set up by Fong Lee around 1916 just north of the Atlantic Hotel. It operated until 1923.

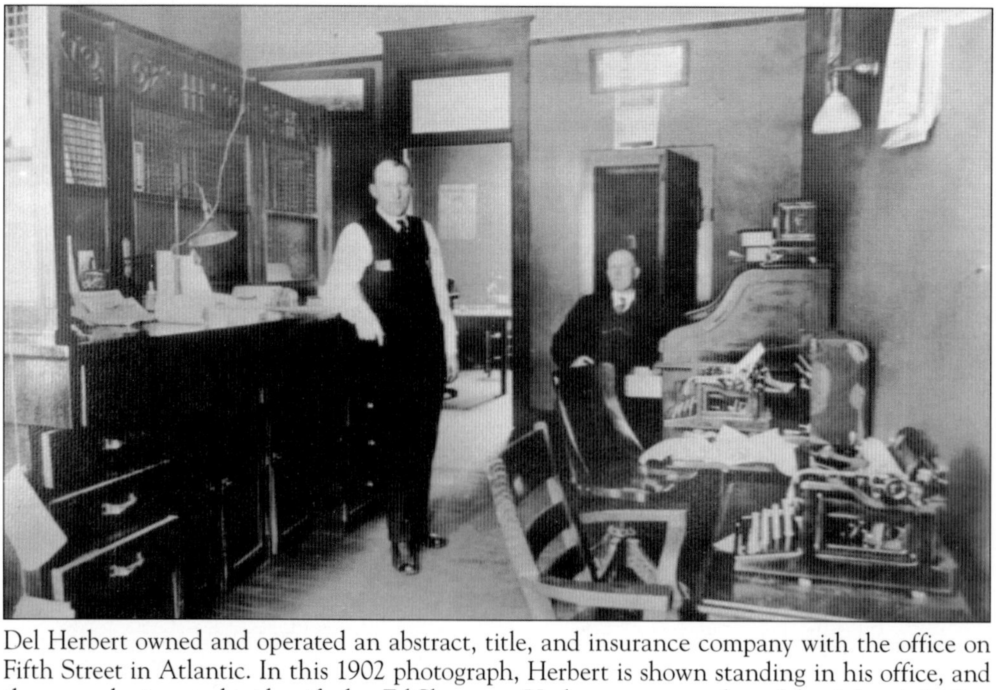

Del Herbert owned and operated an abstract, title, and insurance company with the office on Fifth Street in Atlantic. In this 1902 photograph, Herbert is shown standing in his office, and the man who is seated is identified as Ed Shannon. Herbert was a member of the Atlantic Riding Club and was an avid golfer.

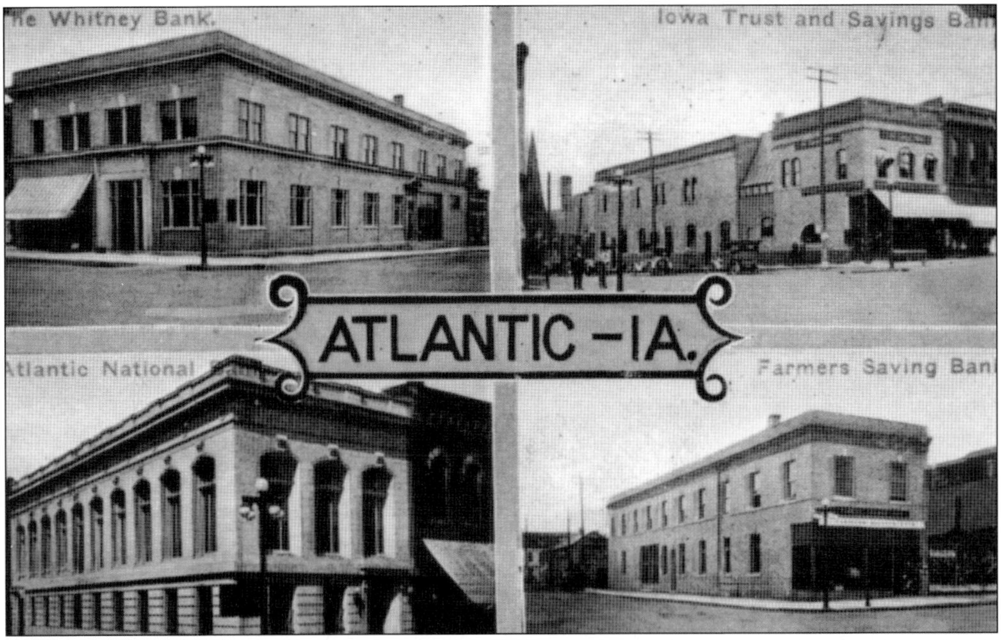

Atlantic had several banks and its share of interesting stories about them. Atlantic's first bank was owned by Loring and Bennett. They had a very successful operation but left town suddenly, taking all the bank's assets with them. It is thought that they fled to South America and were never caught. The loss was in the area of $100,000. Later prominent bankers J. C. Yetzer and A. W. Dickerson ended up in the penitentiary at Fort Madison when it was discovered that the bank was $500,000 short. The above postcard shows several Atlantic banks, and the photograph below shows the Whitney Bank. In October 1929, three men invaded the Whitney Bank, ordered everyone to lie on the floor, and robbed the bank of $40,000. Oscar Otto, then a cashier and later president of the bank, reported that he took one look at the guns and lay down so hard he bounced.

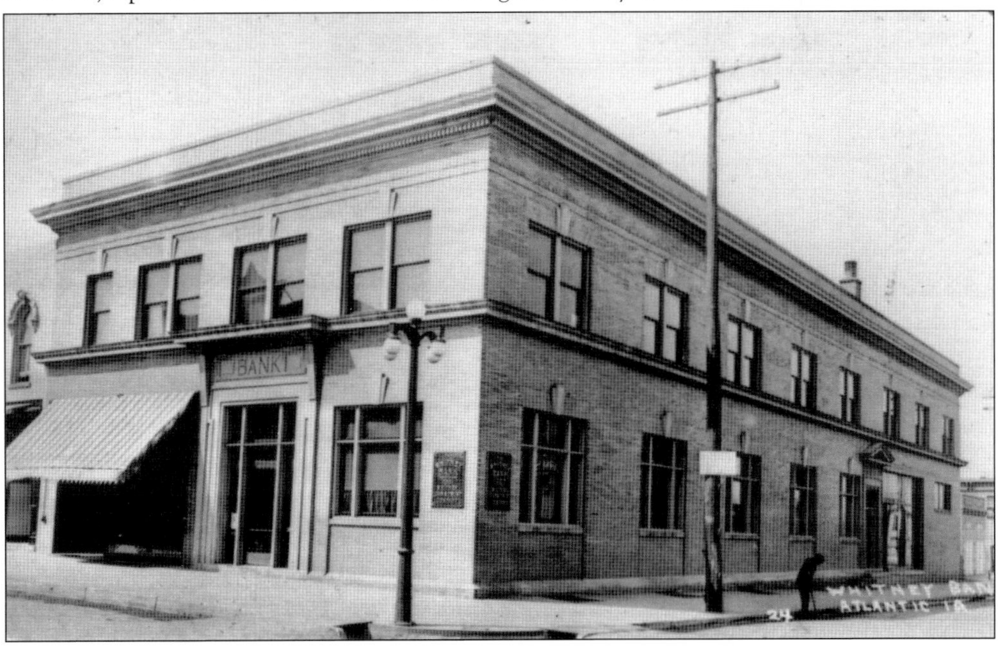

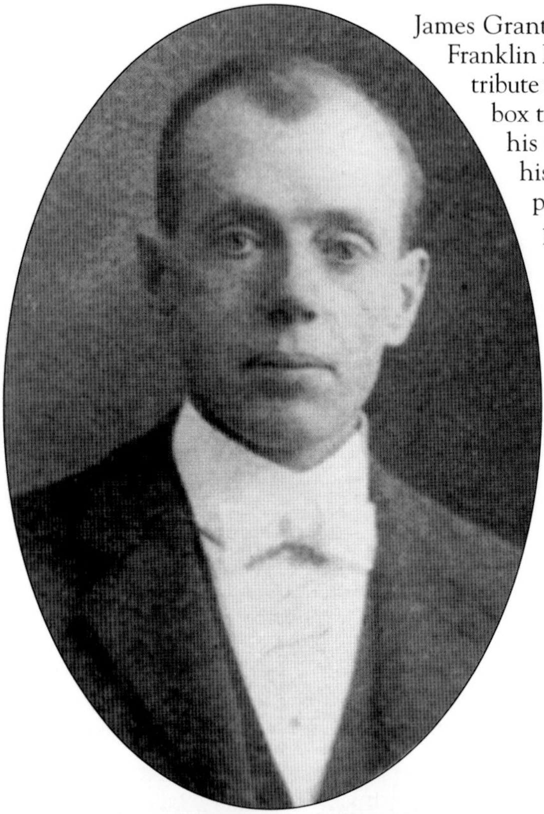

James Grant Whitney was the eldest surviving son of Franklin H. and Ella Grant Whitney. James was a real tribute to his famous father. At age 14, he stood on a box to work as a teller in his father's bank. Upon his father's death, the bank failed. James and his brother Thomas worked until they could pay off the debt to depositors. They not only paid back 100 percent of the deposits, but they added six percent interest.

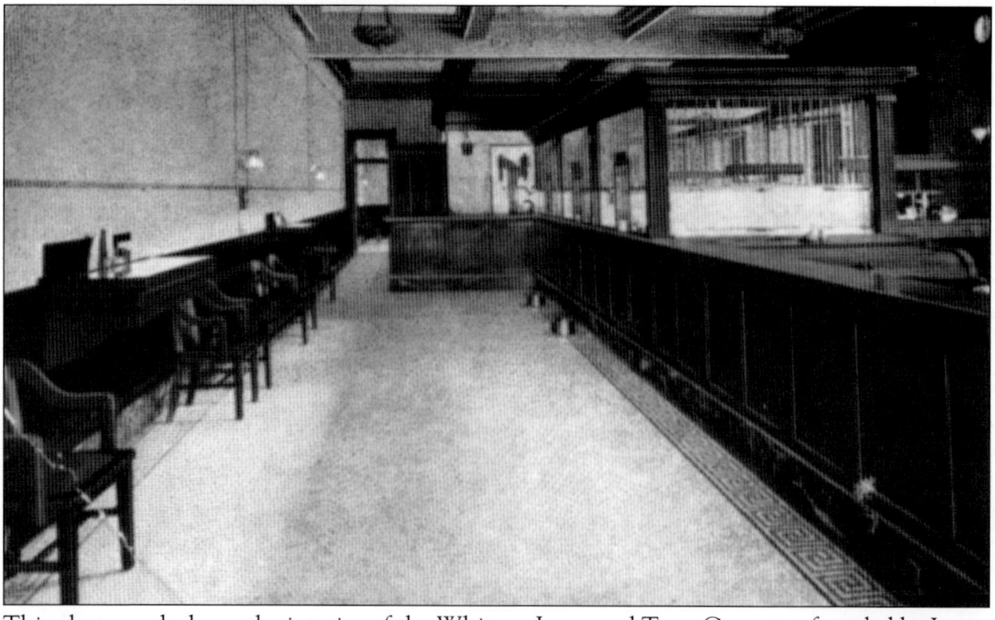

This photograph shows the interior of the Whitney Loan and Trust Company founded by James G. and Thomas H. Whitney, the sons of Franklin H. Whitney. James G. served as president of this bank until his death. He was most proud of the honor given him by the electorate of Atlantic of 50 consecutive years in the office of city treasurer.

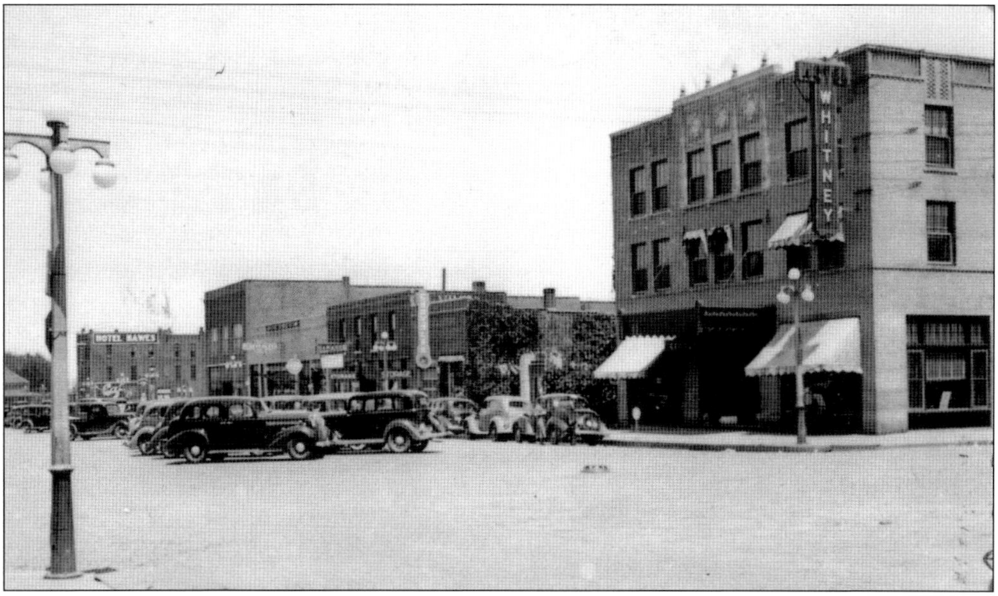

Atlantic has always had an abundance of hotels, and many were quite elegant. One of the later hotels was the Whitney. In 1929, Boss Hotels wanted to build in Atlantic. Knowing the city's history, the company wanted to name their hotel in honor of James Whitney, the longtime city treasurer and son of the city founder. However, Whitney declined the offer, feeling that it should be named to honor his father. As a compromise to honor both men, the hotel was named The Whitney.

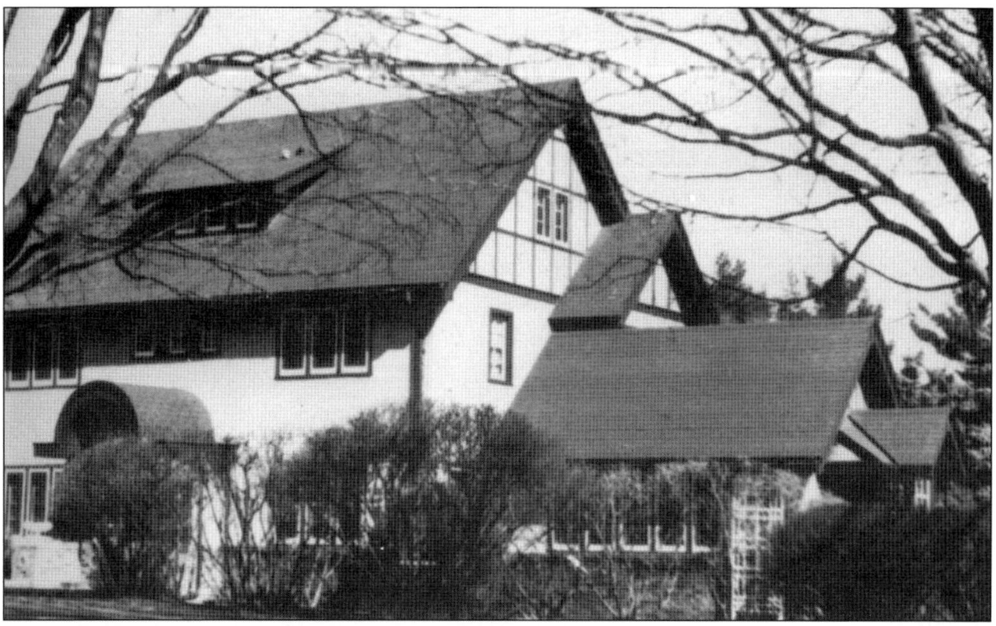

James G. Whitney married Nellie Milner in 1889. While the Whitneys first lived in a very modest home, they were later financially able to build this large home in a beautifully landscaped area at 706 Spruce Street. They named the house Elmhurst. Nellie maintained a household staff and led a very active social life. They also kept a summer home, Jinelma, in the resort area of Lake Okoboji in northwest Iowa.

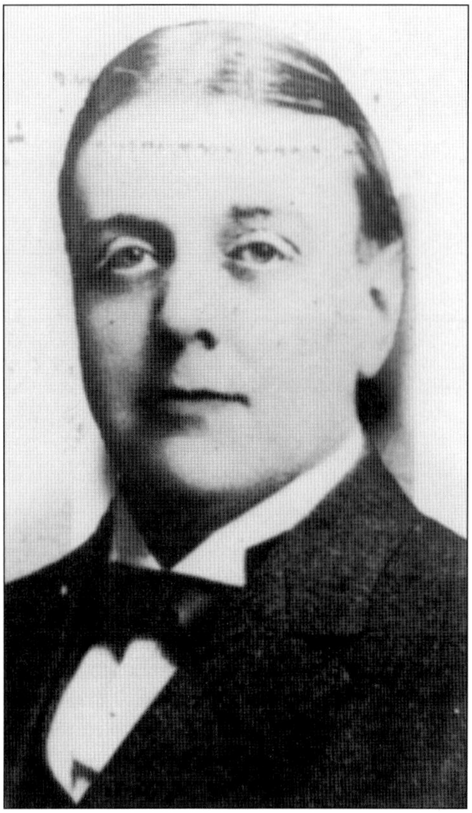

Thomas Hayes Whitney, Franklin H. Whitney's younger son, was born in 1877 and joined his father's bank upon his high school graduation in 1894. Thomas Hayes followed the banking profession all his life, but he had many other varied interests, including music, literature, and the sciences. He maintained a private library of 1,000 volumes, kept daily meteorological records, and contributed articles to ornithology journals.

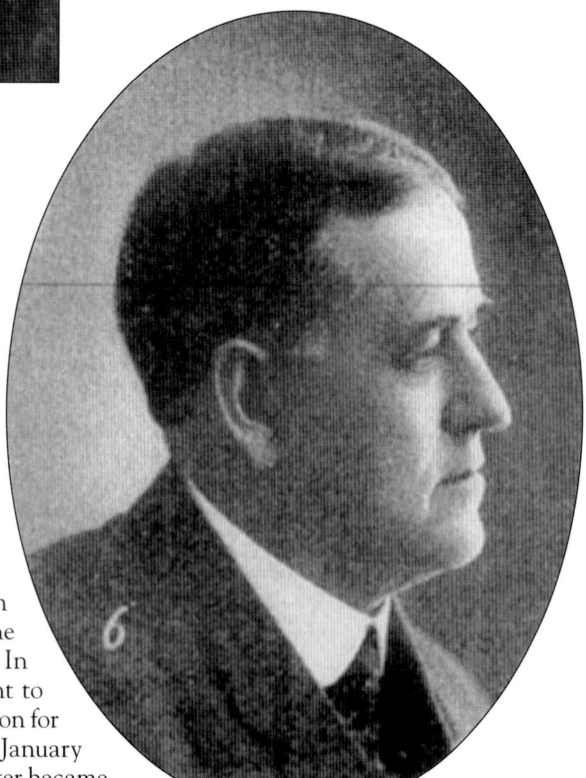

Charles F. Chase came to Atlantic in 1880 and became managing editor of the *Atlantic Daily and Weekly Democrat*. In 1893, Charles received an appointment to serve as postmaster. He filled this position for four years. Chase died at his desk on January 27, 1927. His son Edwin Percy Chase later became associated with the newspaper business.

Edwin Percy Chase, better known as E. P. Chase, brought fame to his hometown of Atlantic when his 1933 editorial, "Where Is Our Money?," won the Pulitzer Prize for editorial writing in 1934. Appropriately, the last line of the article read, "We spent it." Chase was editor of the *Atlantic News-Telegraph* at that time.

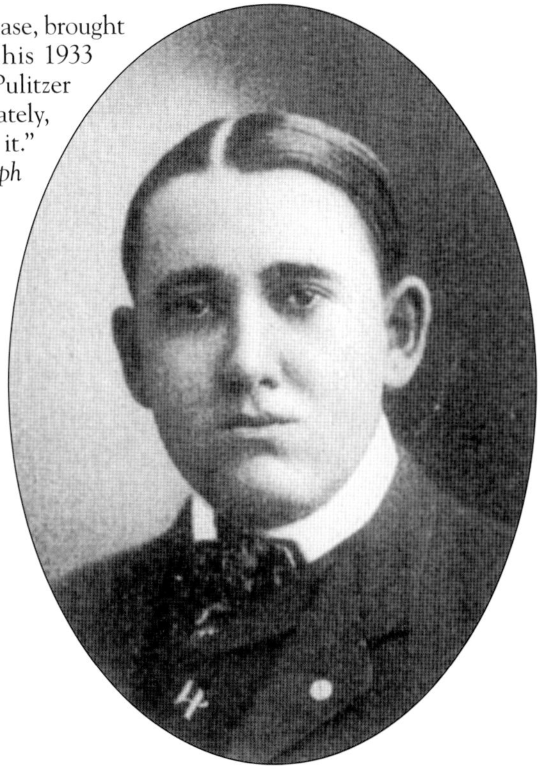

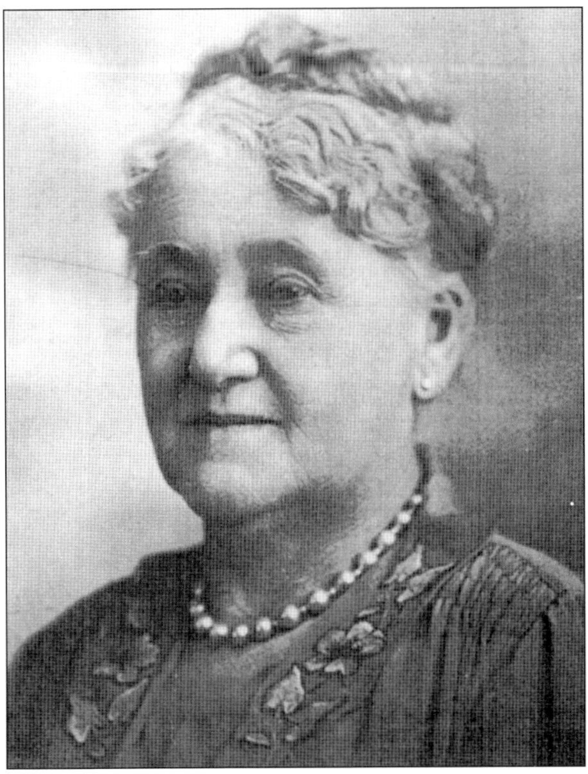

Ruth Catherine Ann Chase, mother of E. P. Chase of Pulitzer fame, was typical of many wives and mothers in early-20th-century Atlantic. In a published tribute to Ruth, her son wrote, "Were it not for the mothers of men, were it not for the world's good women, its institutions would disintegrate and decay. What there is good in a world which has wandered too far afield from its ideals, is kept alive by its mothers."

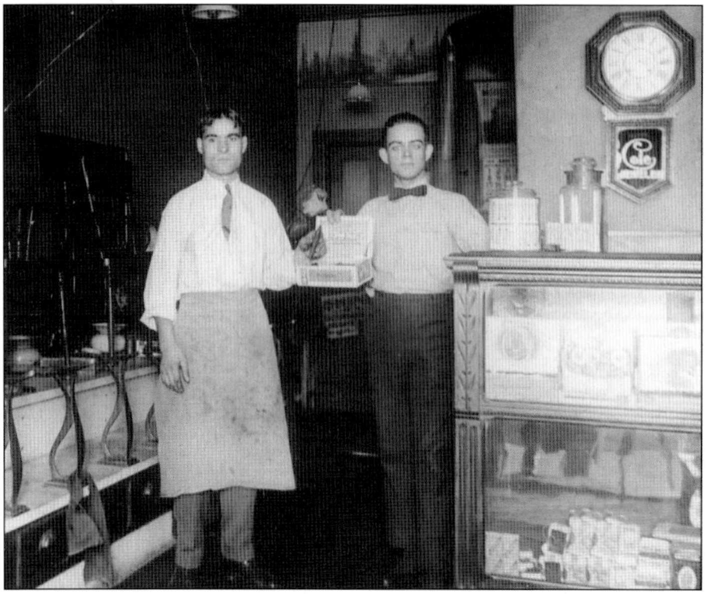

As a young man, Chris Yeanos left his homeland of Greece to come to the United States in 1905. Yeanos recalled that seeing the *Statue of Liberty* in New York Harbor was a great thing. He operated a shoe shine parlor, magazine, and newspaper stand at 516 Chestnut Street. In this photograph, Yeanos is on the left holding a box of the cigars that he also sold. The man on the right is not positively identified but could be his brother.

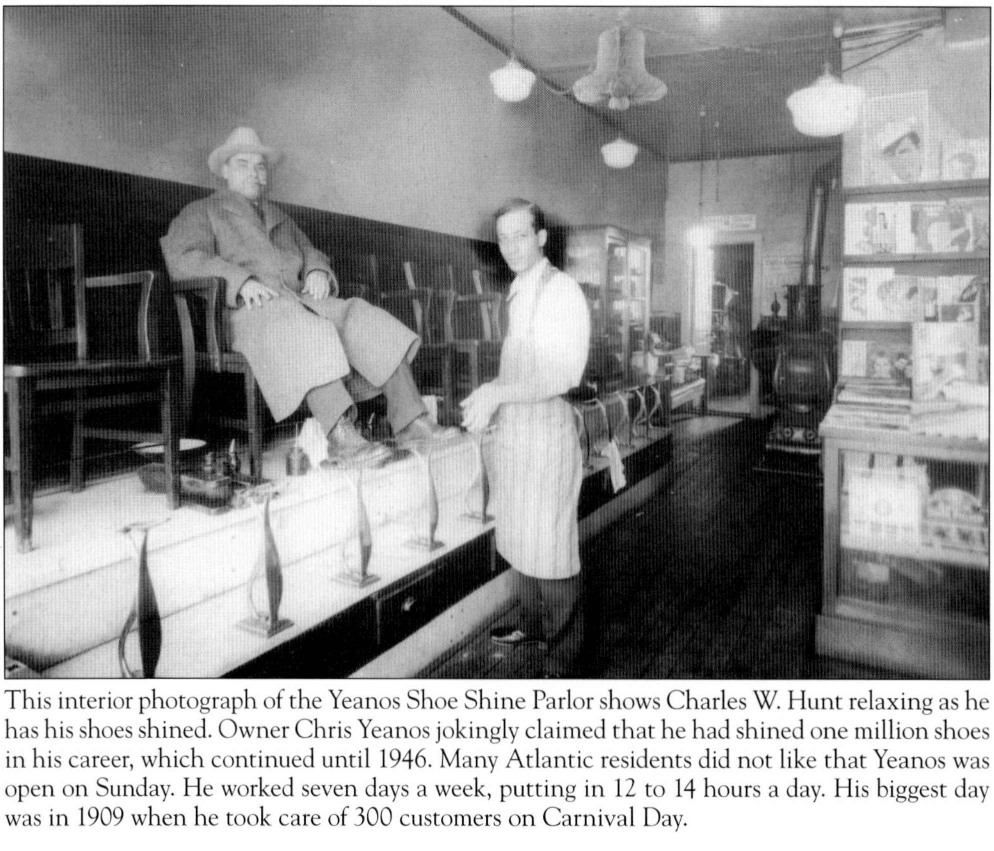

This interior photograph of the Yeanos Shoe Shine Parlor shows Charles W. Hunt relaxing as he has his shoes shined. Owner Chris Yeanos jokingly claimed that he had shined one million shoes in his career, which continued until 1946. Many Atlantic residents did not like that Yeanos was open on Sunday. He worked seven days a week, putting in 12 to 14 hours a day. His biggest day was in 1909 when he took care of 300 customers on Carnival Day.

In 1913, Costas Papathakos was on route to Omaha to look at locations for a new confectionery store. The train stopped in Atlantic to take on passengers, coal, and water. Papathakos took a walk up Chestnut Street and met Chris Yeanos, a fellow countryman from Greece. They talked so long that Papathakos missed his train. Two days later, he had bought a building at 509 Chestnut Street, and in December 1913, the Costas Confectionery was open for business.

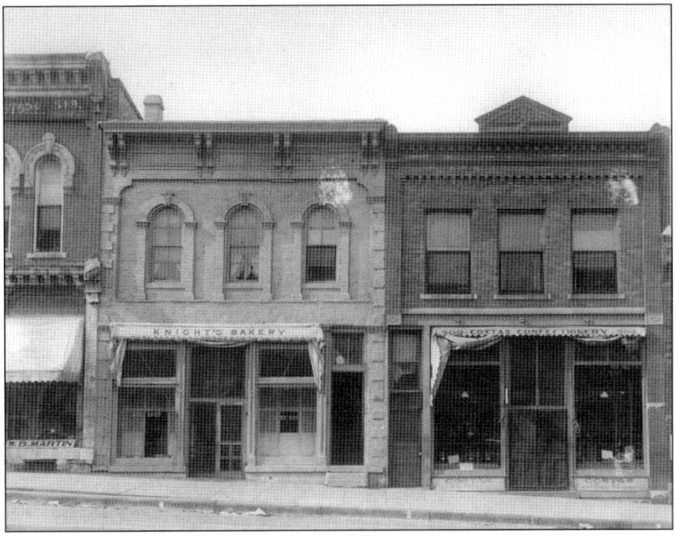

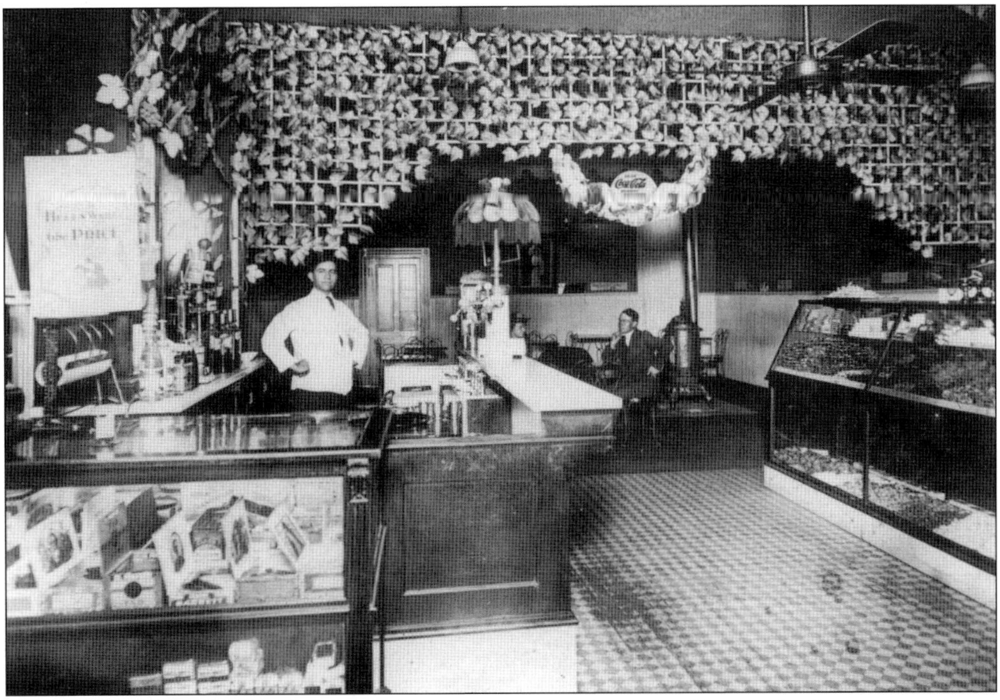

Costas Papathakos is shown behind the counter of his shop, the Costas Confectionery. Costas knew the process for making excellent candy, but time did not allow him to make it from his own recipes except at Christmastime when he made taffy, peanut clusters, and candy canes. When he set up his business in 1913, he had to take out a mortgage. By 1916, he had the mortgage paid off and he married Mary Lianos of Greece. Costas had a photograph taken of the store interior to send to the Lianos family in Greece so that they would know Mary married well. (Courtesy of Jane Papathakos.)

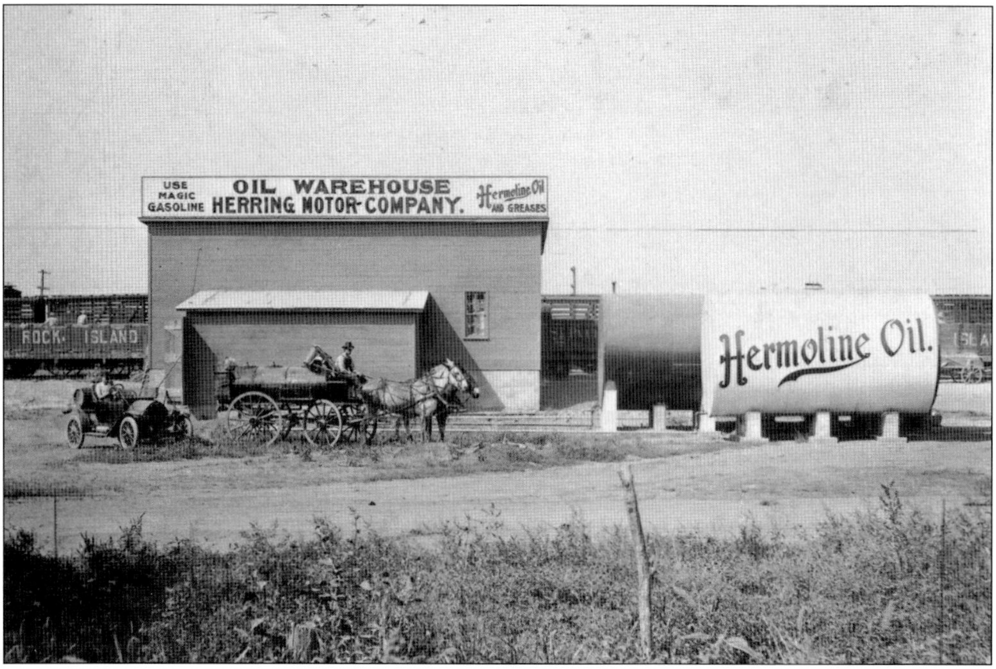

In 1907, the Atlantic Automobile Company was formed by Clyde Herring. Model Ts were shipped from the Ford factory and arrived at the Rock Island depot partially assembled. Cars were removed from crates at the depot, and the wheels were attached. They were then towed to the company's building at Third and Poplar Streets, where assembly would be completed. The Atlantic Automobile Company building (below), along with the filling station (above), covered an entire half block. The massive company building was erected at a cost of $200,000.

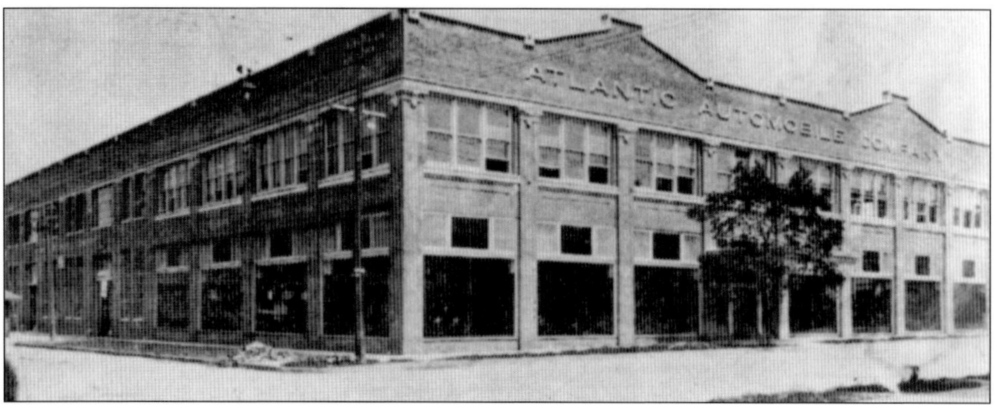

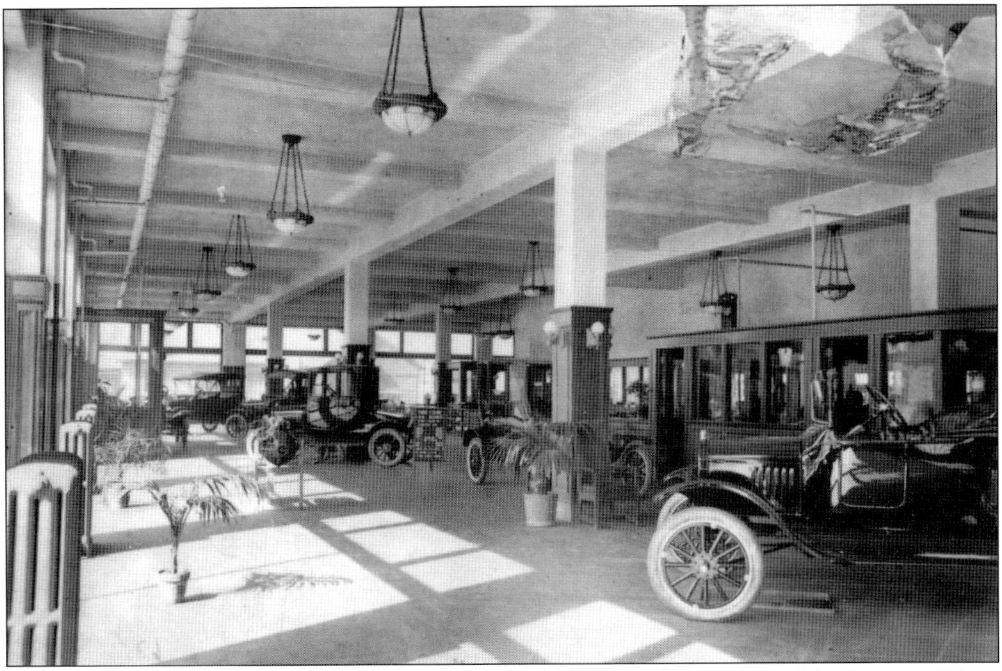

The interior of the Atlantic Automobile Company included an elaborate, heated display area. When the cars had been assembled, they were moved into this showroom to be sold. The showroom was very unusual for its day in that it featured elaborate chandeliers, huge plate-glass windows, and potted plants. Owner Clyde Herring was the Ford Motor Company agent for the state of Iowa. He was so successful that by 1910, he had acquired $3 million worth of Des Moines real estate.

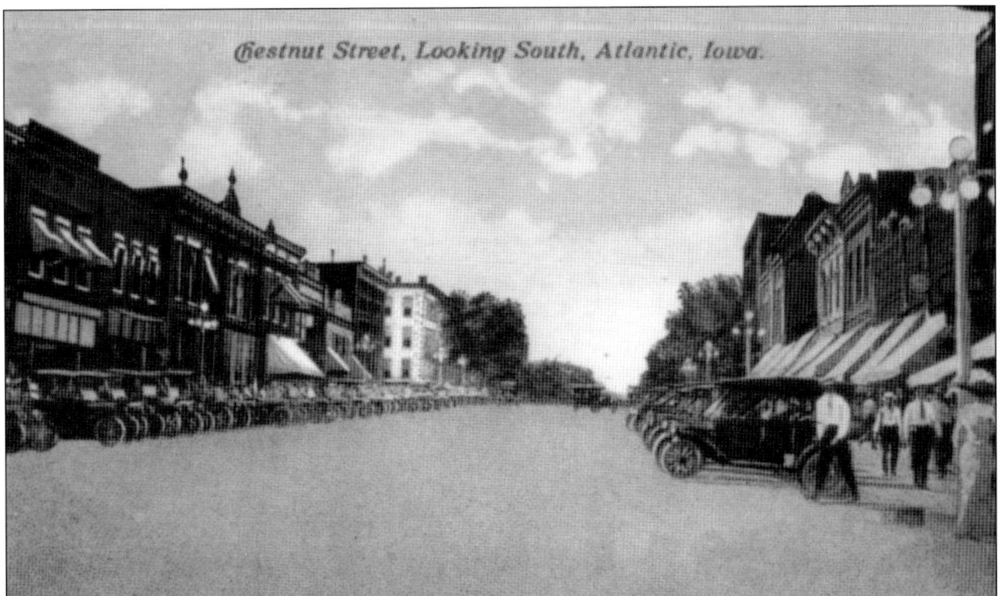

From time to time, Ford Model Ts from the Atlantic Automobile Company would be displayed on both sides of Chestnut Street. This was a promotion by the company to provide a better opportunity for prospective buyers to view the vehicles. When many more Atlantic streets were paved, car sales increased at a rapid rate. It was a prosperous business to be in at the time.

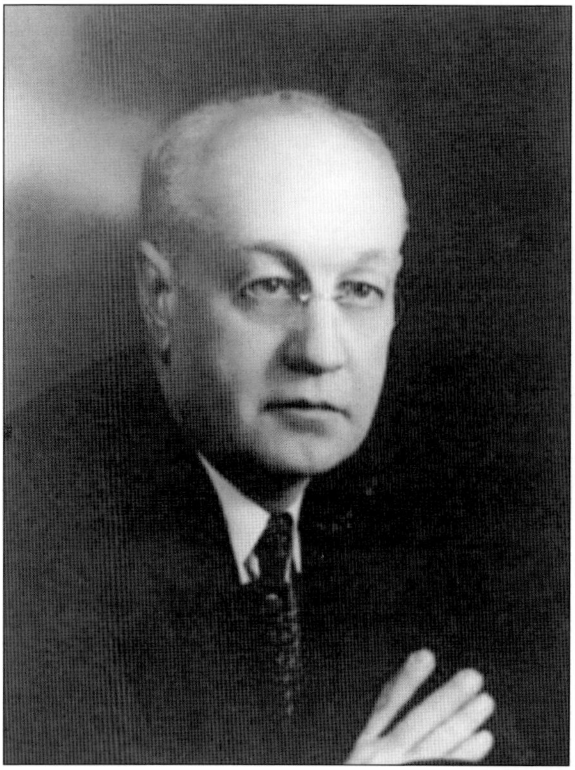

Clyde LaVerne Herring, an Atlantic businessman, served as both Iowa governor and U.S. senator. He was the subject of a cover story for a 1935 issue of *Time* magazine. In 1932, Herring was elected governor of Iowa on the Democratic ticket, only the second Democrat to be so elected since the founding of the Republican Party in 1854.

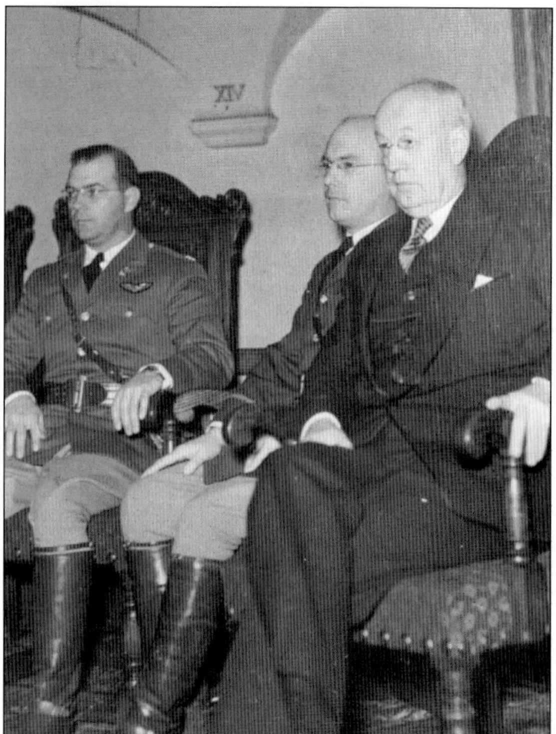

This photograph was taken at St. Ambrose Cathedral on Thanksgiving Day. The men, from left to right, are Lt. Col. W. Gatschel, Gen. Charles H. Grahl, and Gov. Clyde Herring (1932–1935). After serving two terms as governor, Herring was elected to the U.S. Senate in 1936. Following his term as senator, he returned to the automotive business. He was named by Pres. Franklin D. Roosevelt as assistant administrator of the Office of Price Administration, the wartime price regulatory agency. (Courtesy of the State Historical Society of Iowa.)

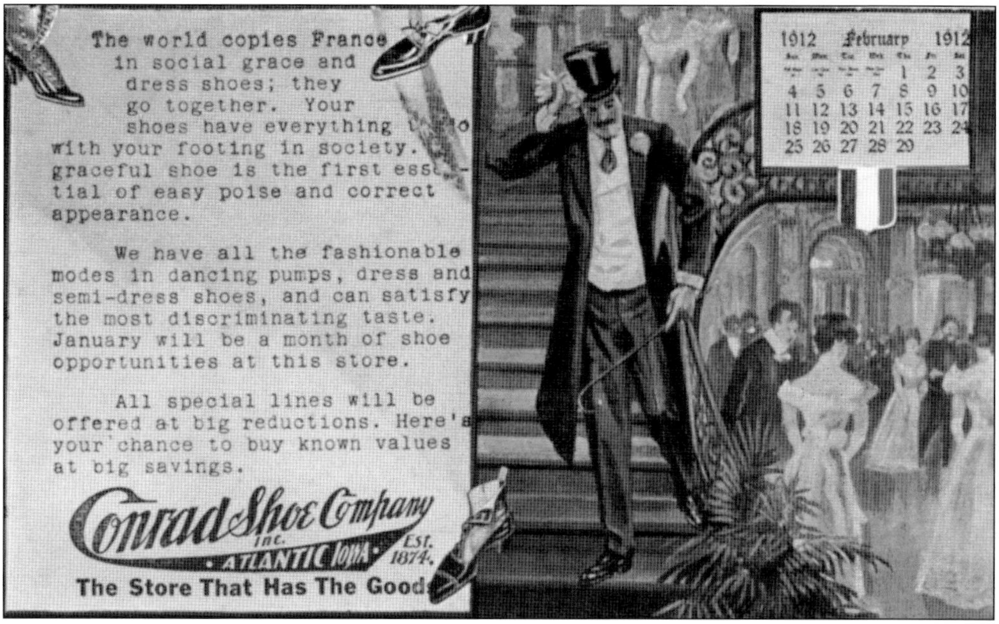

Many businesses in the early 1900s were quick to realize the power of advertising. On March 3, 1878, Congress had established second-class postal rates, which provided an incentive for businesses to use the U.S. mail to advertise their wares. Printing companies flourished as enterprises developed postcards, flyers, and calendars promoting their products. The advertising card above is for the Conrad Shoe Company of Atlantic. It proudly claims to be "The Store that Has the Goods." The card below advertises J. A. Giffen Furniture and Undertaking. The creative, flowery card reads, "A good book, a billowy armchair, and the peace of one's own fireside, is better than a throne."

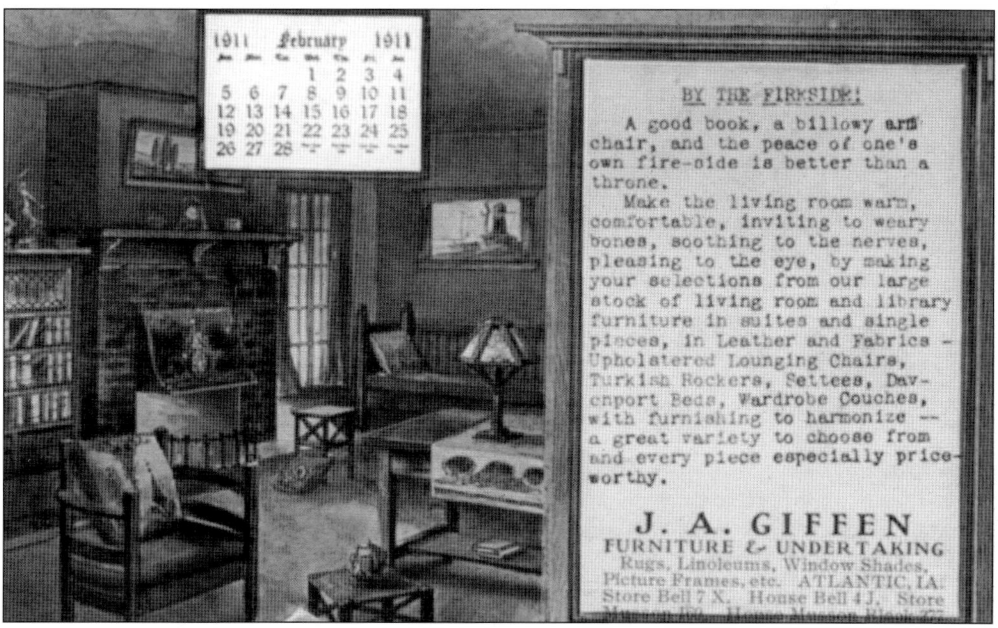

H. M. Boorman,

Attorney and Counseler at Law.
Attorney for Atlantic National Bank, Exchange Bank, Marne. Ex-Cashier Atlantic National Bank.

Dr. U. S. Mullins.

PHYSICIAN AND SURGEON.

Opera House Block.

C. T. Wornom,

Justice of the Peace and Notary Public

Collections Promptly Attended to.
First hallway north of Post Office.

J. L. Winne,

FUNERAL DIRECTOR

AND EMBALMER.

Full Line of Furniture. 315 Chestnut St.

C. P. Meredith,

Agricultural Implements.

Coal, Lime, Cement, Etc.

Northwestern Machine Shops,

H. D. JACOBSON, Prop.

GENERAL & BICYCLE REPAIRING

Model Making a Specialty.

Commercial Hotel,

Best $1 a day house in the city. Good barn in connection.

C. M. WILLEY, Proprietor.

LESTER L. TILDEN,

Safe Insurance

Against Fire, Lightning and Tornadoes
In Reliable Stock Companies.

ATLANTIC, IOWA.

The city of Atlantic is located on the Nishnabotna river, and on the C. R. I & P. Ry. at the junction of the Griswold and Audubon branches of the same road in Cass county, of which it is the judicial seat. It is 63 miles northeast of Omaha, 82 west of Des Moines and 440 west of Chicago. The town was laid out in 1868 and building commenced the same year. The town was incorporated in 1870. The city has gas and electric plants, the streets being lighted by electricity. The water works, which are of the Holly, high-pressure system are complete in every respect and have a capacity of 3,000,000 gallons per day. Water of unequalled purity is obtained from artesian wells.

Atlantic is the trade center of a large and prosperous agricultural district and is supplied with 13 churches, 4 banks, 3 regular newspapers, THE CASS COUNTY DEMOCRAT, The Telegraph and Messenger. There are here a number of elevators, flour mills, foundry and machine shops, a planning mill, broom factory, bottling works, creamery, corn canning factory, a tank station of the Standard Oil Co., brick yards, opera house, etc. The city has two private and four public schools. An excellent fire department furnishes protection against fires. Large shipments of hogs, cattle, sheep, grain, flour, fruit, potatoes, canned corn and peas are made from this point. The principal secret societies have lodges here; the Masons, Odd Fellows and Woodmen having fine buildings.

The city is beautifully situated on the sides and tops of several gently rolling hills and is surrounded by some of the finest farming land in the world. The streets are wide, well graded and drained and have plenty of shade trees. The city has risen rapidly in population and commercial importance until it now ranks as one of the most important and prosperous cities in southwestern Iowa. It now has a population of over 5000 souls. Atlantic offers exceptional opportunities to manufacturing concerns and mercantile establishments. Good farming lands can be purchased at from $35 to $75 per acre.

If you want to know more about Cass County farm lands and loans write

J. F. HUBBARD,
FARM LOANS.
ATLANTIC, - - - IOWA.

Brownie Patent Flour

MADE BY

ATLANTIC ROLLER MILLS

Manufacturers of Flour, Feed and Meal

S. E. Grant,

ATLANTIC MARBLE WORKS,

DEALER IN

Marble and Granite.

R. M. Westphalen,

Dealer in

FRESH, SALT AND SMOKED MEATS.

Eggers Bros.

Watches, Clocks, Diamonds,
Silverware, Jewelry, Etc.

Fine Watch and Jewelry Repairing a Specialty.

P. Zetterberg,

Fine Merchant Tailor,

East Fourth Street.

Goodale & Rasmussen,

CONTRACTORS AND BUILDERS.
Water Tanks of All Kinds.
Plans and Specifications Furnished.

The Delmonico

LUNCH and ICE CREAM PARLOR.

Franklin & Arn, Props.

CLARENCE HEDGES

Palace Livery

Cor. 5th & Walnut St.

B. & O. Illustrated Letter Head. Printed by The Democrat. Fine Commercial and Society Printers, Atlantic, Iowa. Mail Orders Solicited.

The *Democrat* printed this early advertisement around 1900. It contains interesting information about Atlantic and was sponsored by several concerns. This type of promotion actually served as stationery since the back of the page was used for business correspondence. In this way, owners could take care of business and, at the same time, promote Atlantic. The message on this letterhead was sent from J. L. Winne, a furniture dealer and funeral director, to a Des Moines firm from which he ordered a no. 39 cradle.

Four

Building a City

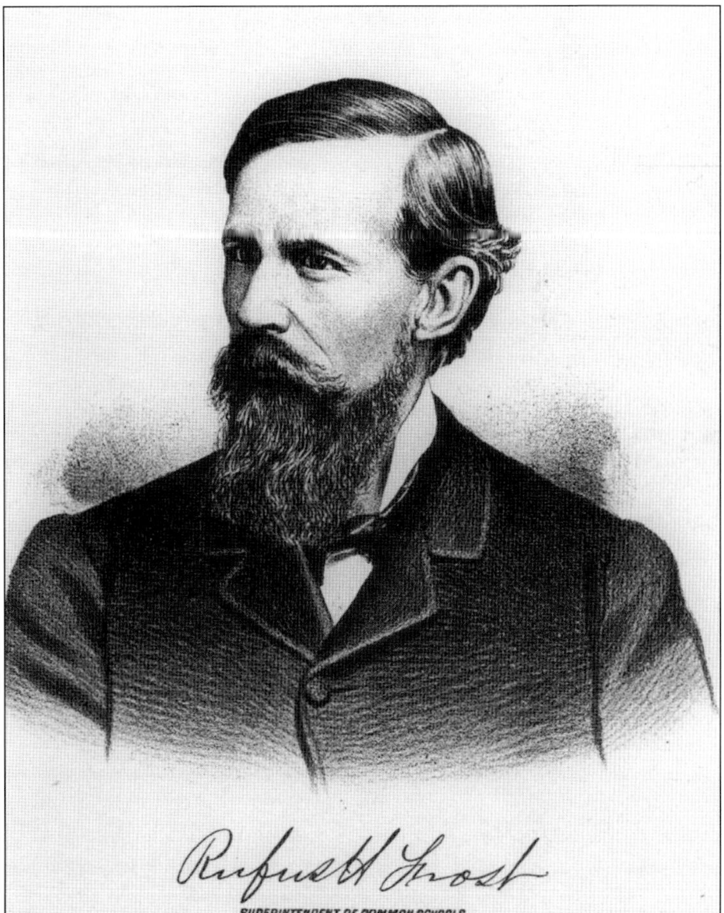

Rufus H. Frost came to Atlantic in 1876 to accept the position of principal at West Side School. Frost was highly praised as an educator and as a man of sterling integrity. After serving at West Side for three years, he was elected as the superintendent of schools for Cass County, a position to which he was repeatedly reelected. His wife, Julia Stanard Frost, was an accomplished teacher.

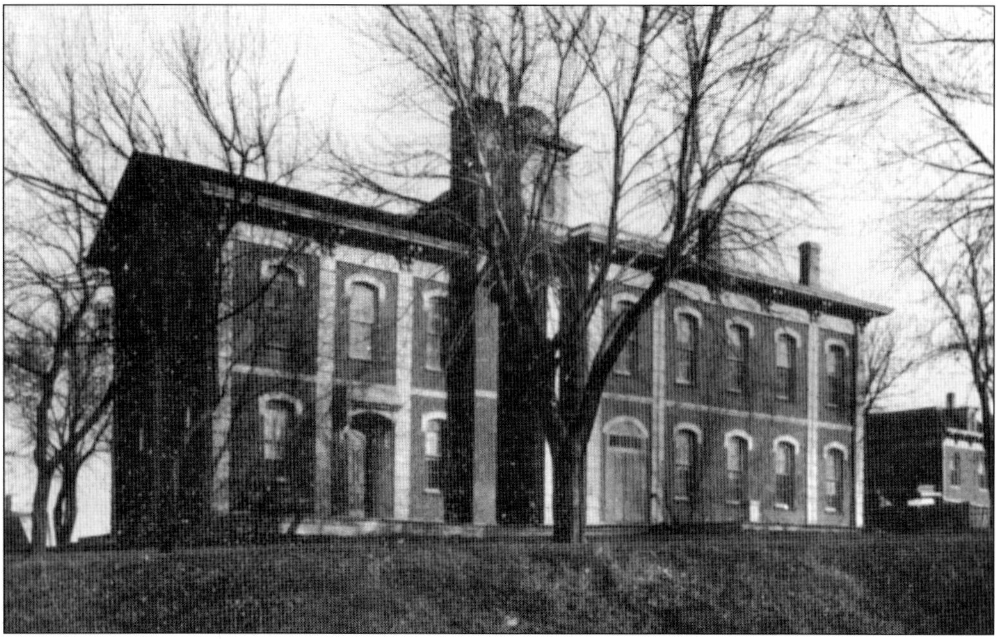

In 1870, the first school board was elected and moved immediately to purchase land on the east side of town for the erection of a school. The Neimeyer brothers were awarded the contract with a completion price of $9,288. Atlantic's first school building, the East Side School (above) was finished and occupied in January 1871. It was built on a hill, and the structure is prominent in many early panoramic views of the town. S. R. Manning served as principal and was assisted by his wife, along with Lucy Terry and S. V. K. Towne. In 1875, the West Side School (below) was built at a cost of $6,000. The teachers were Ada Duncan, Kate and Madge Tupper, and Alice Baugh. Rufus H. Frost served as principal.

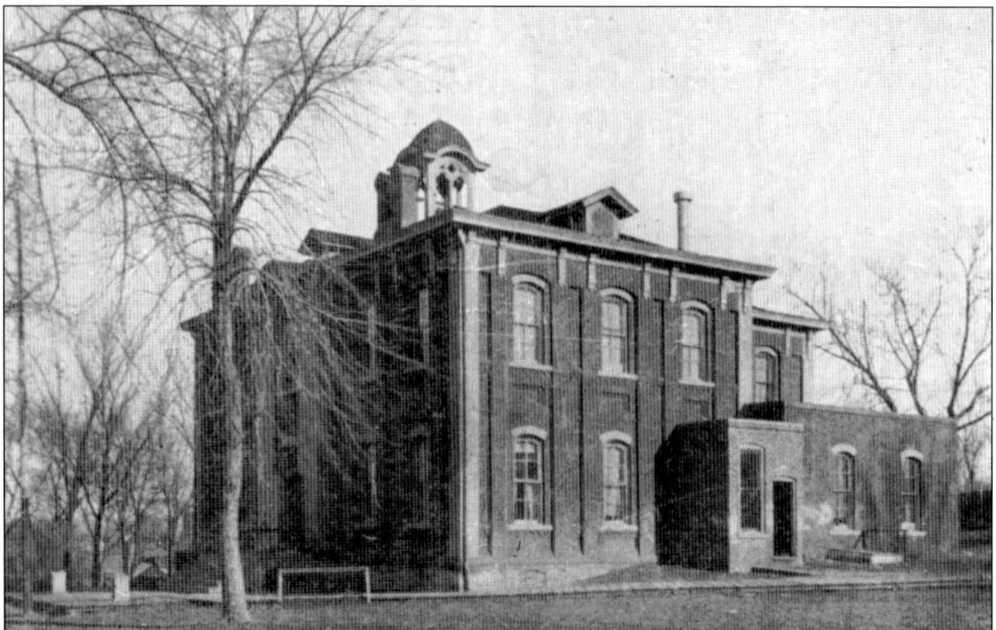

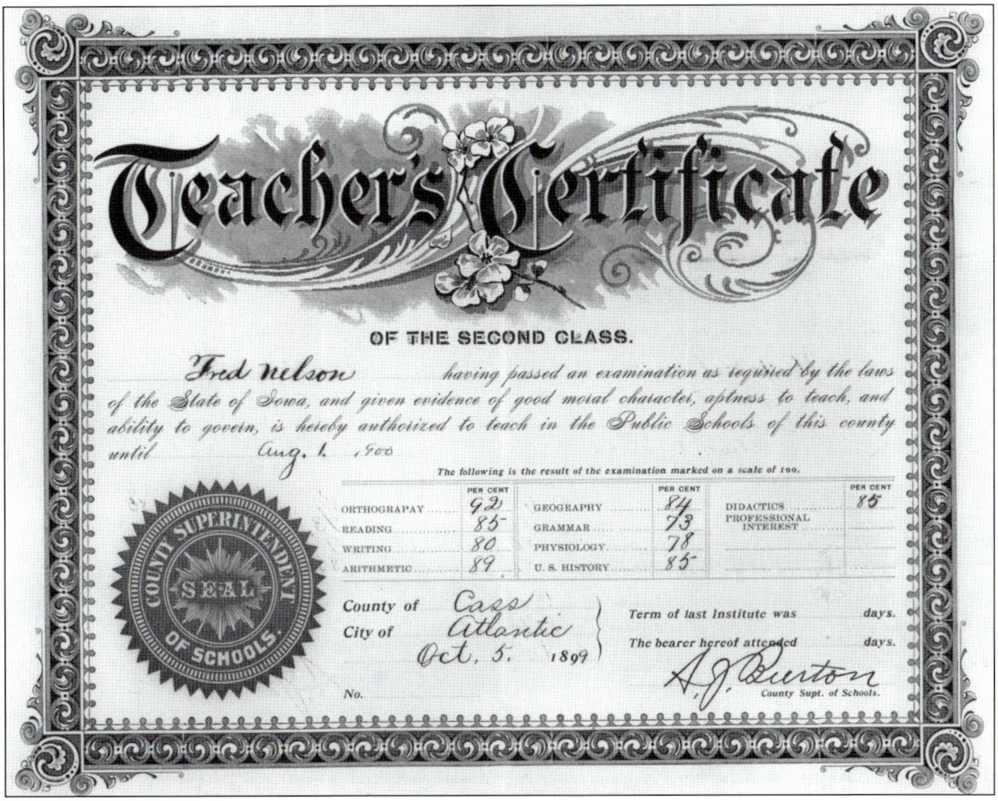

Teacher's Certificate

OF THE SECOND CLASS.

Fred Nelson having passed an examination as required by the laws of the State of Iowa, and given evidence of good moral character, aptness to teach, and ability to govern, is hereby authorized to teach in the Public Schools of this county until Aug. 1. 1900

The following is the result of the examination marked on a scale of 100.

	PER CENT		PER CENT		PER CENT
ORTHOGRAPAY	92	GEOGRAPHY	84	DIDACTICS	85
READING	85	GRAMMAR	73	PROFESSIONAL INTEREST	
WRITING	80	PHYSIOLOGY	78		
ARITHMETIC	89	U. S. HISTORY	85		

COUNTY SUPERINTENDENT SEAL OF SCHOOLS

County of Cass
City of Atlantic
Oct. 5. 1899

Term of last Institute was days.
The bearer hereof attended days.

No.

A. J. Burton
County Supt. of Schools.

In order to teach in Iowa, a person was required to hold a teaching certificate. This certificate was presented by A. J. Burton, county superintendent of schools, to Fred Nelson in October 1899 and was good only until August 1900. It states that the recipient must have good moral character, an aptness to teach, and the ability to govern.

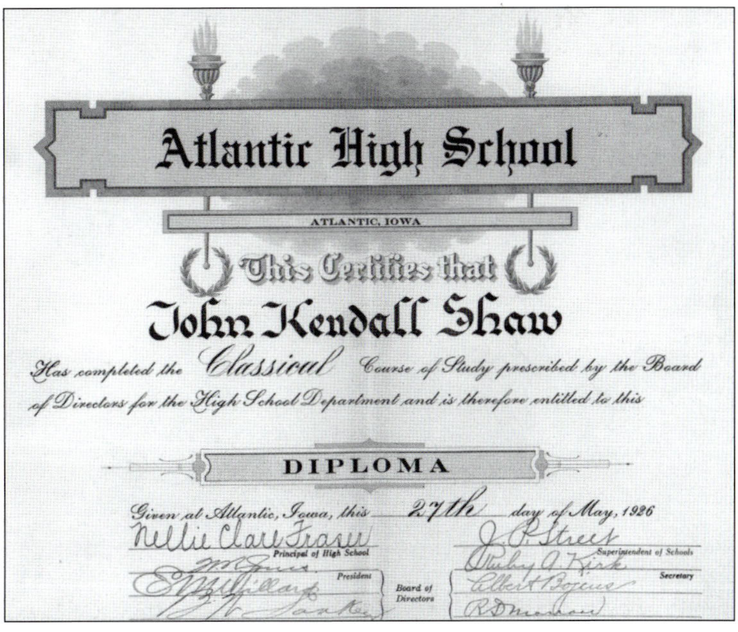

Atlantic High School

ATLANTIC, IOWA

This Certifies that

John Kendall Shaw

Has completed the Classical Course of Study prescribed by the Board of Directors for the High School Department and is therefore entitled to this

DIPLOMA

Given at Atlantic, Iowa, this 27th day of May, 1926

Nellie Claire Fraser — Principal of High School
J. P. Street — Superintendent of Schools
President
Board of Directors
Ruby A. Kirk — Secretary
Albert Bojens

John Kendall Shaw's diploma is typical of documents presented to graduating seniors in the early 1900s in Iowa. The high school program is defined as the "classical course of study." This diploma was presented to Shaw on May 27, 1926, by Atlantic High School principal Nellie Claire Fraser.

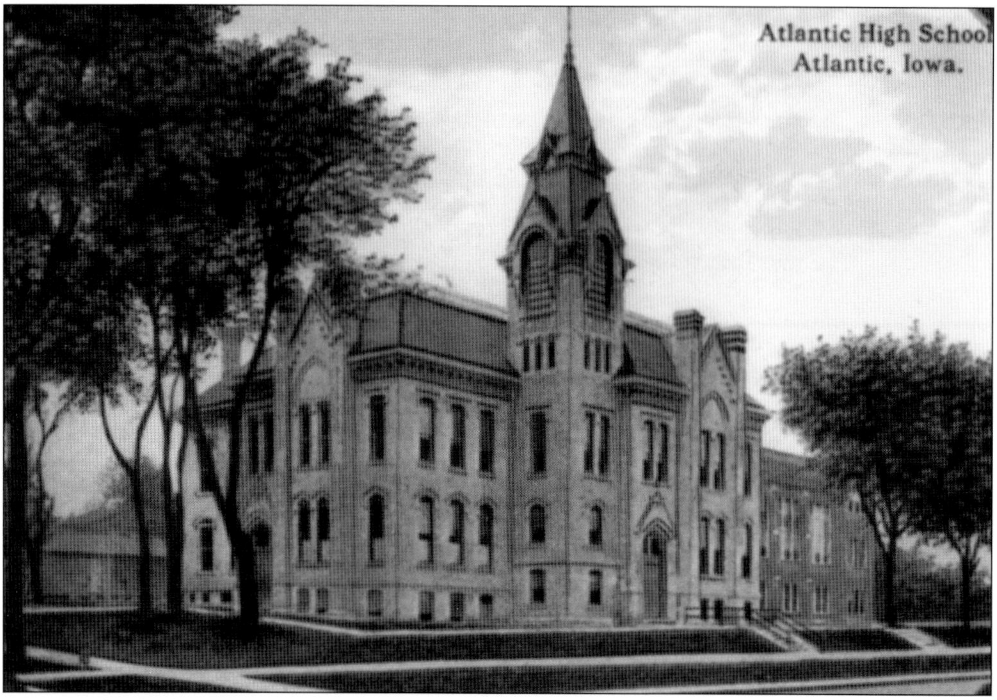

In 1877, this high school was built with tuition set at $6 per term. Books were provided free of charge to families who could not afford to buy them. An early superintendent's pay was $600 per year, and teachers' pay ran from $37 to $50 per month. It should come as no surprise that one of the members of the first school board in Atlantic was Franklin H. Whitney.

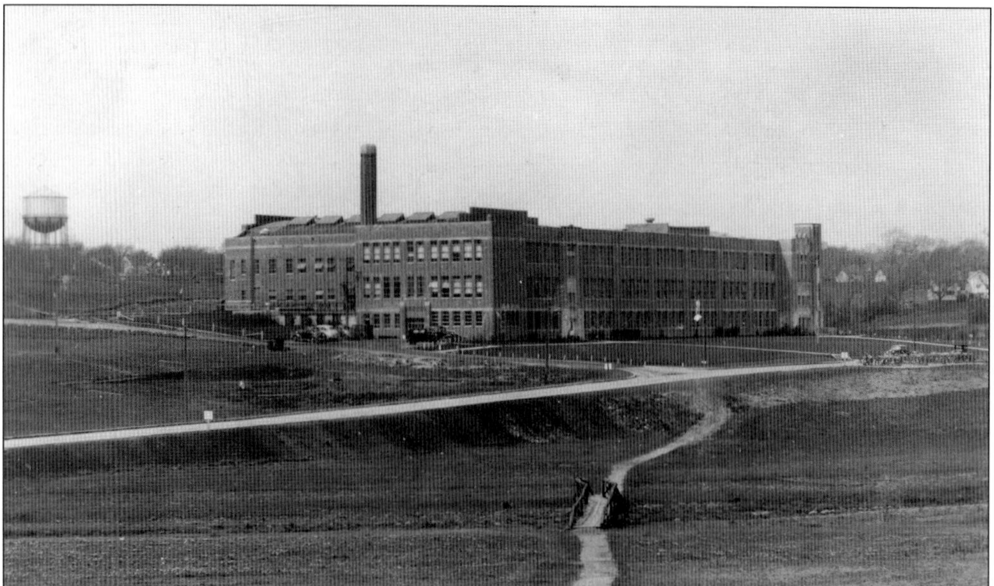

In 1935, Atlantic voted to construct a new junior-senior high school. This building was dedicated on July 30, 1937, and cost $330,000. In the 1950s, the Atlantic School District became known as the Atlantic Community School District with the addition of the Pymosa and Marne Districts as well as a number of small country schools. By 1967, the school was valued at $3,050,000.

This photograph of the 29 Atlantic graduating seniors of the 1911 class shows the formality with which high school graduation was associated at the time. The girls as well as the boys are attired in their caps and gowns with a tie obviously being required dress for the occasion. The photographs were taken and then artfully arranged by Hal H. Egbert of the Egbert Studio.

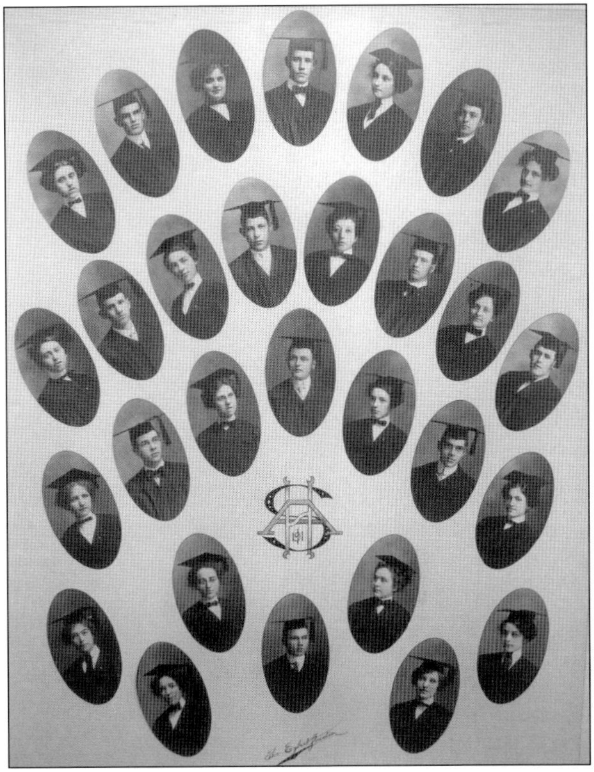

This photograph is of the 1901 Atlantic High School football team. The players are, from left to right, (first row) Rasty Owen, Joe Bruff, and Bill McFadddon; (second row) Buck Jones, ? Ashton, Bert Laird, Jim Wycoff, and Earl Wilson; (third row) Roy Camblin, Max Ross, Earl Hodges, and Ross Camblin; (fourth row) Frank Libby, Ruppert Lee, Soccer Vale, Jack Flemming, and Professor Laartz.

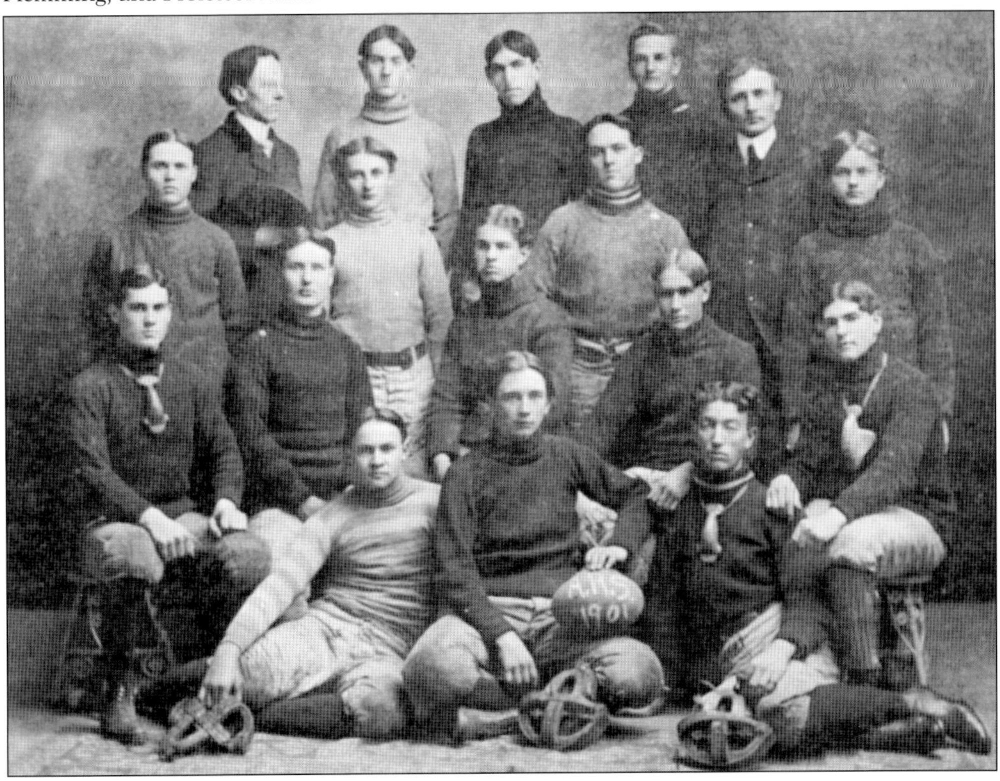

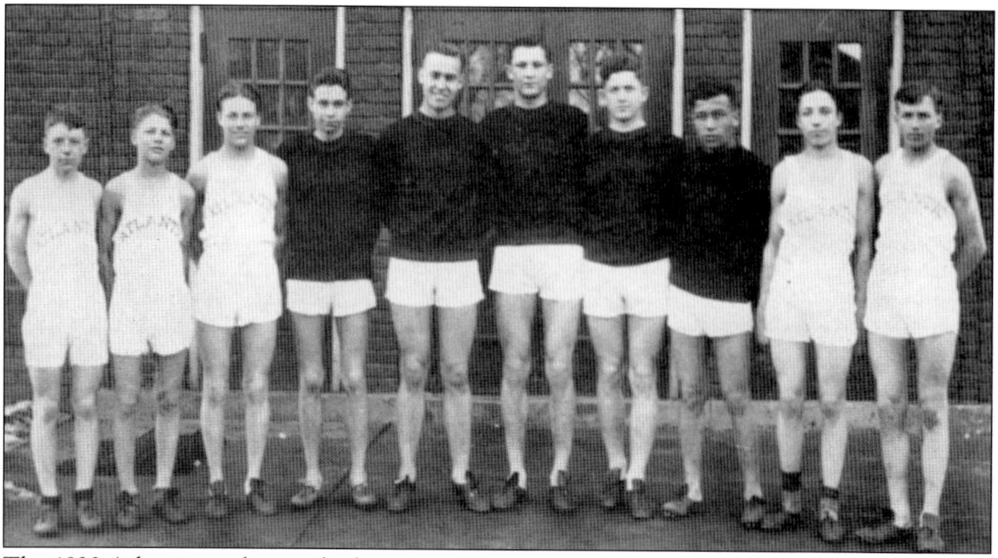

The 1930 Atlantic track team had a successful season with a number of new recruits and eight regulars. In 1929, John Smoller was captain of the team and had set a conference record with a discus throw of 109 feet, 4 inches. This Atlantic team was considered to be one of the best in southwest Iowa. The team members from left to right are Russell Miller, Edward Williams, Wayne Joyce, Charles Rudolph, John Smoller, Ronald Skoda, William Allender, Nacho Manriquez, Maurice Joyce, and John Wheatley.

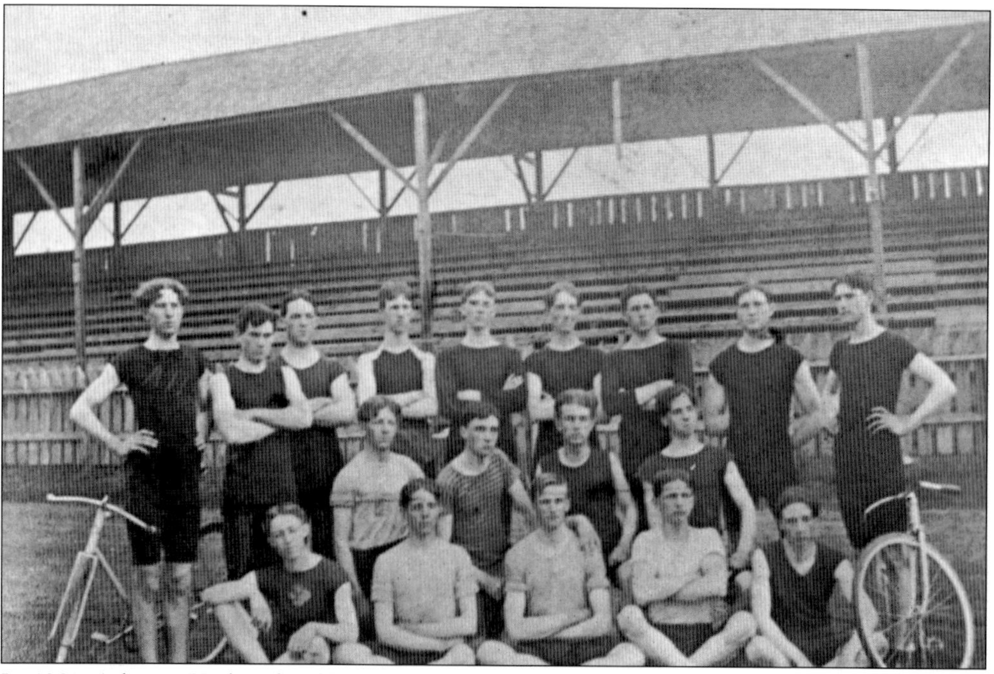

In 1901, Atlantic High School had a track and cycle club. The team held track meets at the fairgrounds on Fifth Street. Members of the team were Karl Steinke, George Taylor, Will Wilson, Bert Laird, Earl Fox, John Jones, Joe Bruff, Charles Hully, Earl Low, John O'Connell, Earl Hodge, George Johnson, Shirley Allen, Ed Mumby, Lou Low, Rupert Lee, and Delmar Herbert (standing at far left).

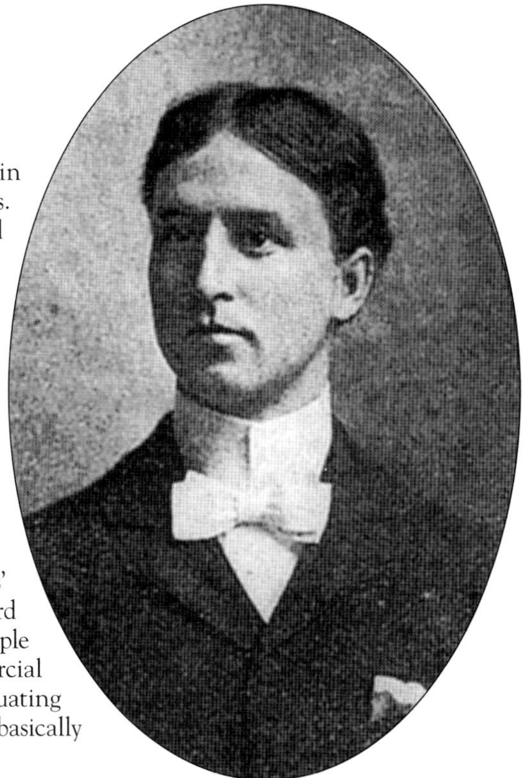

Prof. J. S. McMiniemee, at right, was born in Denison, Iowa, in 1874 but moved to Illinois. He attended the Illinois Normal School and graduated from Dixon Business College, Northern Illinois College of Shorthand and Typing, and Illinois College of Drawing and Penmanship. McMiniemee was considered to be one of the best teachers of penmanship in the country. He resigned his position at Princeton High School in Illinois to organize the Atlantic Commercial College. Due to the high standing of the institution and McMiniemee's excellent reputation, the school could not meet the demand for first-class office help. The fact that the Merchants' Association of Atlantic advanced $270 toward the rent for the schoolrooms shows that the people of Atlantic appreciated a professional commercial college. Below is a photograph of an early graduating class. Each graduate wears a beautiful hairstyle, basically like her classmates but amazingly individual.

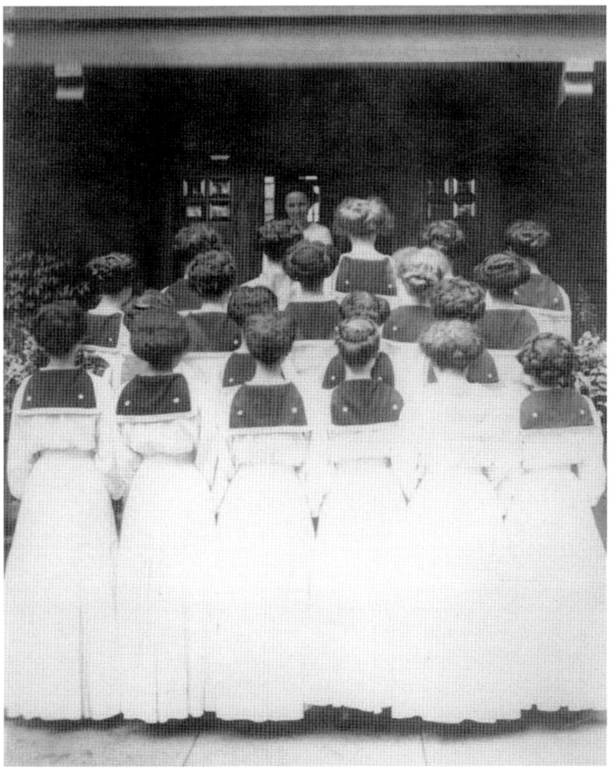

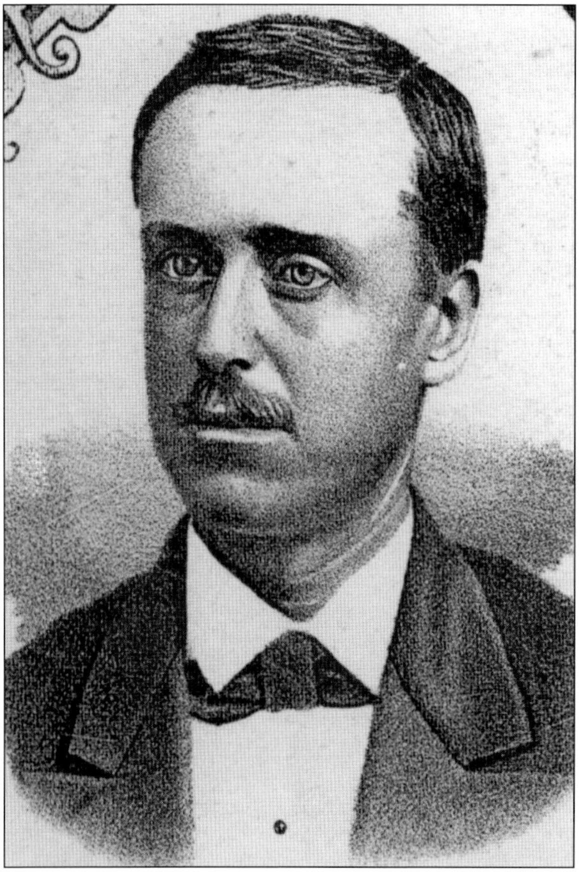

Dr. J. M. Emmert graduated with a medical degree from Jefferson Medical College in Philadelphia in 1872 and moved to Atlantic in 1874. Always interested in politics, he served as an Iowa representative at the 1884 National Democratic Convention that nominated Grover Cleveland for president. Emmert was a member of the Iowa State Medical Society and became its president in 1889. He was elected as a Democratic state senator in 1897.

In 1902, Dr. J. M. Emmert read the oration for the State of Iowa before the American Medical Society meeting in Saratoga, New York. Emmert was the medical examiner for a number of East Coast insurance companies. He was a member of many civic organizations in Atlantic, including all four Masonic groups, and lived at 601 Oak Street.

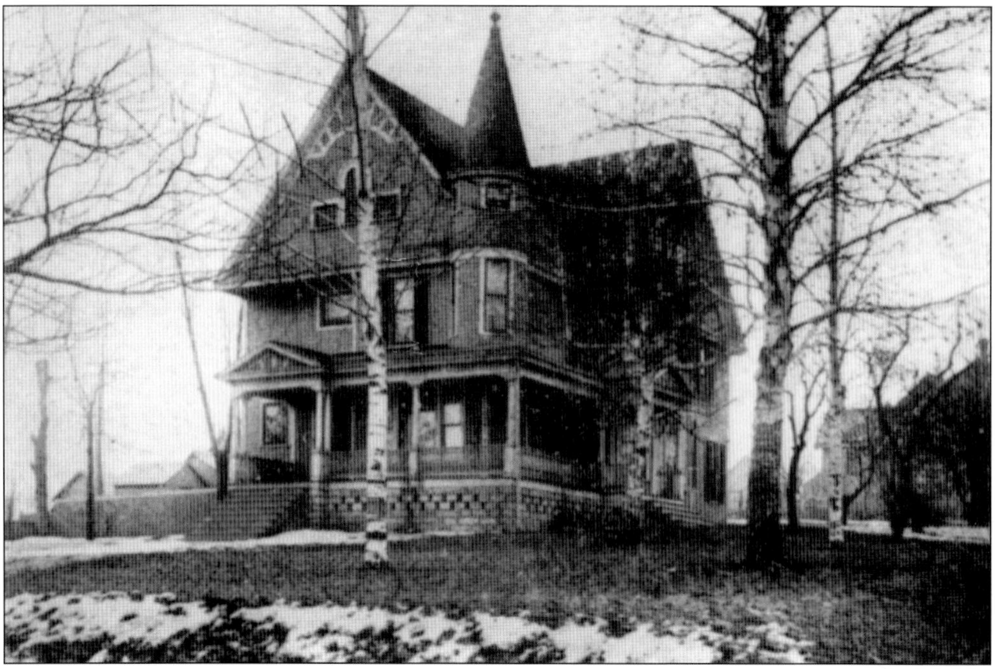

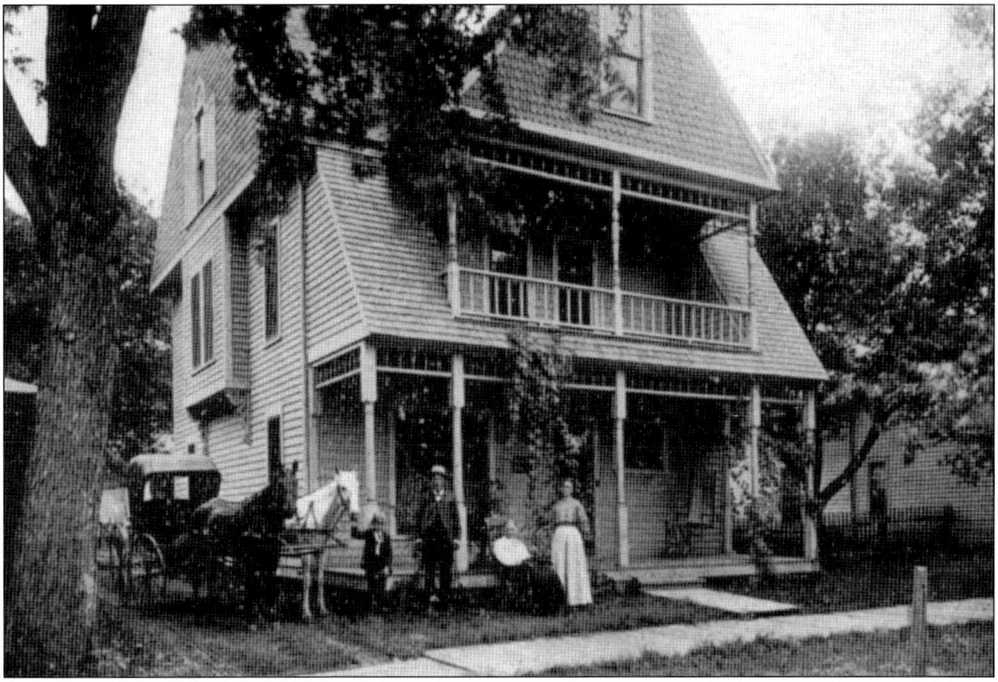

This is the home of Dr. William C. Egan. As a boy of 15, Egan wanted to fight in the Civil War. Although his physician father was opposed, William enlisted, fought at Morgan's Run, was wounded, and, due to disability, was discharged in April 1864. He took up the study of medicine, graduated from Rush Medical College in Chicago, and moved to Atlantic in June 1877. Egan set up a medical practice, became a prominent doctor, and served as Cass County coroner for many years.

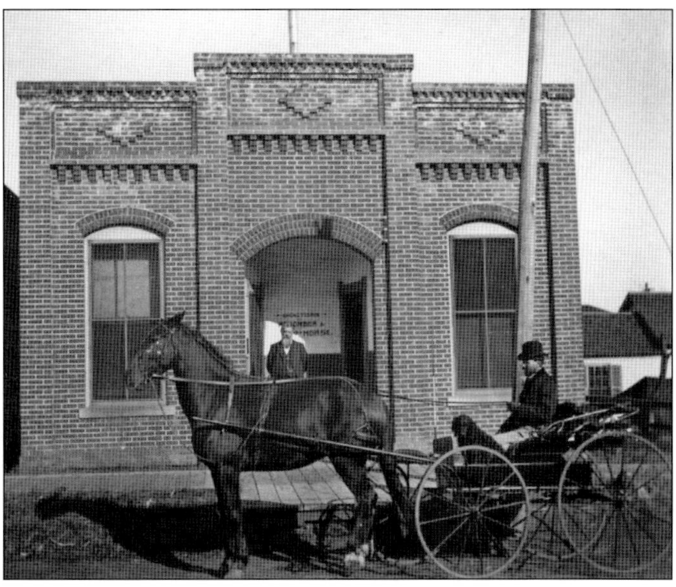

Beginning in 1879, Dr. A. P. Macomber, shown here standing in the doorway, practiced medicine in Atlantic. He also served as president of the State of Iowa Homeopathic Medical Society. His wife was in practice with him and specialized in the diseases of women and children. The horse and carriage in front of the office shows J. W. Cuykendall and his dog, Duke. Duke appears several times in the vintage photographs in this book. (Courtesy of the State Historical Society of Iowa.)

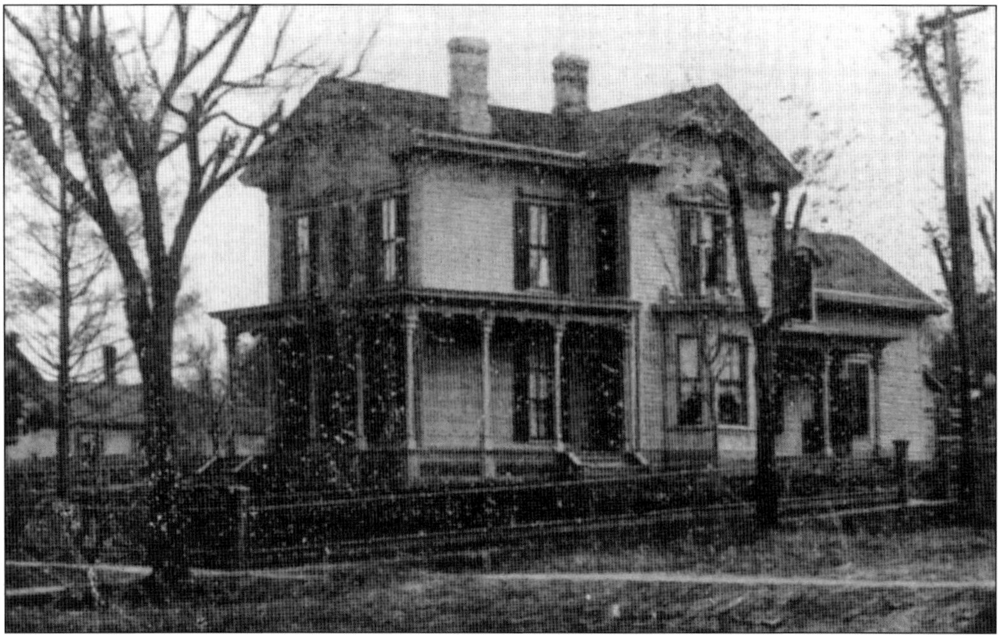

In 1903, this home of druggist and former mayor J. B. Jones (above) was purchased by the newly formed Atlantic Hospital Association and designated as the first hospital in Atlantic. Located at Fifth and Oak Streets, it could accommodate 10 patients. Around 1910, the hospital (below) was enlarged by the addition of 16 rooms. It provided courses and rooms for student nurses. Several nurses sit on the steps in the later image. Management was turned over to the Atlantic Hospital Corporation in 1916.

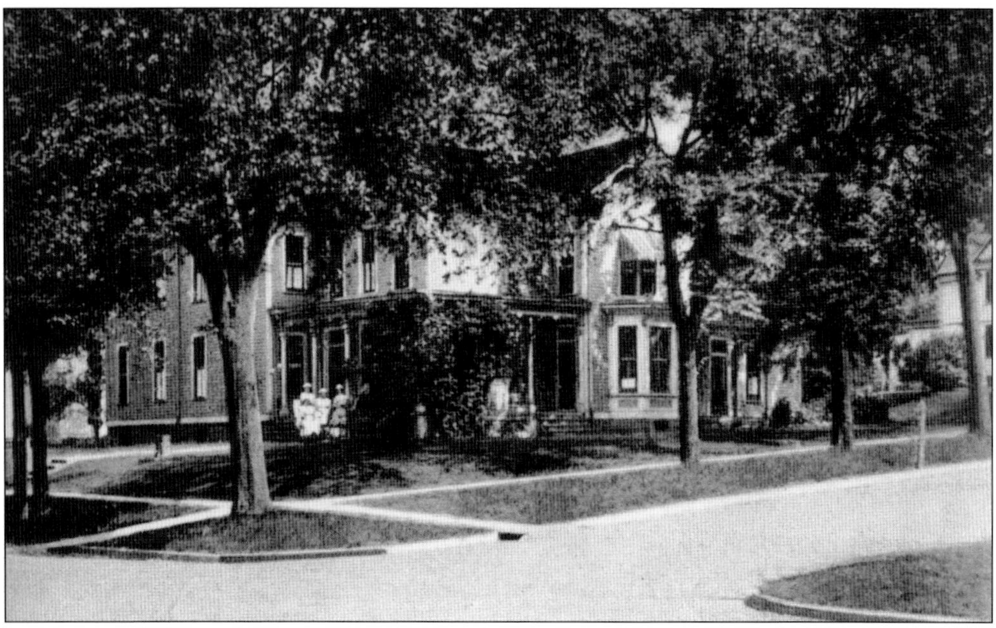

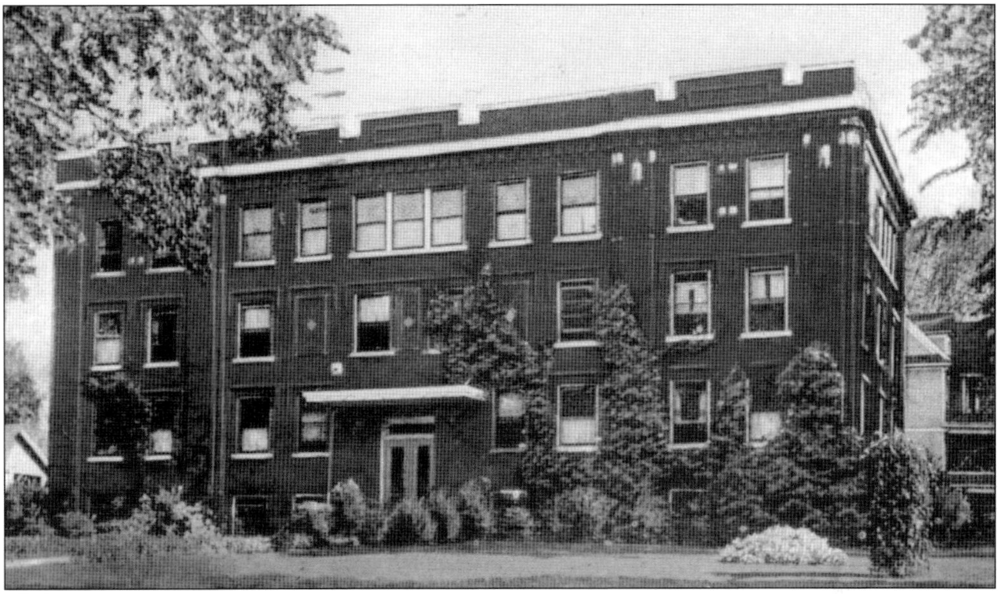

Atlantic's second hospital was a big improvement over the original one. The substantial brick structure was erected in 1916. Connected with it was a school for nurses, and as at the first hospital, space was set aside to be used as a residence for the student nurses until another building was purchased for that purpose. This photograph was taken in 1918.

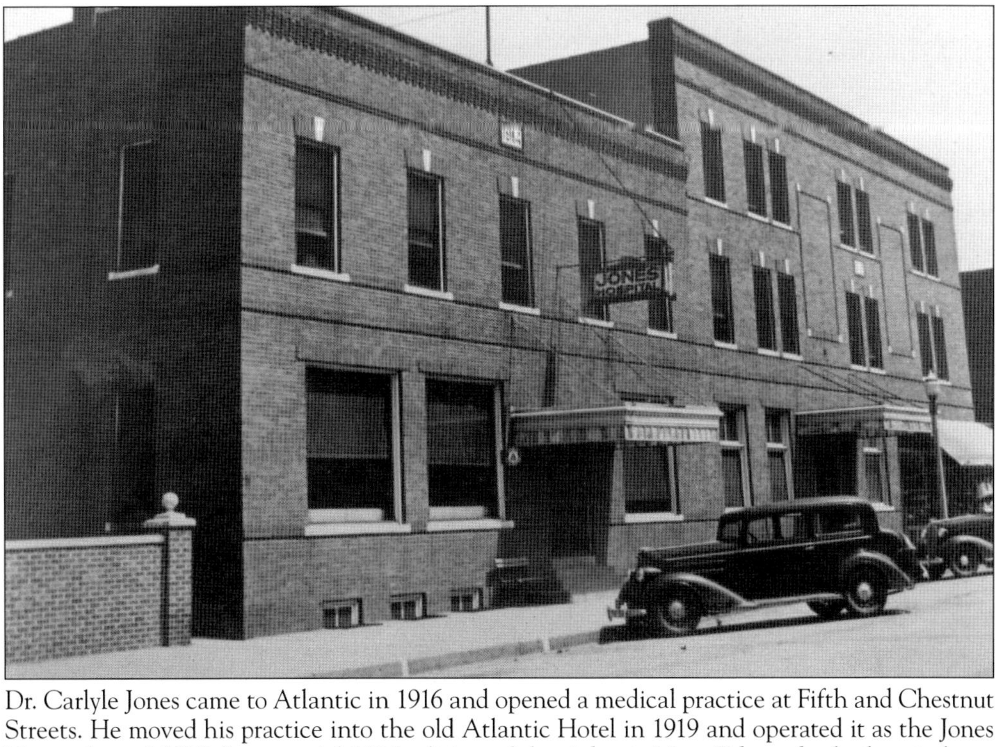

Dr. Carlyle Jones came to Atlantic in 1916 and opened a medical practice at Fifth and Chestnut Streets. He moved his practice into the old Atlantic Hotel in 1919 and operated it as the Jones Hospital until 1939. In a special 1929 edition of the *Atlantic News-Telegraph*, the hospital was reported to have 35 patient rooms, eight nurses, three doctors, and several rooms where patients' family members could stay when necessary.

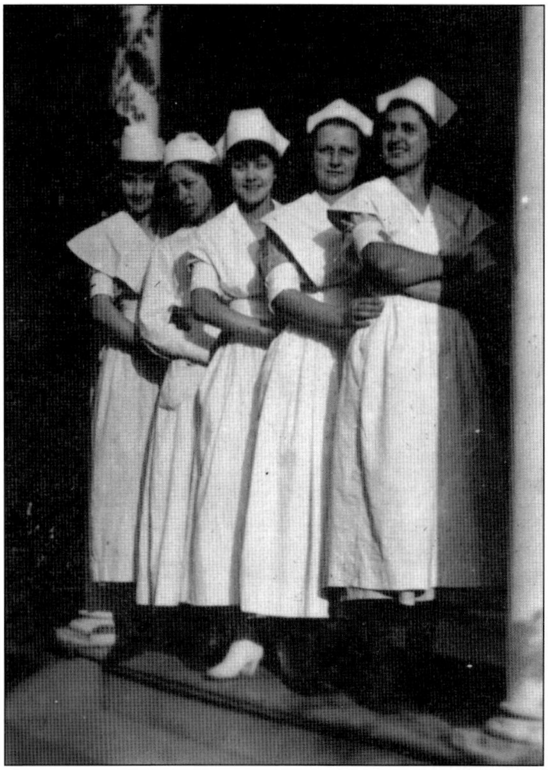

Five nurses at the Atlantic Hospital are shown enjoying some leisure time as they pose for the photographer on the hospital steps at Fifth and Oak Streets. From left to right they are identified as Lee McCauley, Ann ?, Elsie ?, unidentified, and Beryl ? .

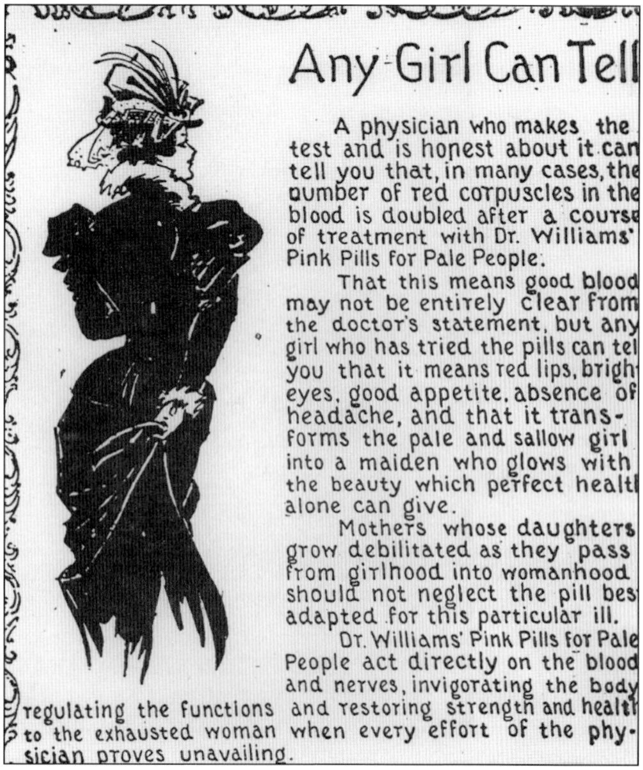

This 1890s advertisement from an early Atlantic newspaper advocates the use of an over-the-counter remedy that promises to make a "pale and sallow girl into a maiden who glows." This amazing remedy was called "Dr. William's Pink Pills for Pale People." Such remedies were often sold by traveling salesmen who knew how to entice a country audience with their outlandish claims.

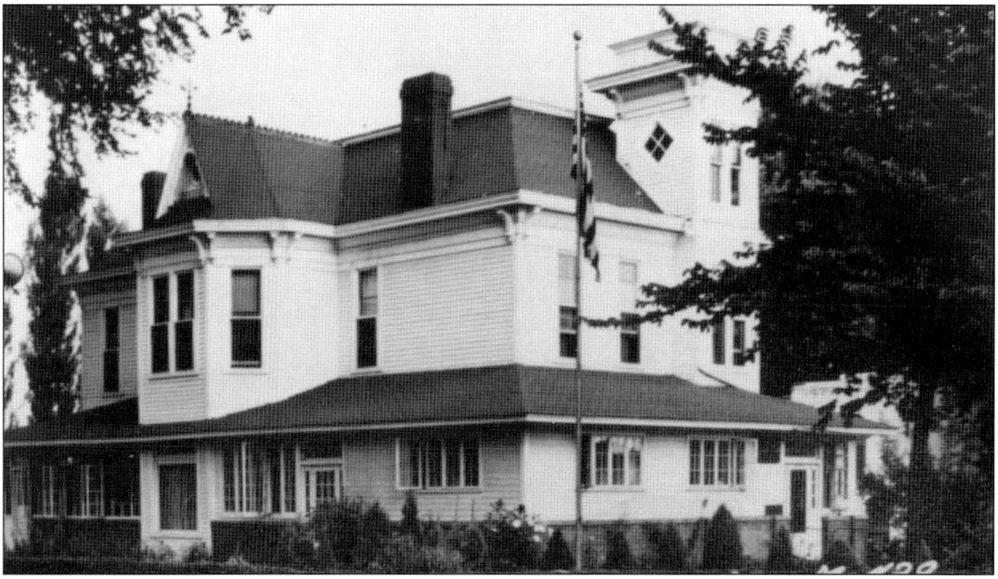

Dr. Schwendemann owned this house from 1938 until his death in the early 1970s. He had a very successful chiropractic practice with his office and examining rooms in the closed-off areas of the porches. Built by Samuel Franklin Martin in 1872, the home is located at Fifth and Poplar Streets and is on the National Register of Historic Places.

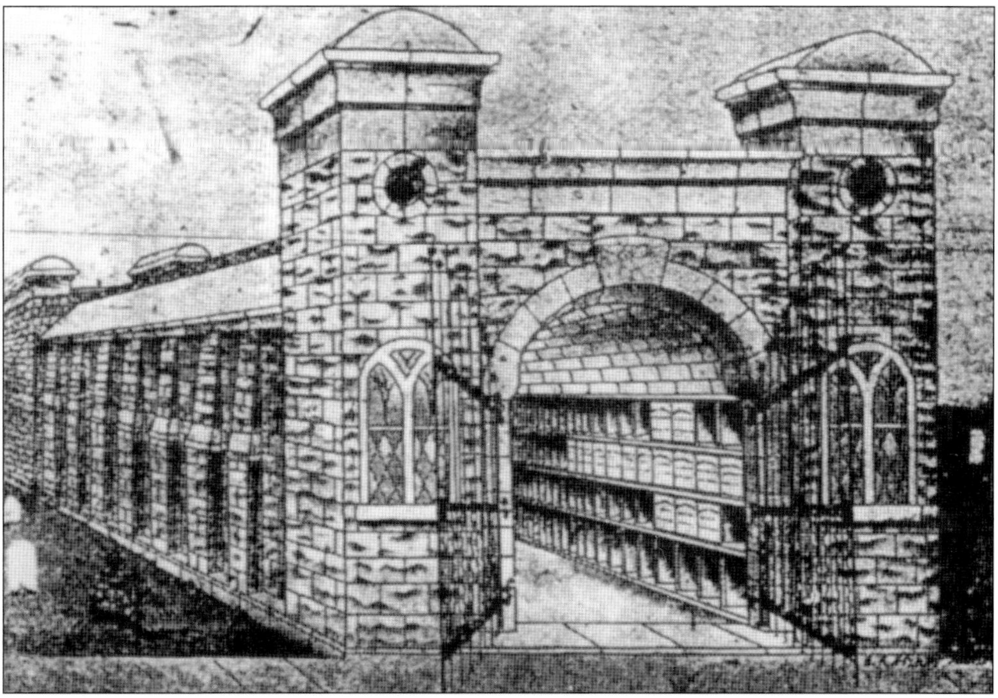

In 1909, the U. S. Mausoleum Company, with C. A. Rinehart and A. L. Baker as representatives, sold crypts in the newly erected Atlantic mausoleum for $8 each. The firm soon failed and the business was taken over by the Atlantic Cemetery Association. Later crypts sold for $125 each. Although this early information claimed that the building would "stand for all time," the structure was razed in 1968 due to severe deterioration.

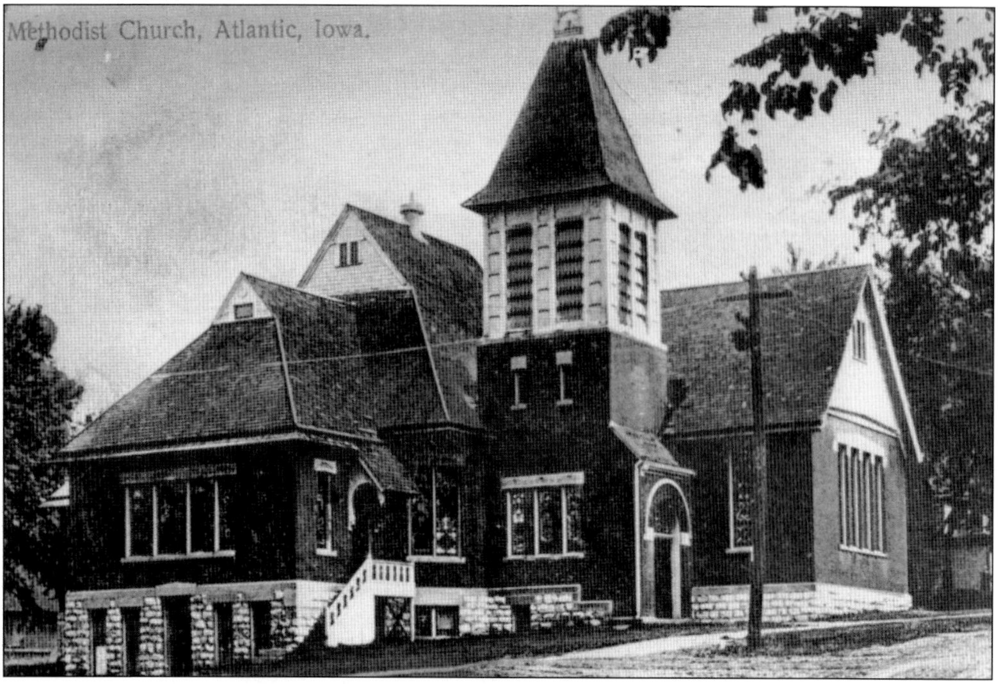

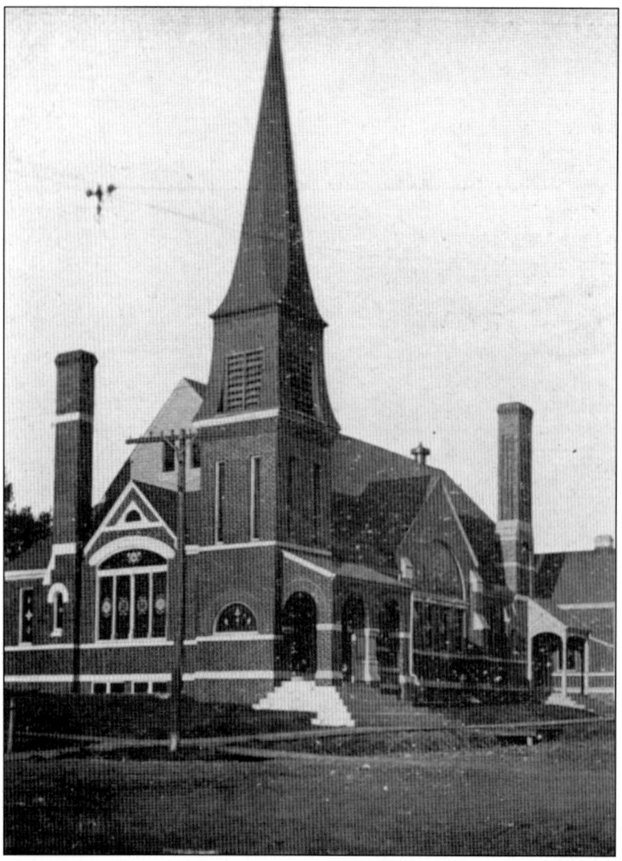

The Methodists were the first religious group to form in Atlantic. In the fall of 1867, a group met in the home of Ebenezer Herbert. Charter members included the Montgomery, Sharp, Pittman, Everett, McKibbon, Needles, McWaid, and Herbert families. The first frame courthouse served as the meeting place, and the first pastor was Rev. William Abraham. The present church was erected in 1924 at 800 Poplar Street and by 1968 was valued at $250,000.

The First Congregational Church of Atlantic was organized in 1869 with a charter membership of eight persons. The Reverend E. S. Hill was the first pastor and served for 36 years. The first bells pealed in 1870 at the church located at Fifth and Walnut Streets.

The St. Peter and Paul Church began in Atlantic under the leadership of Rev. Father Moynaghan. The first church was erected at Sixth and Locust Streets. The congregation grew rapidly, and, in 1893, the cornerstone for a new building was laid. One of the priests who served the church was Rev. Father P. N. McDermott, better known as "Father Pat." He was a chaplain in World War I and later became the national chaplain for the American Legion.

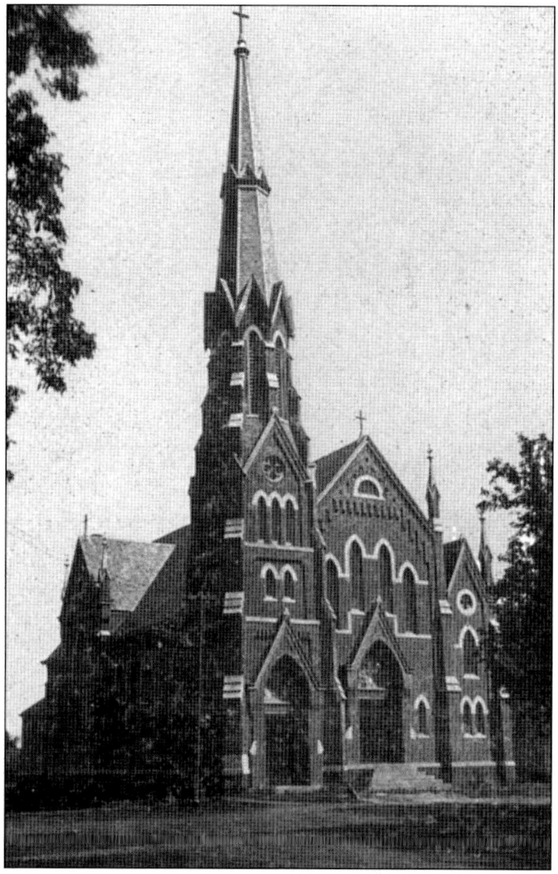

The Presbyterians held their first services in the Park Hotel in 1875. The church was organized with 18 members under the guidance of Rev. R. T. McCrea. In 1877, they built their first church at Sixth and Walnut Streets. The Baptists were organized in 1869 by C. C. Baird, a missionary. There was a great rivalry among the different denominations in Atlantic. The story is told that while the Presbyterians were singing "Will There Be Any Stars in My Crown?" the Baptists down the street were singing "No, Not One!"

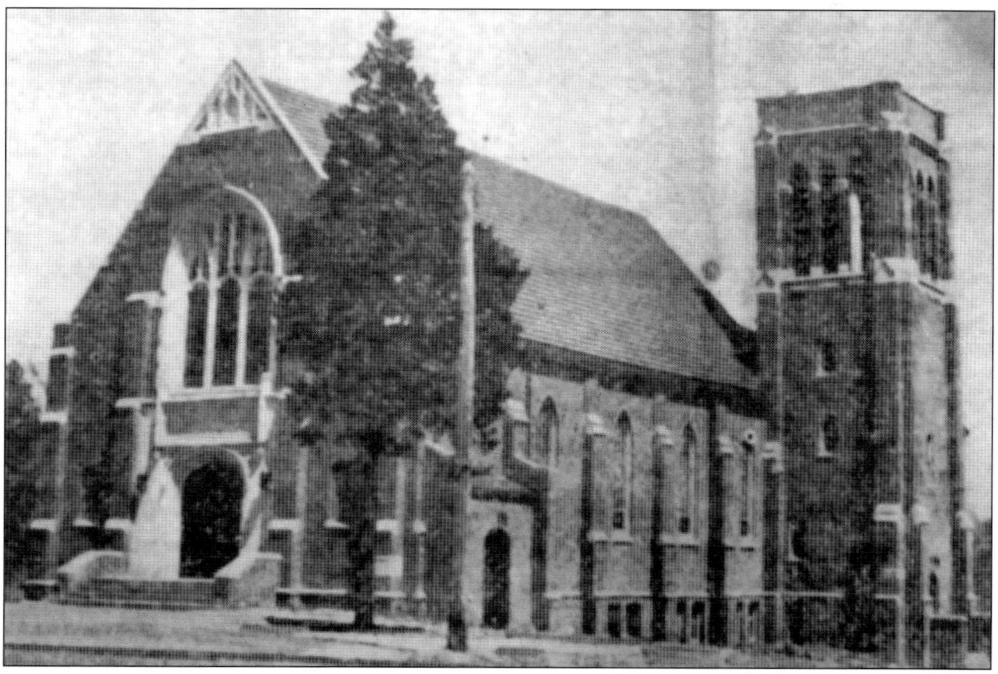

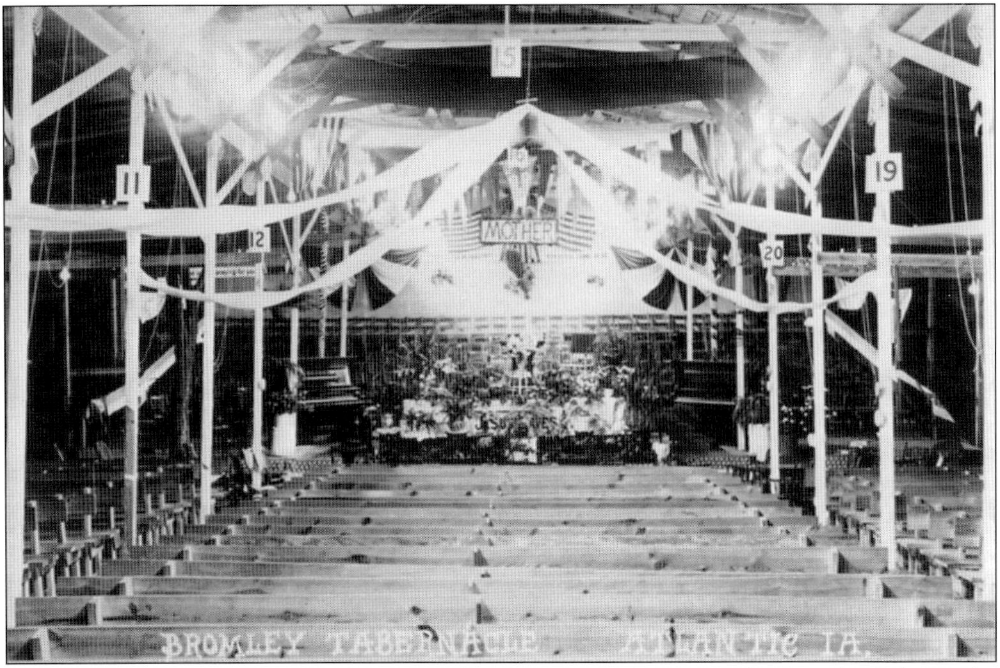

One of the most unusual and ambitious undertakings in Atlantic was the Bromley Tabernacle. This elaborate, temporary, tent-like structure, located at 801 Poplar, was erected in one day. This enormous structure could hold 2,000 people and was divided into 24 sections, each with its own usher. It featured a choir of 200 voices and was nondenominational. Dr. Henry W. Bromley, one of the world's foremost evangelists, was the preacher and remained in Atlantic for several weeks to preside over evangelical meetings in October 1915.

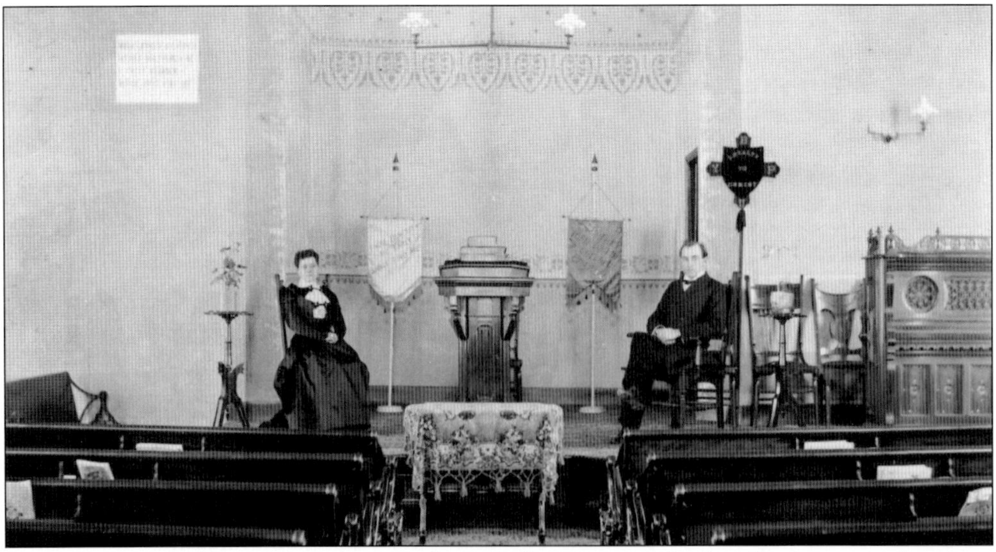

This photograph shows the interior of what is believed to be the first Presbyterian church in Atlantic. Several signs and banners are on display, including "What kind of church would our church be if every member were just like me?"; "Those that seek Me early will find Me"; "The Lord loveth a cheerful giver"; and "Loyalty to Christ." (Courtesy of the State Historical Society of Iowa.)

Five

Enjoying the Social Scene

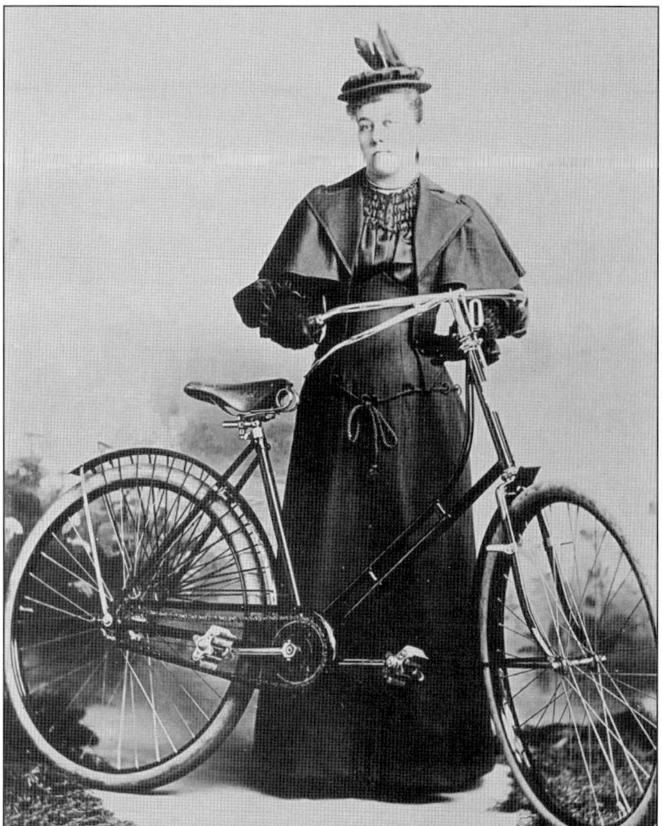

The lady in this 1900 photograph is Mrs. Sara Cuykendall. The velocipede was in vogue in 1900, and while Sara is posed as if to take a ride, the fine fabric of her ensemble and the rich detail of her dress, hat, and gloves make her readiness to ride the cycle questionable. The chain guard would be of some help in this regard. (Courtesy of the State Historical Society of Iowa.)

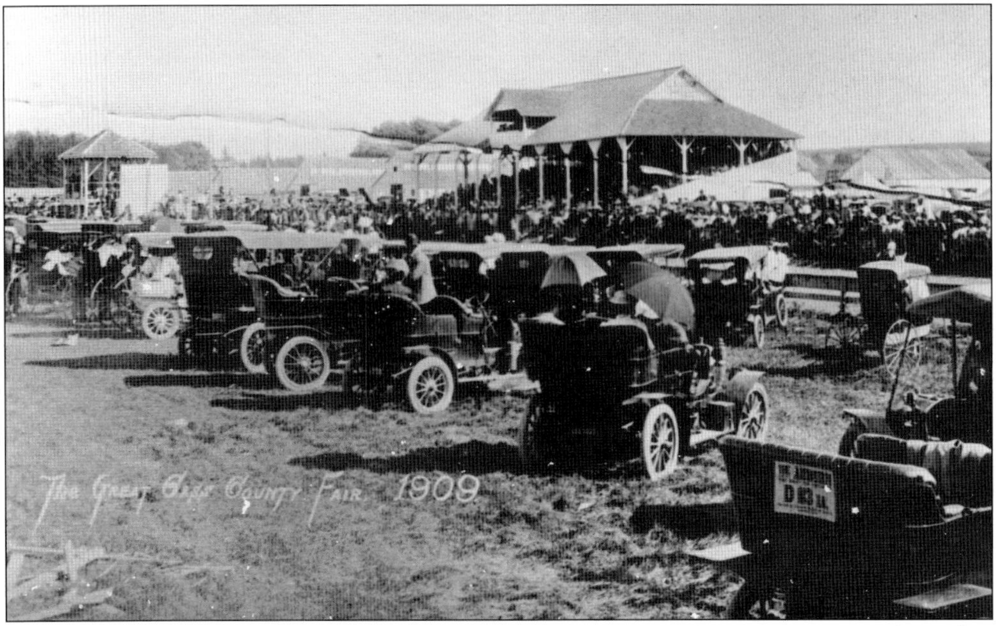

The Cass County Agricultural Society was organized in 1869, and a committee was formed to select a site for the first fair. Land in the northwest part of the city was chosen for "the biggest exhibition of pumpkins and pigs ever shown in southwest Iowa." The first board was formed in 1871 with John Keyes as its president. In 1921, the fair association moved the fairgrounds to the present site adjacent to Sunnyside Park.

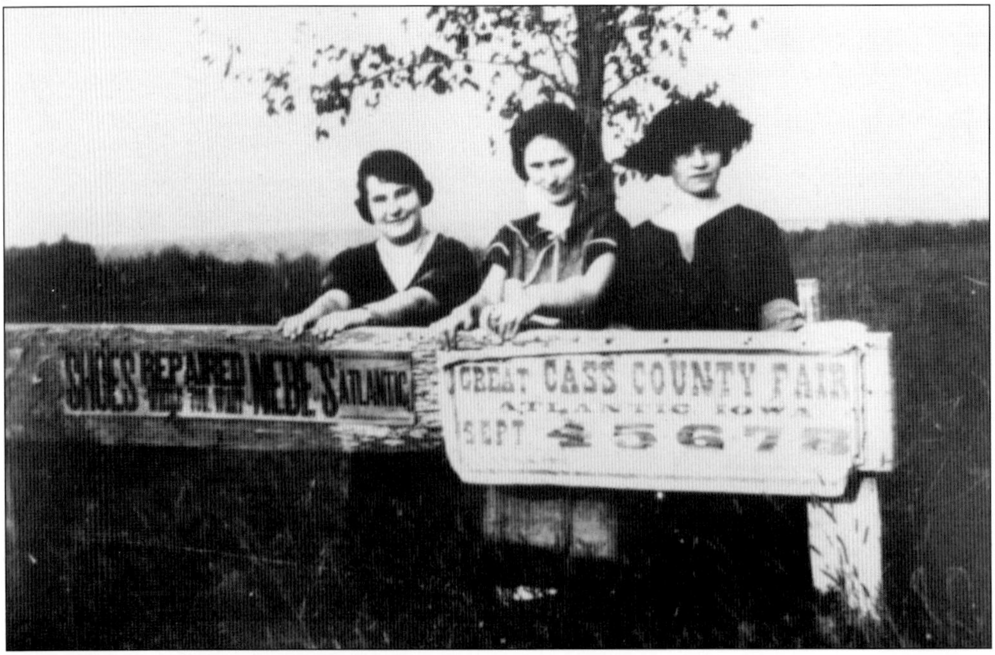

Early fairs featured vaudeville and circus acts, harness races, trotting and pacing, pony races, running races, a band concert, and a huge fireworks display. The three ladies shown here in the early 1900s are advertising the Nebe Shoe Store as well as the Great Cass County Fair. Frank M. Nebe opened the Nebe Shoe Store in Atlantic in 1899.

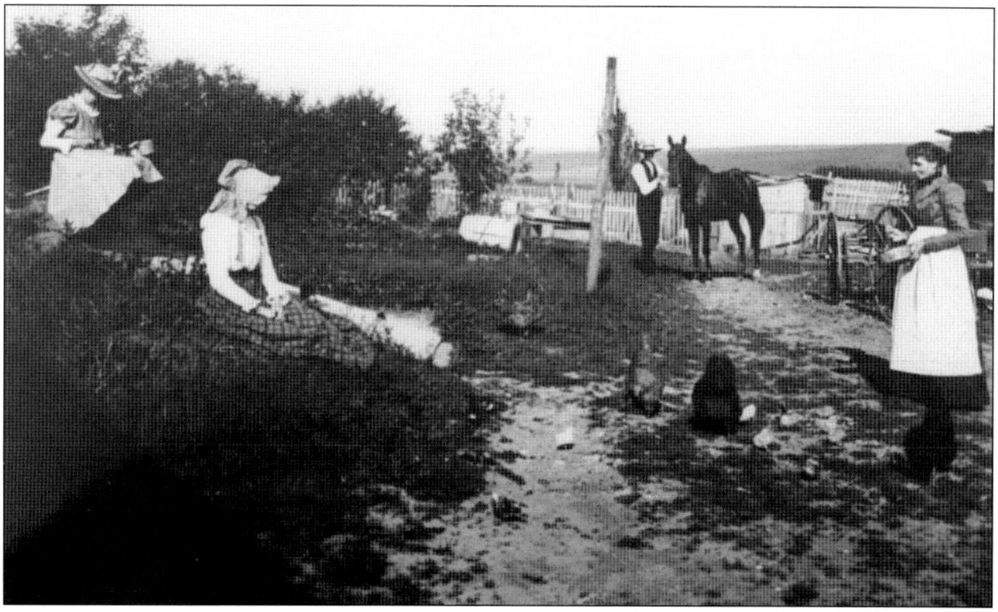

In the late 1890s, the Atlantic Farmers Institute was formed. This organization predated the Farm Bureau. The purpose of the organization was to further the interests of rural life, help farmers stay abreast of new farming methods and machinery, and provide housewives with useful information. The group had its own board of directors who supervised informative programs. Meetings were held in the Cass County Courthouse. (Courtesy of the State Historical Society of Iowa.)

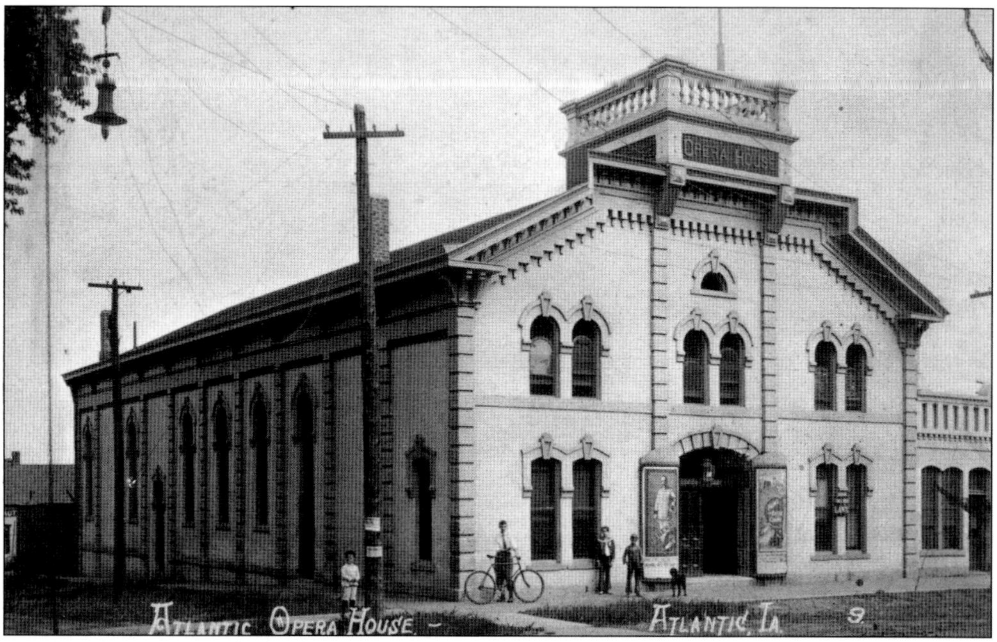

In 1880, H. E. Bacon built the Bacon Opera House, which immediately became the center of social activity in Atlantic. Traveling theatrical companies sometimes stayed in town for several performances. The Opera House could seat 600 and hosted many famous personages. It had its own orchestra and its own company of players. The first talking picture was presented at the opera house in January 1929. This building is now home to the Atlantic Theatres.

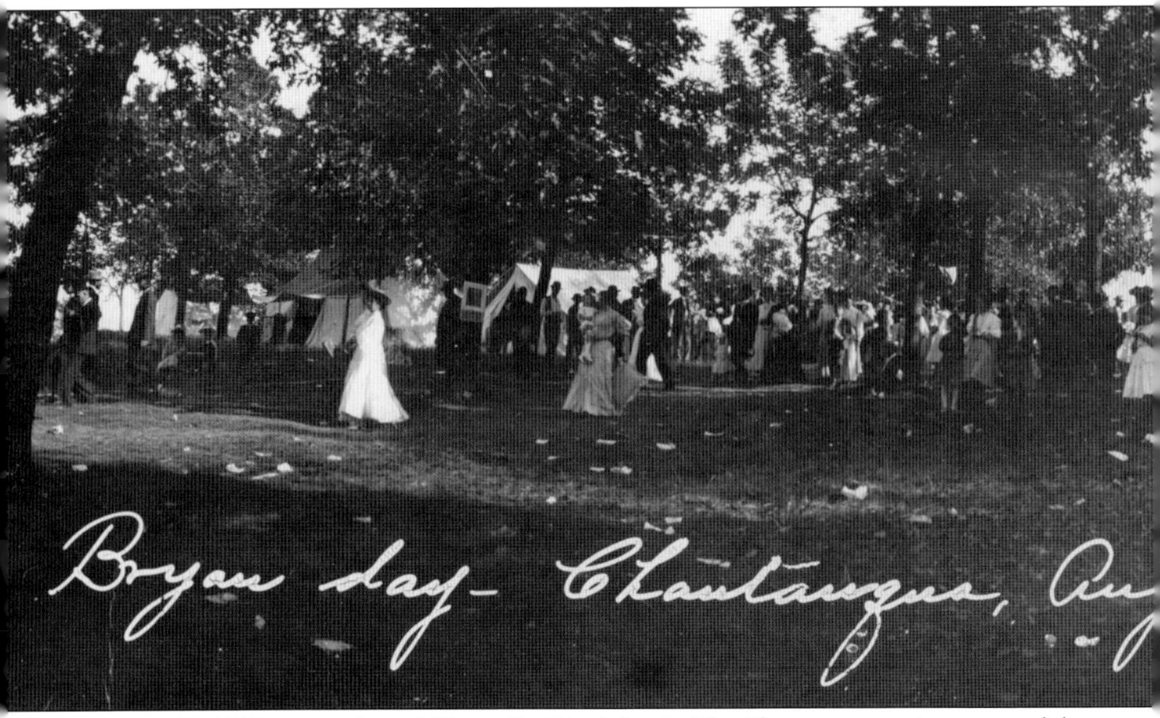

August 22, 1907, was proclaimed "Bryan Day" in Atlantic. The Chautauqua was in town, and the main speaker for the program was William Jennings Bryan, famous for his speech entitled, "Cross of Gold." Bryan's advocacy of free coinage of silver won him national acclaim. His main speech for Atlantic's 1907 program was entitled, "The Old World and Its Ways." Bryan was a popular

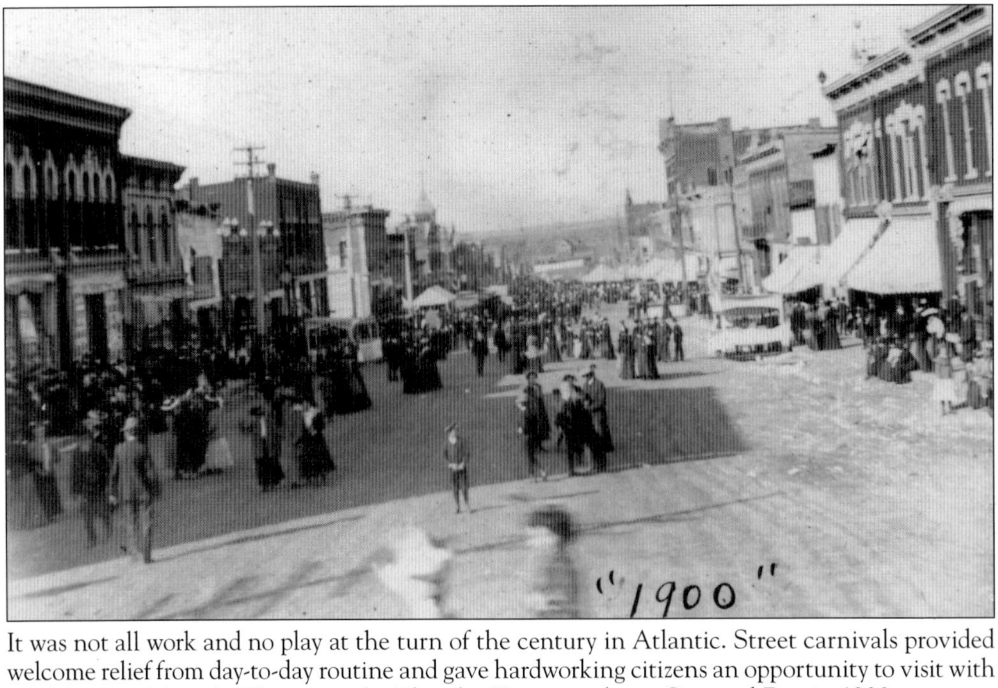

It was not all work and no play at the turn of the century in Atlantic. Street carnivals provided welcome relief from day-to-day routine and gave hardworking citizens an opportunity to visit with neighbors and friends. This image by Theodor Krogman shows Carnival Day in 1900.

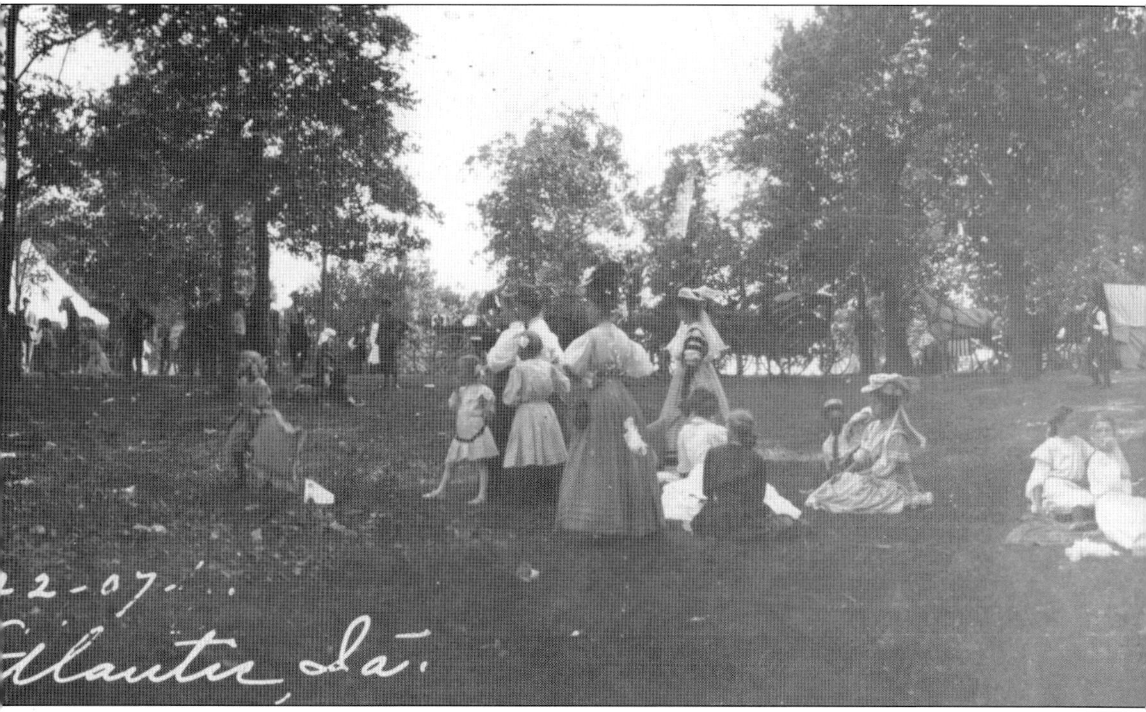

speaker on the Chautauqua circuit for 30 years. Having been a candidate for the presidency of the United States on three occasions—1896, 1900, and 1908—he was nationally known. Bryan was against the teaching of evolution and joined the prosecution team in the John Scopes trial in Tennessee in 1925.

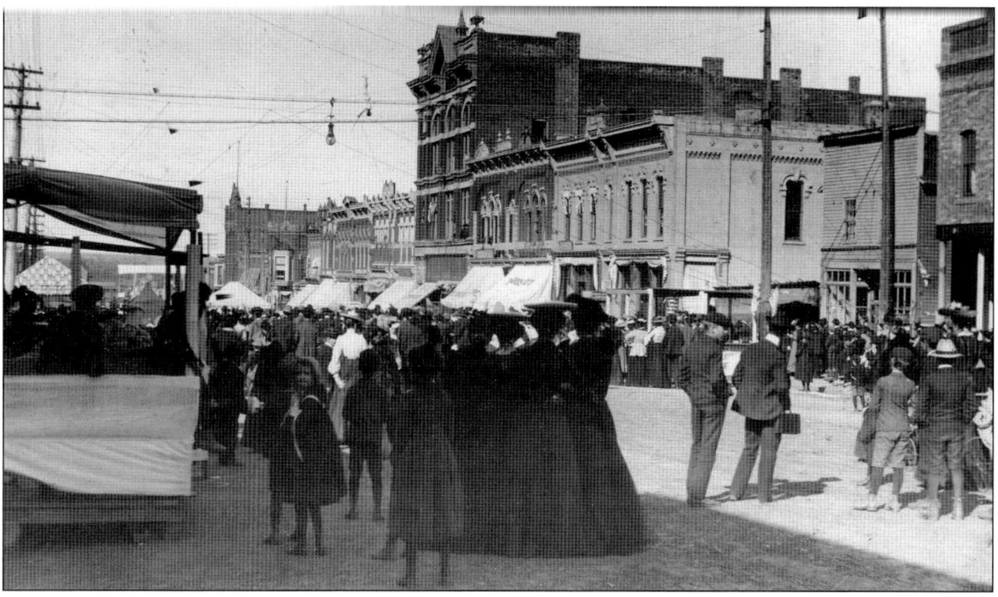

As seen in this Krogman photograph, booths were set up on both sides of Chestnut Street on Carnival Day. There was plenty of opportunity to try one's hand at games of chance. Everyone enjoyed the races, games, food, and camaraderie. Huge crowds attended the festivities, and many businesses recorded their most profitable day of the year.

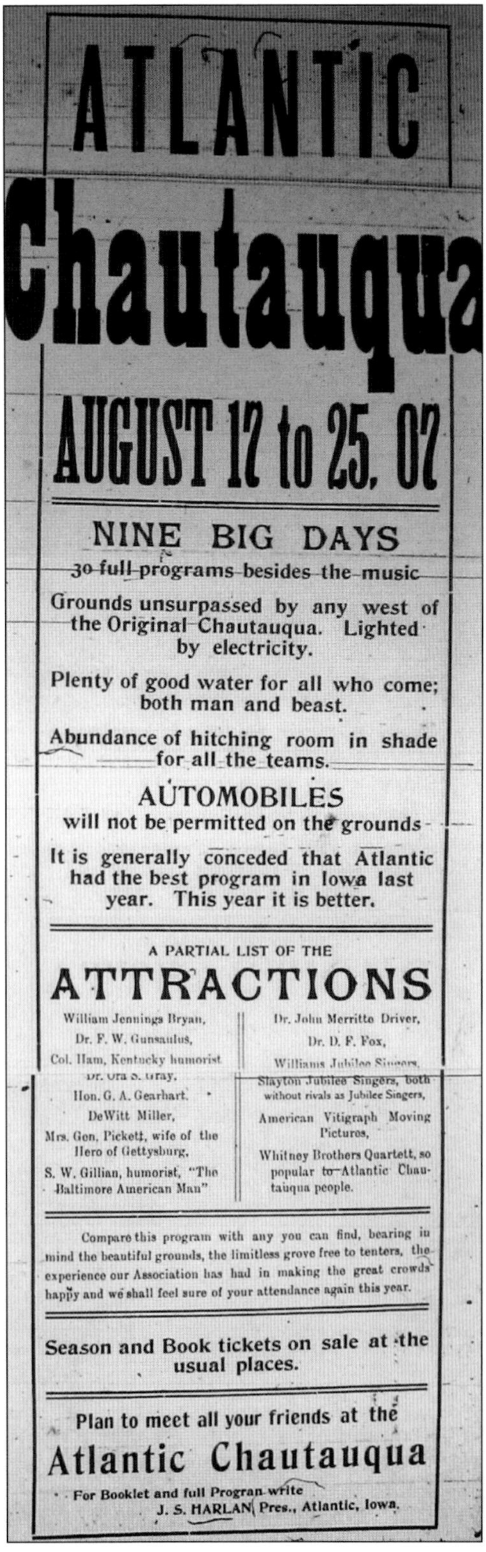

ATLANTIC

Chautauqua

AUGUST 17 to 25, 07

NINE BIG DAYS

30 full programs besides the music

Grounds unsurpassed by any west of the Original Chautauqua. Lighted by electricity.

Plenty of good water for all who come; both man and beast.

Abundance of hitching room in shade for all the teams.

AUTOMOBILES will not be permitted on the grounds

It is generally conceded that Atlantic had the best program in Iowa last year. This year it is better.

A PARTIAL LIST OF THE

ATTRACTIONS

William Jennings Bryan,
Dr. F. W. Gunsaulus,
Col. Ham, Kentucky humorist
Dr. Ora S. Gray,
Hon. G. A. Gearhart,
DeWitt Miller,
Mrs. Gen. Pickett, wife of the Hero of Gettysburg,
S. W. Gillian, humorist, "The Baltimore American Man"

Dr. John Merritte Driver,
Dr. D. F. Fox,
Williams Jubilee Singers,
Slayton Jubilee Singers, both without rivals as Jubilee Singers,
American Vitigraph Moving Pictures,
Whitney Brothers Quartett, so popular to Atlantic Chautauqua people.

Compare this program with any you can find, bearing in mind the beautiful grounds, the limitless grove free to tenters, the experience our Association has had in making the great crowds happy and we shall feel sure of your attendance again this year.

Season and Book tickets on sale at the usual places.

Plan to meet all your friends at the

Atlantic Chautauqua

For Booklet and full Program write
J. S. HARLAN, Pres., Atlantic, Iowa.

In the 1900s, the Chautauqua, an adult educational movement, brought entertainment and culture to rural sections of the country and was an integral part of the Atlantic social scene. People would spend up to 10 days tenting out in Sunnyside Park to be able to participate in the many activities provided by this unique outreach program. One of the famous speakers who visited Atlantic was Booker T. Washington, who spoke in August 1906. The local paper commented, "He told of his own struggles for advancement and how slowly but surely he forged upwards out of the darkness of slavery and ignorance into freedom and education, by his own efforts." Washington was introduced by prominent local attorney H. M. Boorman and was warmly received.

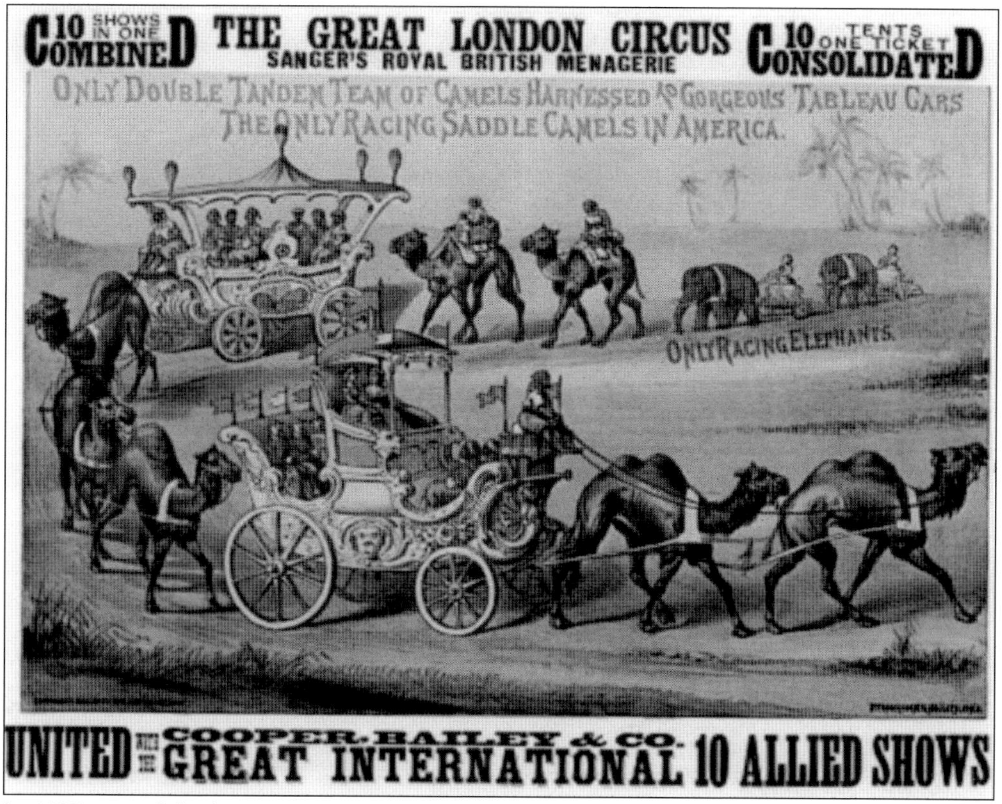

In 1875, one of the largest crowds ever seen in Atlantic came to attend Howe's Great London Circus. The *Atlantic News-Telegraph* reported, "The show was splendid with the exception of that bareback rider. She was almost as bare as the horse she rode." At later dates, the Barnum and Bailey and Ringling Brothers Circuses came to Atlantic. Animals would be unloaded at the depot and paraded through town on their way to the circus site.

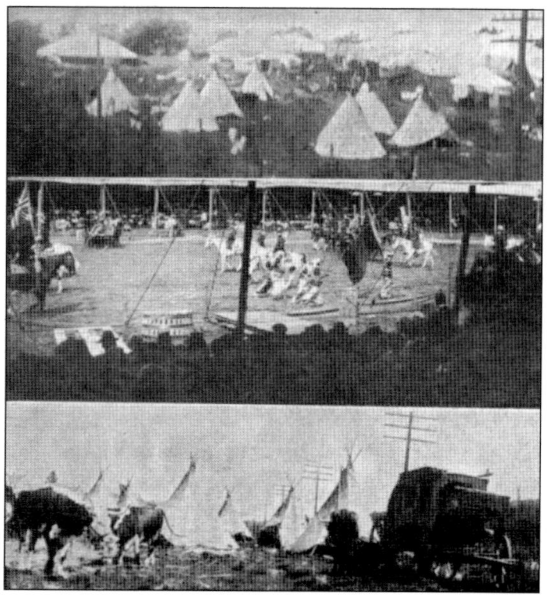

On August 29, 1898, Buffalo Bill Cody arrived in Atlantic with his popular Wild West Show. He wore his trademark white hat, deerskin jacket covered with medals, and highly polished leather boots. What a sight he was with his long white hair and carefully trimmed goatee as he arrived in the outdoor arena astride his magnificent horse. The show was replete with cowboys, Indians, buffalo, and wild horses.

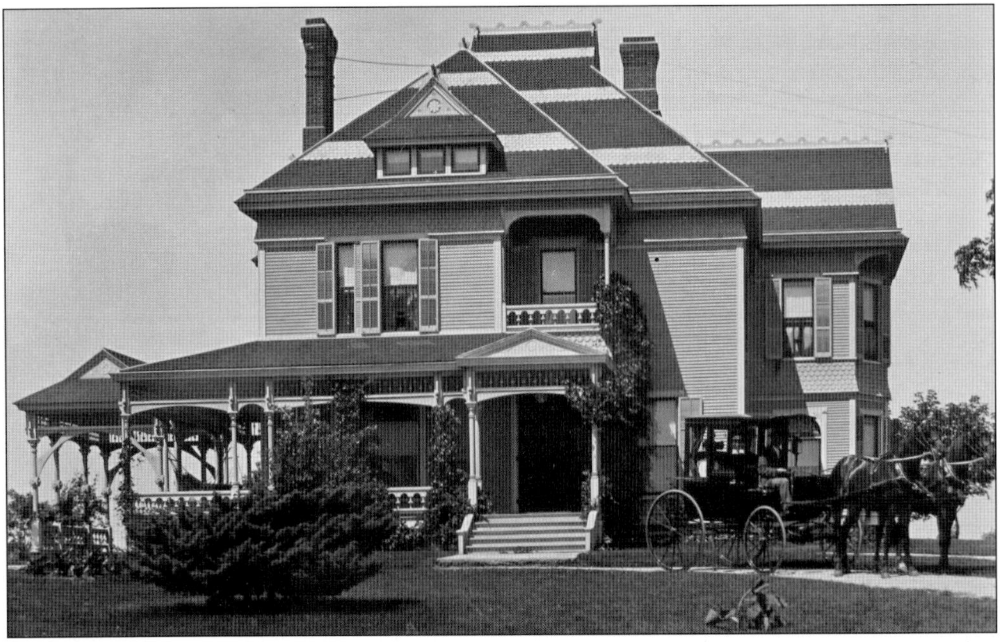

This imposing edifice, built in the Queen Anne style, is the J. W. Cuykendall home located at Fourteenth and Chestnut Streets. The house, called Lyndhurst, was built in 1890. The Cuykendalls purchased the house in 1901. It was used extensively for business and social gatherings in the early 20th century. (Courtesy of the State Historical Society of Iowa.)

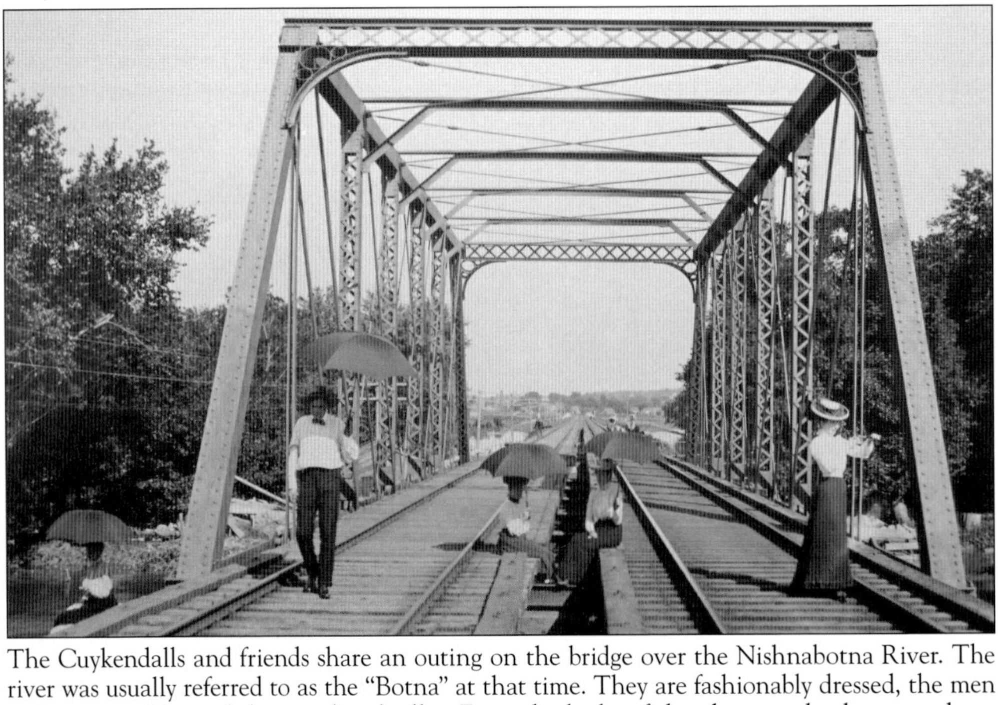

The Cuykendalls and friends share an outing on the bridge over the Nishnabotna River. The river was usually referred to as the "Botna" at that time. They are fashionably dressed, the men and women alike with hats and umbrellas. From the looks of the photograph, they must have known the train schedule, since they have made themselves quite at home in the middle of the bridge. (Courtesy of the State Historical Society of Iowa.)

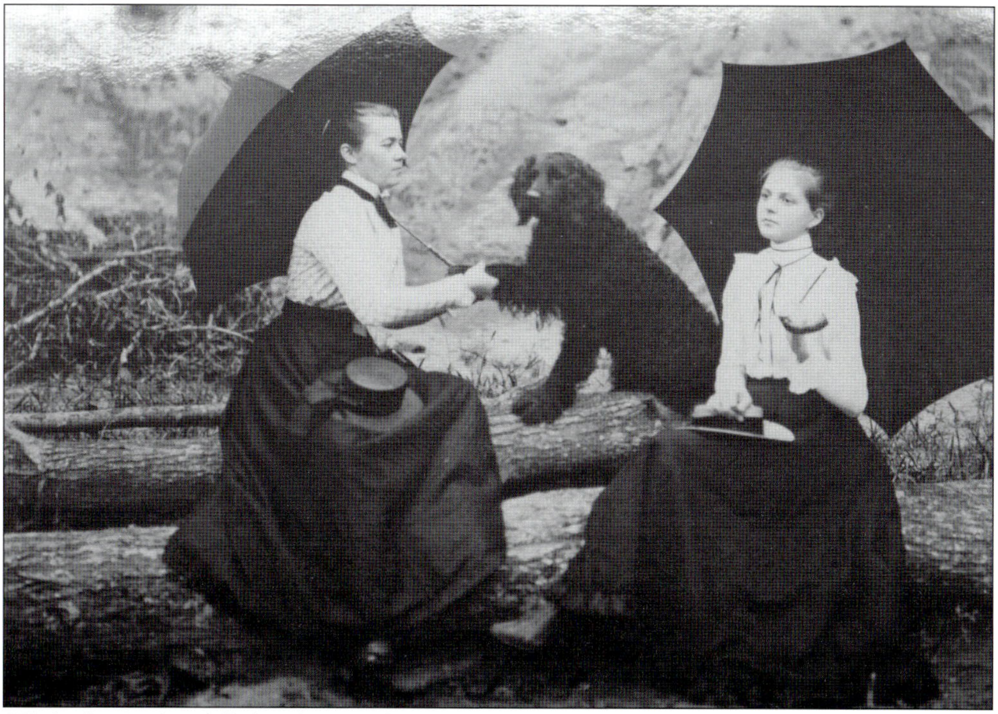

While the Cuykendalls lived a very formal lifestyle at the turn of the century in Atlantic, they obviously knew the benefits of fresh air and sunshine. The above photograph is of Sara (left) and Virginia Cuykendall. The family dog, Duke, is getting a warm welcome from his mistress. The photograph below is the Cuykendalls at Oak Camp No. 39 in 1900, with the ever-present Duke. One of the women is fixing her hair while another pours coffee. Keeping up appearances was obviously a high priority as the men have on ties and the women are all beautifully dressed for the camping trip. (Courtesy of the State Historical Society of Iowa.)

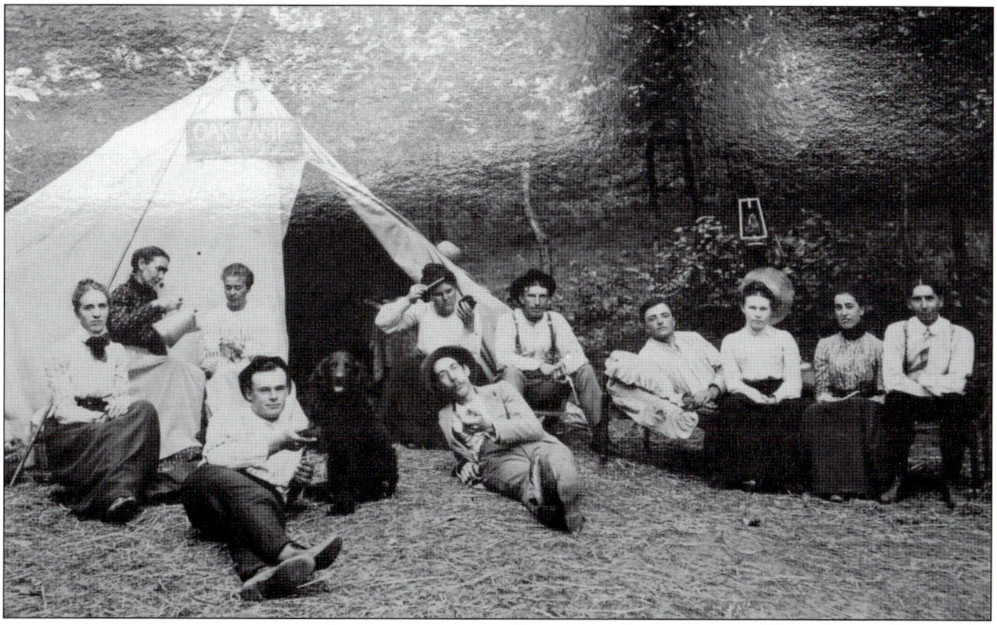

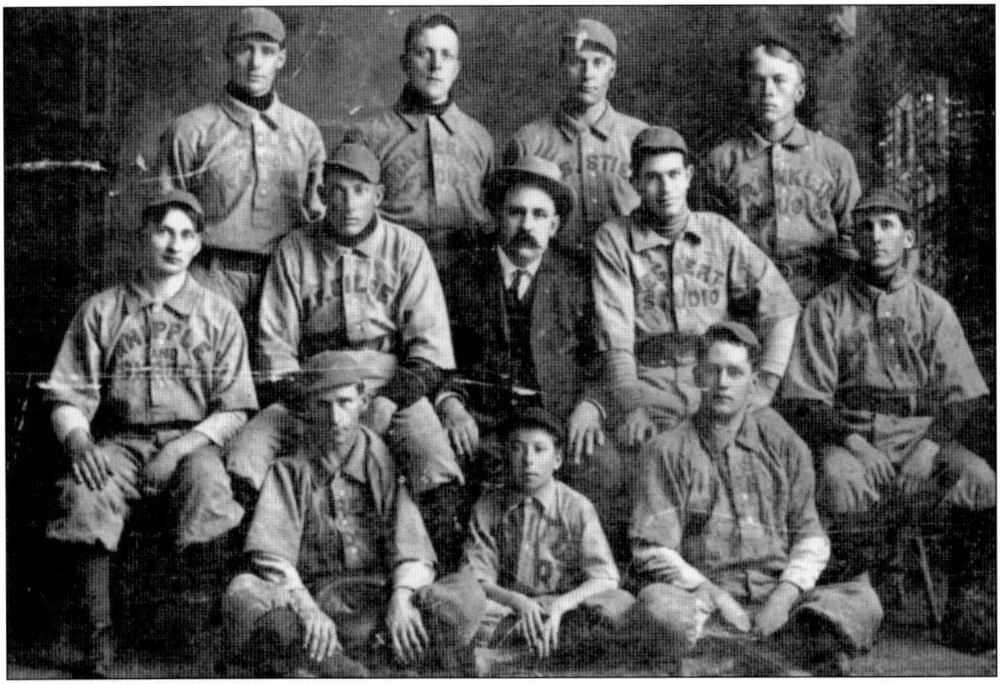

The Merchant Greys were the pride of Atlantic baseball followers in the early years of the century, attracting crowds of over 500 at each game. This picture of the 1906 team first appeared in the June 8, 1906, issue of the *Daily Democrat*. Team members are, from left to right, (first row) Harry Franklin, Dave Bardtman (bat boy), and Roy White; (second row) Max Ross, Bill Timm, Bill Williams (manager), Frank Barnhart, and George Franklin; (third row) Dale Morrow, B. Bercher, Wilbur Herbert, and Charles Whitcomb. The names on the uniforms are business sponsors.

Atlantic's Carnegie Library was built in 1903 at a cost of $12,500. The majority of the funds for this project came from well-known philanthropist Andrew Carnegie. J. A. McWaid was the mayor of Atlantic in 1903 and the first chairman of the library board. This building still houses the Atlantic Public Library in 2010.

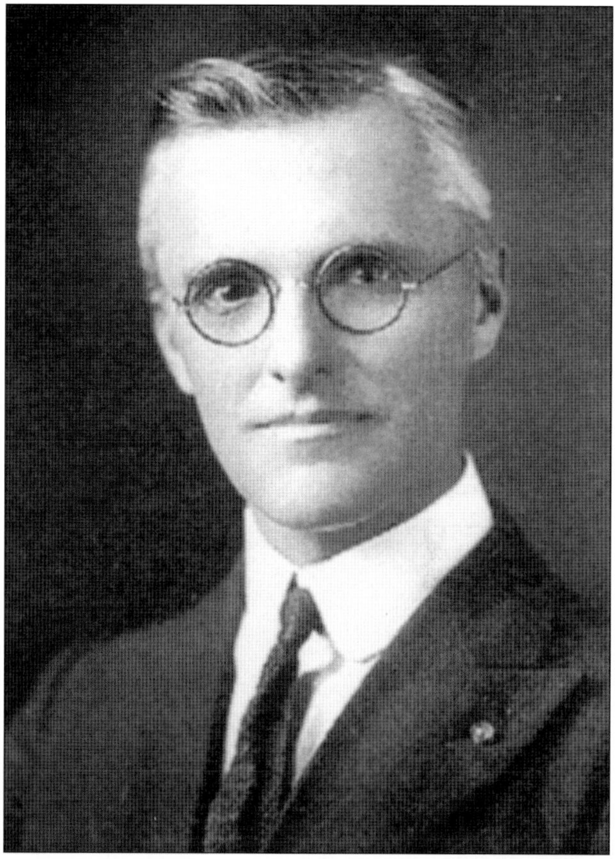

Frank Pellett gave up his law practice in Missouri to move to Atlantic in 1907, where he purchased a small farm on the northeast side of Atlantic and lived the life of a naturalist. He was interested in preserving the land and set aside five acres for the growth of wildflowers and plants that could provide the best food for bees. Pellett became a world authority on the subject of bees and authored many books and articles on the subject. In 1954, the five-acre woodland that Pellett had set aside was dedicated to his memory. In 1978, the area was designated as an Iowa State Preserve. It is known as the Frank Chapman Pellett Memorial Woods.

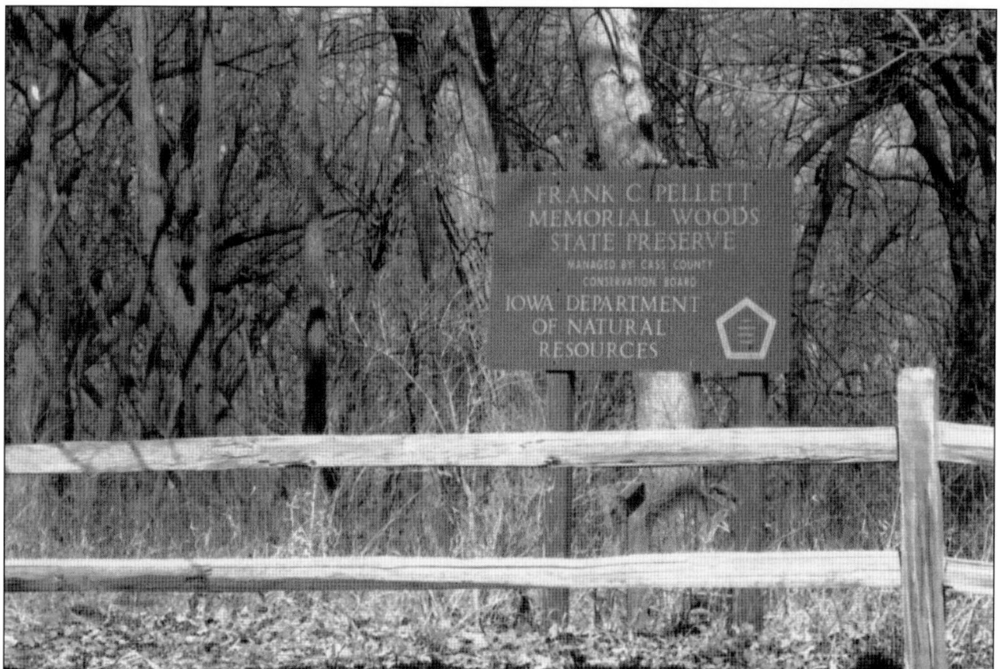

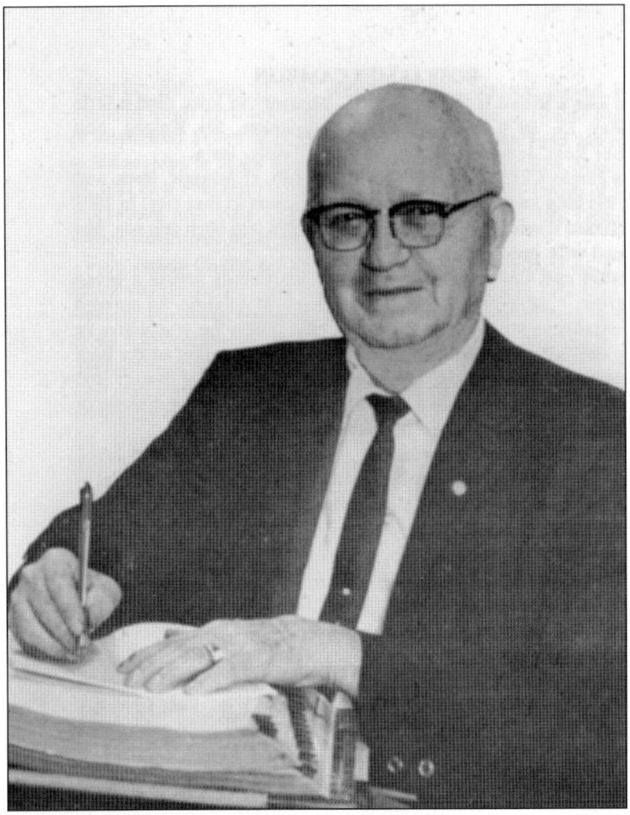

Ross J. Camblin was always associated with Sunnyside Park. He was a member of the original Atlantic Parks Commission in 1919 and continued to serve for 55 years. An expansion of Sunnyside Park was named the Camblin Addition in his honor. Camblin and his wife, Harriett, managed the Calumet Cafe in Atlantic for 40 years.

This photograph shows the entrance to Sunnyside Park before the trees were destroyed by Dutch elm disease. The trees were planted in the 1920s by the Atlantic Lions Club as a tribute to the soldiers of World War I. Each beared a brass shield with the name of a Cass County soldier killed in the war. Only one of the brass plates, that of Max L. Hubbell, is known to have survived.

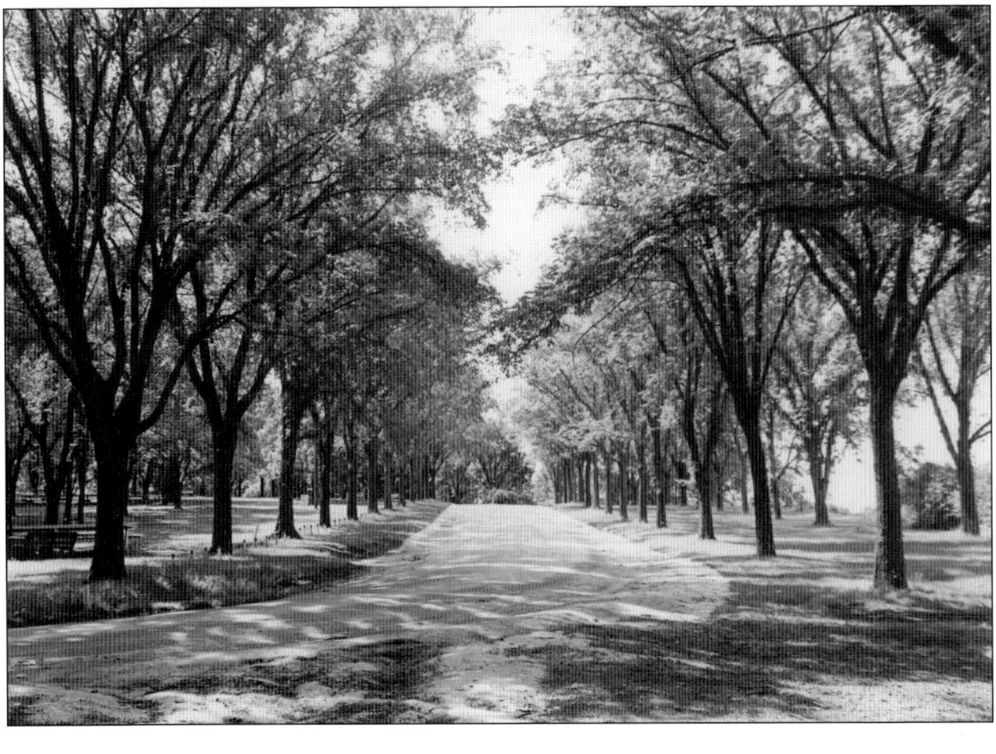

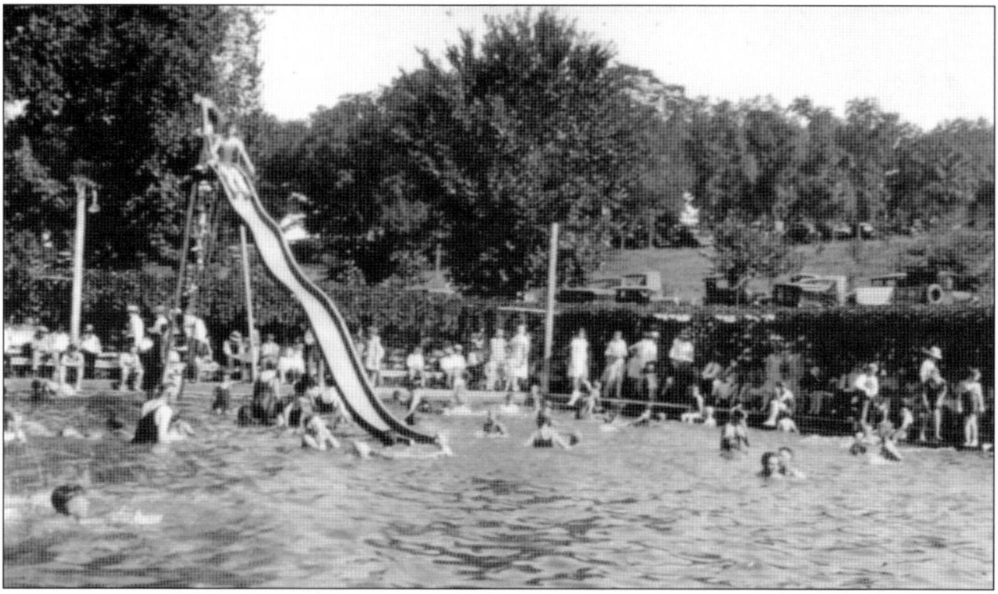

Every town needs recreational sites and no place could be more successful than the pool at Sunnyside Park in the 1930s. This pool was opened in 1938, replacing the previous one. This new pool was part of a WPA (Works Progress Administration) project. Sunnyside could also boast of a picnic area and campsite.

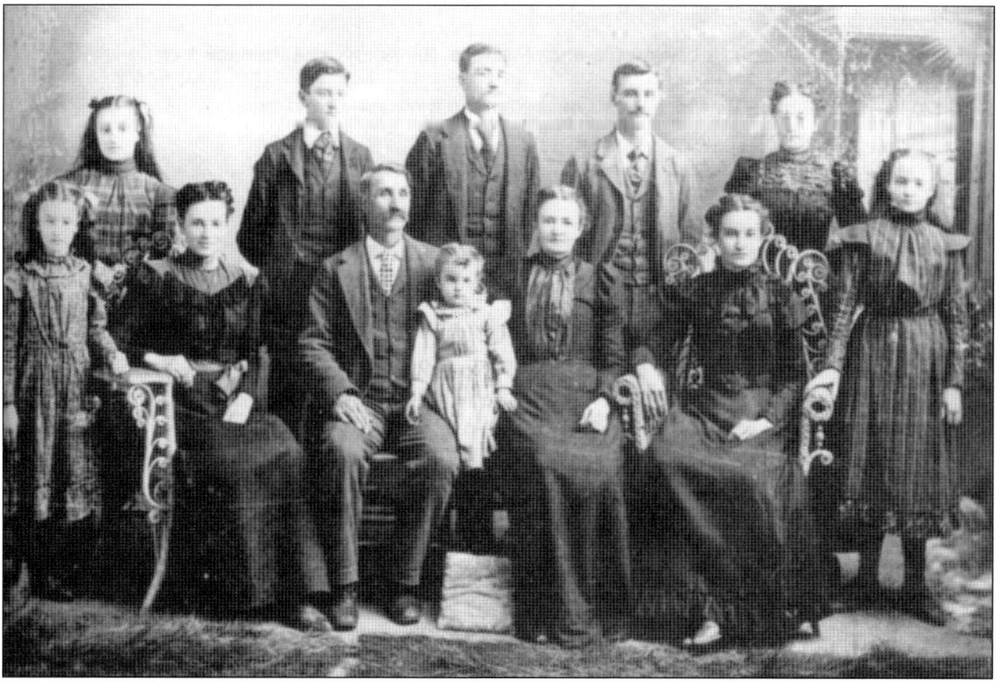

This photograph of the James Henry DeBusk and Lucy Jane Bishop DeBusk family was taken in Atlantic on December 25, 1899. These ancestors of the Atlantic Camblin family are, from left to right, (first row) Mary Ethel, Edna Inez, James Henry DeBusk, Lula Anna, Lucy Jane Bishop DeBusk, Ella May, and Hattie Jane; (second row) Lucy Olive, James Arthur, Lewis Levi, Charles Hayden, and Mamie Cooney.

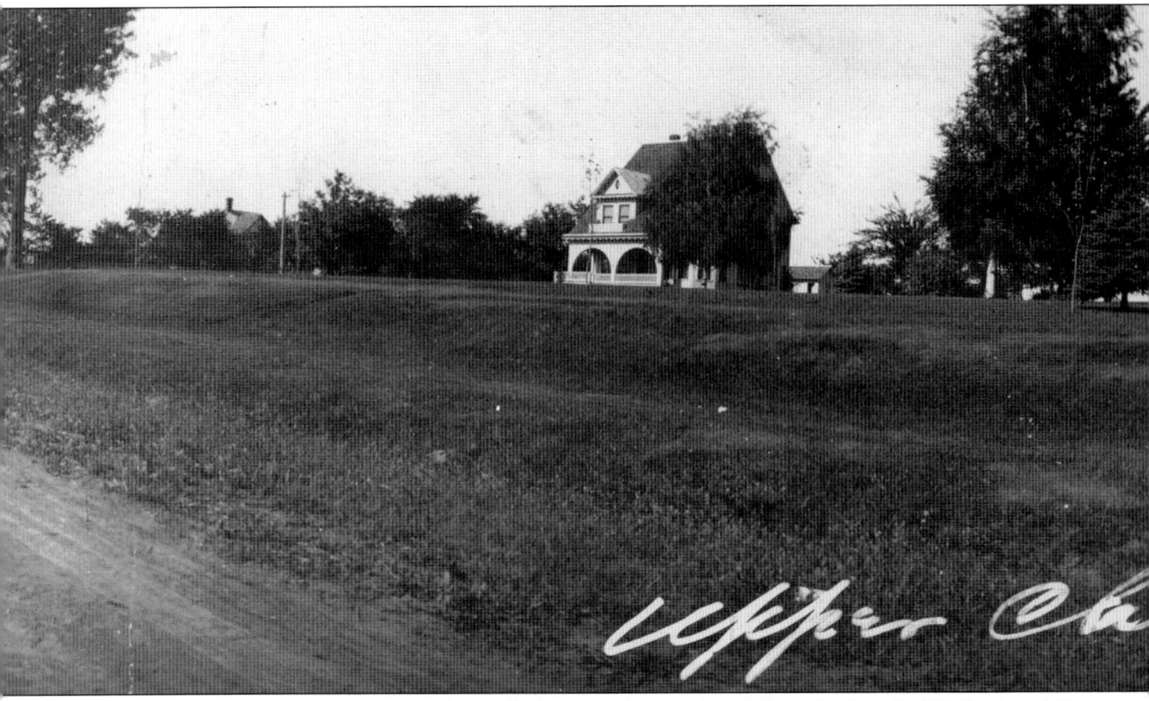

This view of upper Chestnut Street shows the homes of Dr. U. S. Mullins (left) and J. W. Cuykendall, two of the several fine Atlantic houses where the town's social life centered. According to *One Hundred Years of Pioneering and Progress*, a newspaper reported activities like the following, "The Congregationalists will commemorate Longfellow's birthday with a social at Mrs. Julian Phelps'

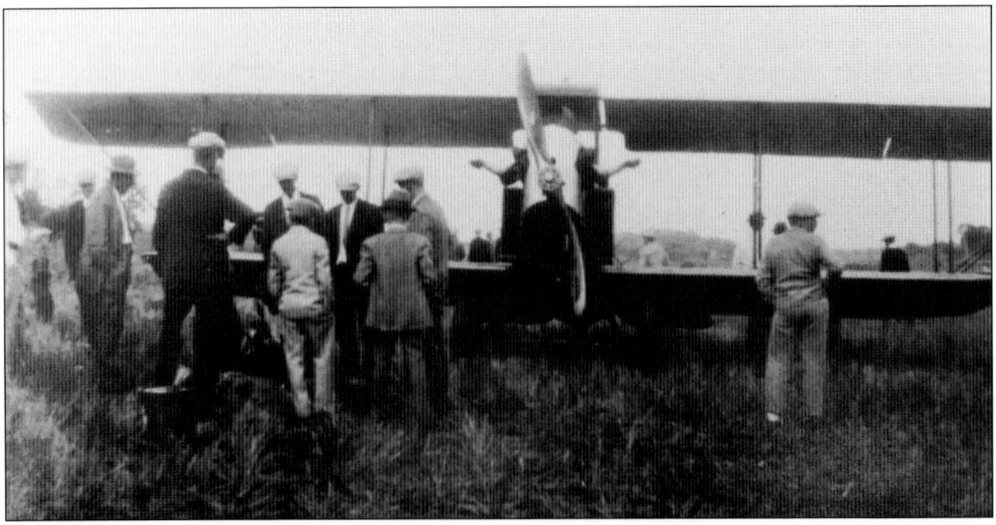

Aerial photographer Adolph Paul, better known as "Frenchie," took many photographs of the city of Atlantic. In this 1906 image, he has gathered quite the crowd of people interested in taking a close-up look at the plane. In 1928, Col. Charles A. Lindbergh flew over Atlantic but didn't circle the city because it was reported that he didn't know where the city was. On May 30, 1931, Amelia Earhart made a forced landing on the Hunt farm south of Atlantic when her Pitcairn Autogyro ran out of gas. She stayed overnight at the Whitney Hotel and resumed her flight at 7:00 a.m. the next day.

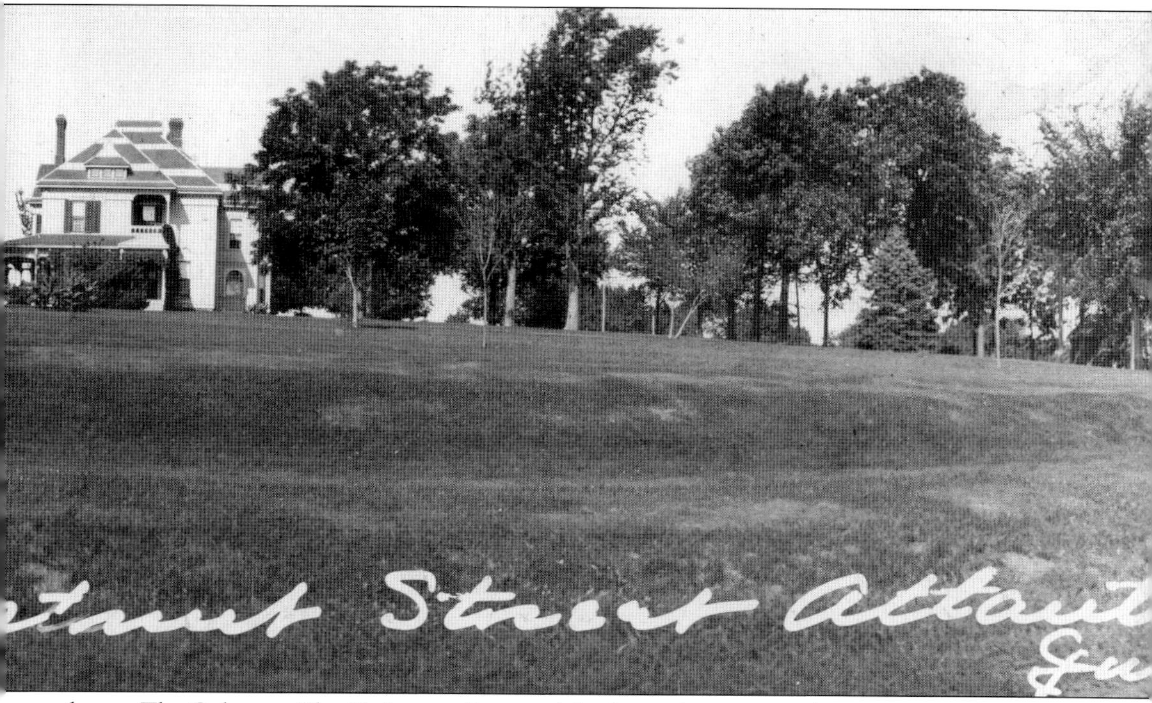

home, The Oaks. . . . The Owls are a literary club whose object is social enjoyment and mental culture. . . . The Knights of Pythias, in 1890, gave a grand ball at the Opera House with 80 guests present. All enjoyed to the highest degree the Light Fantastic. . . . One of the pretty parties of the time was the thimble party given by Mesdames Brown, Brewster, Nebe, and Mae Hewitt."

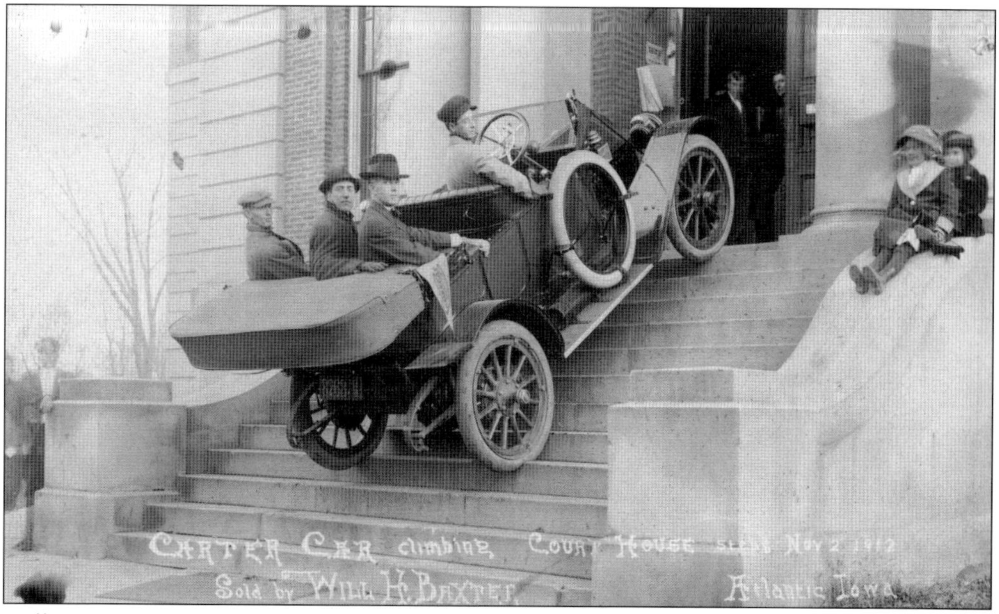

Will H. Baxter sold Carter cars in Atlantic in the early 1900s. He liked to show off the power of his cars by using rather unusual methods. In this 1912 photograph, Baxter, the man in the middle of the back seat, shows how easily the powerful Carter car can climb the steps of the Cass County Courthouse.

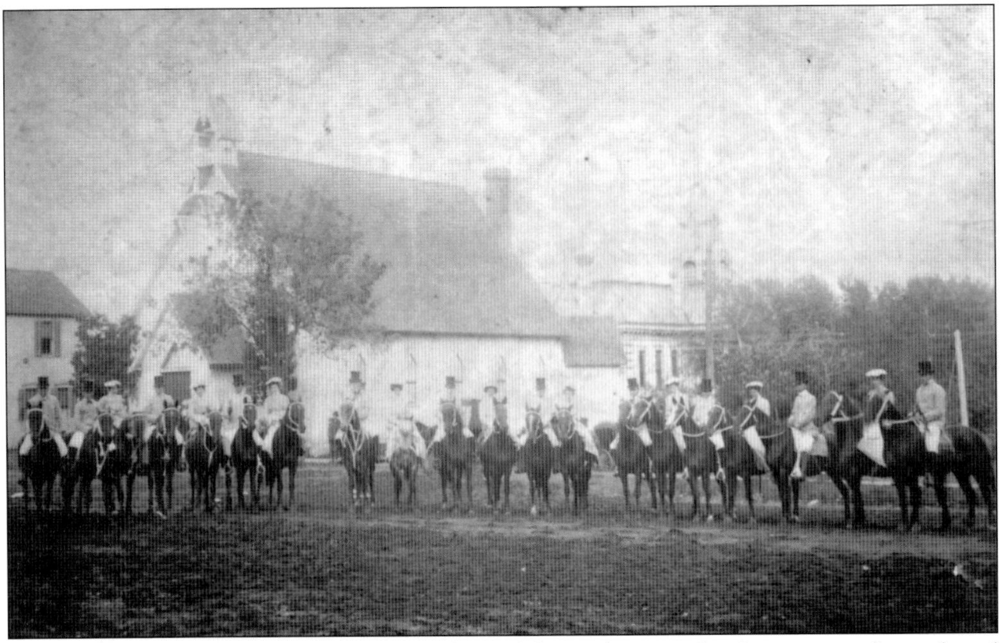

Dressed in formal riding habits, Atlantic Riding Club members stand in formation at Seventh and Chestnut Streets. The Atlantic Presbyterian Church is in the background. In 1902, the owners of a pack of foxhounds would meet at J. A. McWaid's pasture, and everyone would enjoy a good foxhunt. Many interested spectators would follow on foot to watch the riders and hounds.

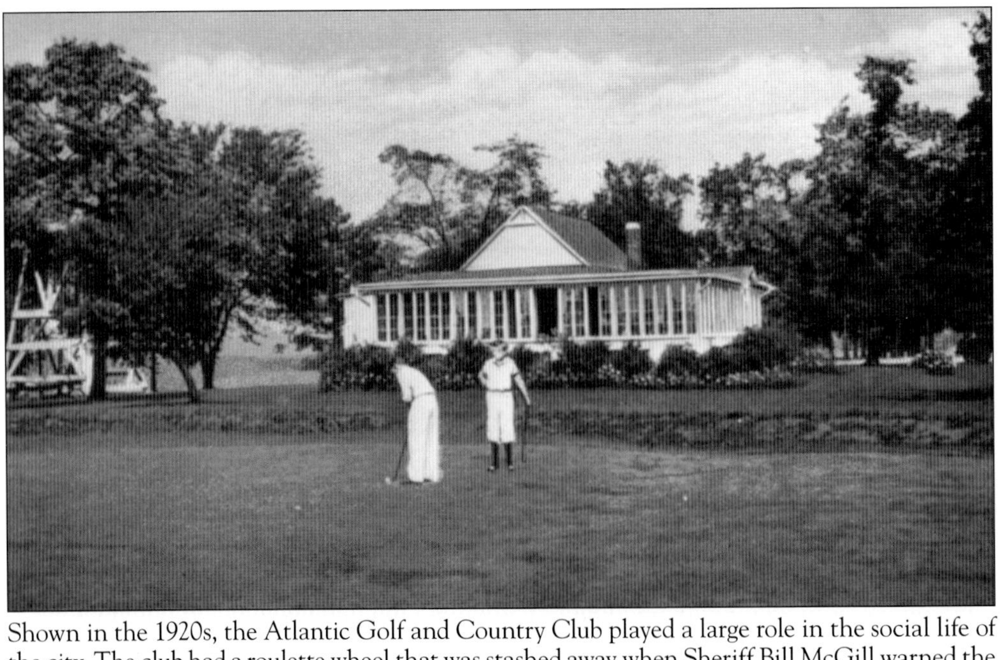

Shown in the 1920s, the Atlantic Golf and Country Club played a large role in the social life of the city. The club had a roulette wheel that was stashed away when Sheriff Bill McGill warned the management that a raid was imminent. In the 1940s, Phyllis Otto of Atlantic won the Women's Western Amateur Golf Tournament in Chicago, beating the famed Babe Didrikson Zaharias.

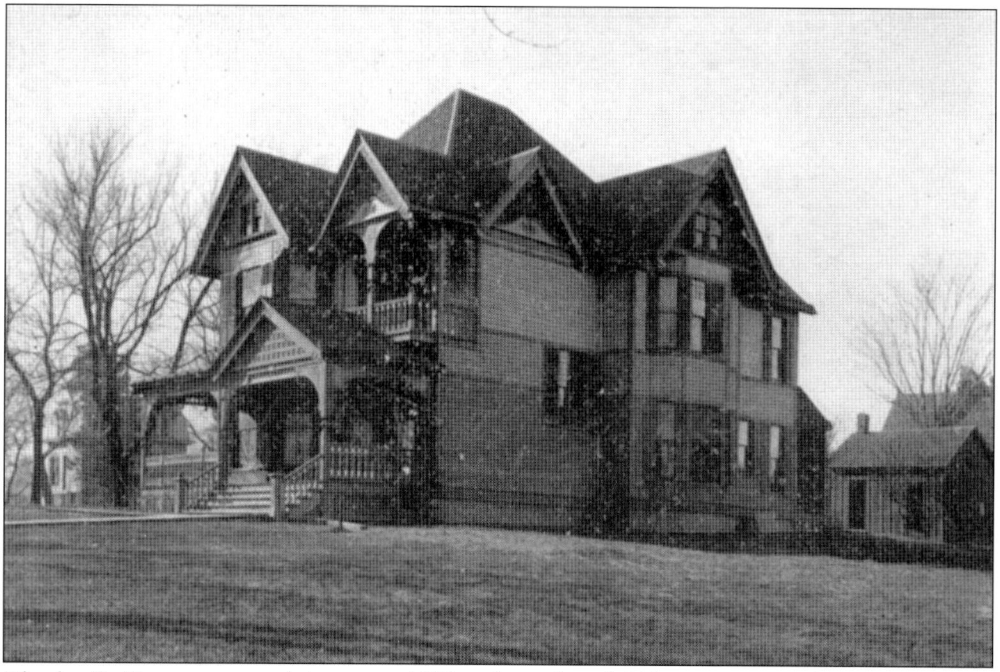

Charles R. Hunt came to Atlantic in 1875 and purchased 280 acres to start his cattle-feeding business and farming venture. He married Fanny Gearheart in 1876. While their home was being built on the farm, they stayed at the Pullman Hotel. The Hunts lived on the farm for 25 years before moving into town, occupying the home shown above at Ninth and Poplar Streets. Cattle feeding has been the mainstay of the Hunt farms through the years. The Hunts had two sons, Fred Roy and Gear. Gear died of what was then called "summer complaint." The photograph below shows Charles R. (on the donkey) and Fanny Hunt (standing to his immediate left) on a trip to Colorado with family and friends.

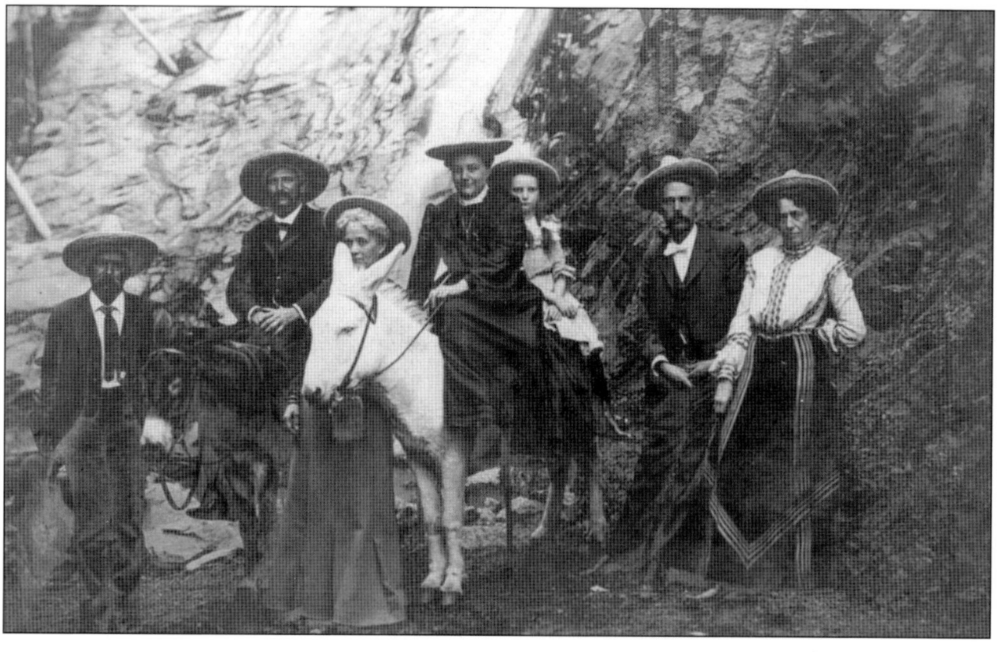

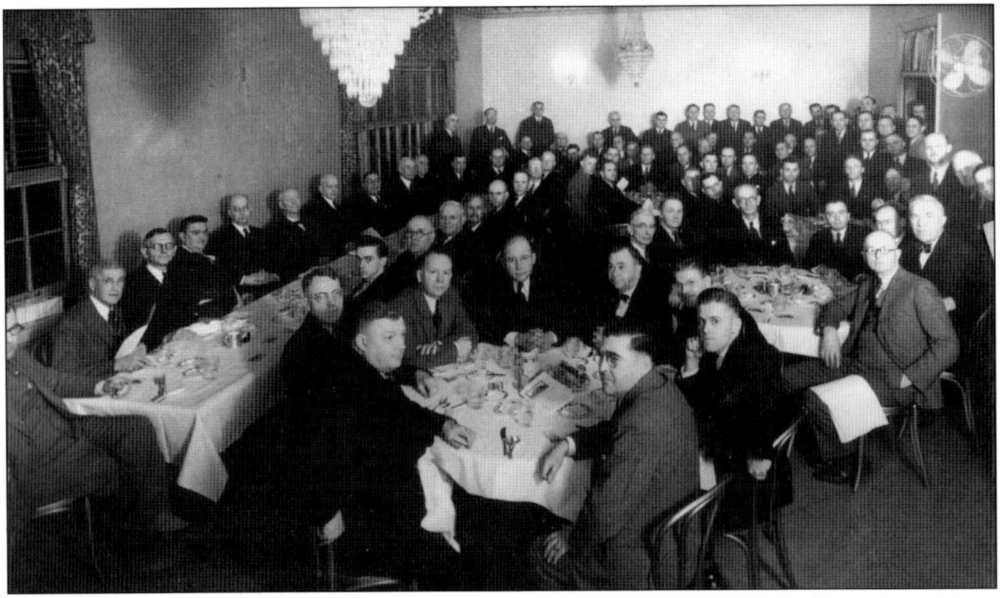

With the completion of the new Cass County Courthouse in 1935, county offices moved from the old Herring Building where they had been operating since the devastating courthouse fire of 1932. Dedication of the new building took place in the Whitney Hotel dining room and was attended by the business and professional elite of the county.

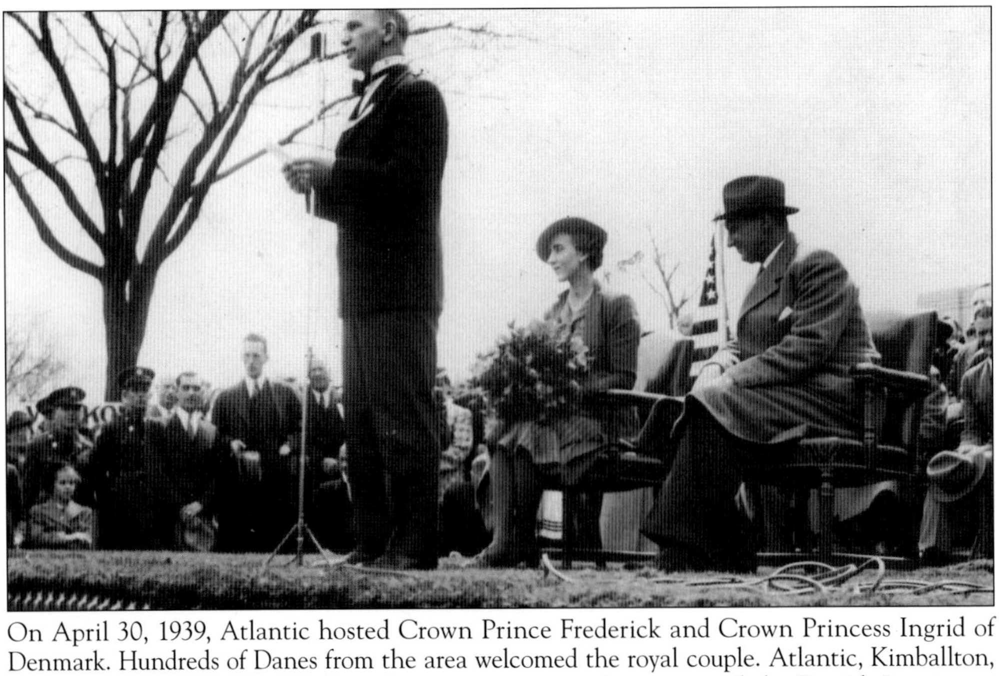

On April 30, 1939, Atlantic hosted Crown Prince Frederick and Crown Princess Ingrid of Denmark. Hundreds of Danes from the area welcomed the royal couple. Atlantic, Kimballton, and Elkhorn welcomed many Danish immigrants over the years, and the Danish Immigrant Museum is located in Elkhorn.

Six

Dealing with Adversity

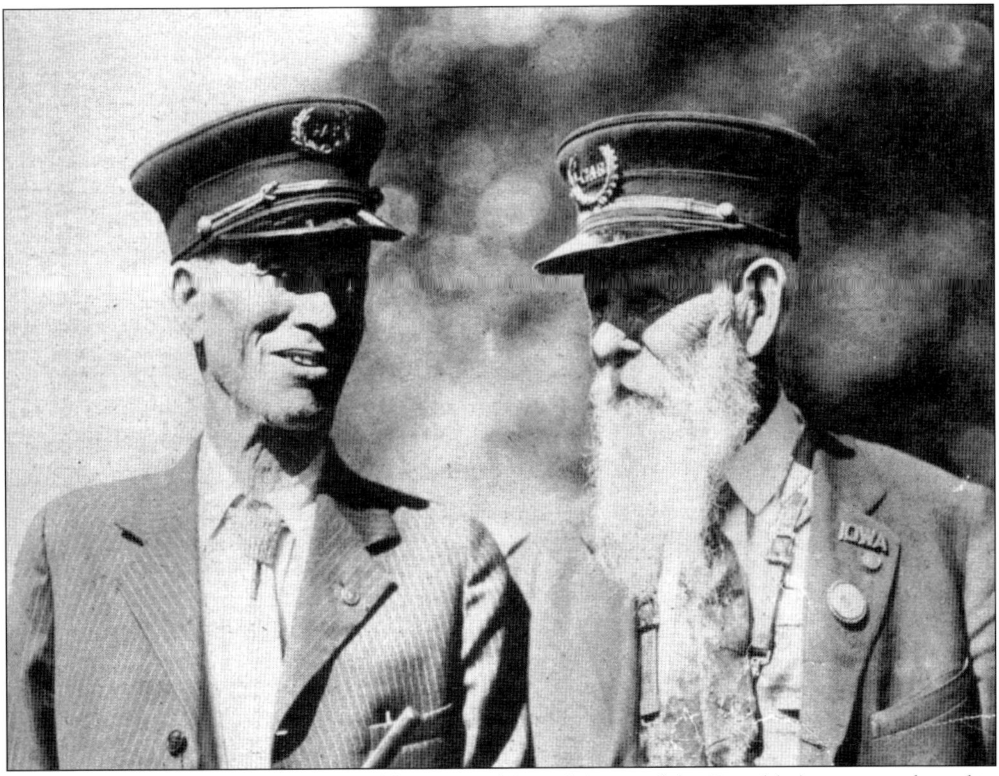

R. S. McGeehon (right) was Iowa's oldest GAR (Grand Army of the Republic) veteran when this 1910s photograph was taken at the Iowa State Fair. R. S. was a master carpenter and came to Atlantic in 1868 and helped build many of Atlantic's first homes. Another McGeehon, Robert D. (most likely a cousin), came to Iowa in July 1852. On September 1, 1852, he returned to Illinois where he married Mary Hoblitt. In the first six months at her new home, Mary McGeehon saw only one other woman. On December 22, 1864, Mary gave birth to the first white girl born in Grove Township.

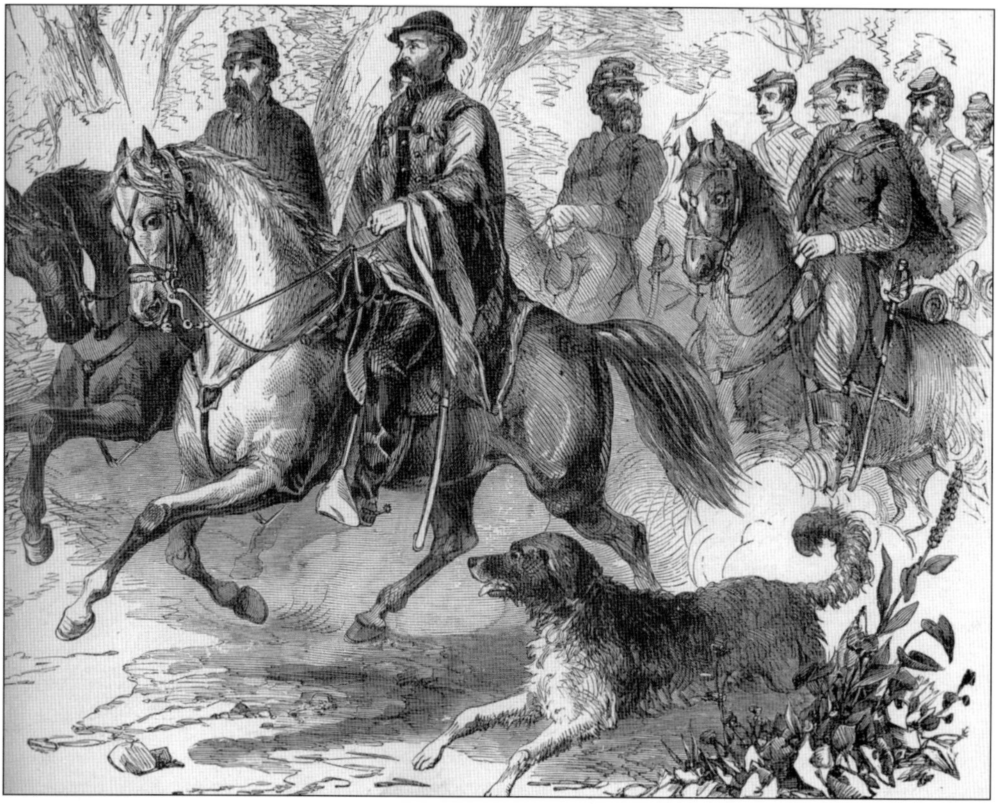

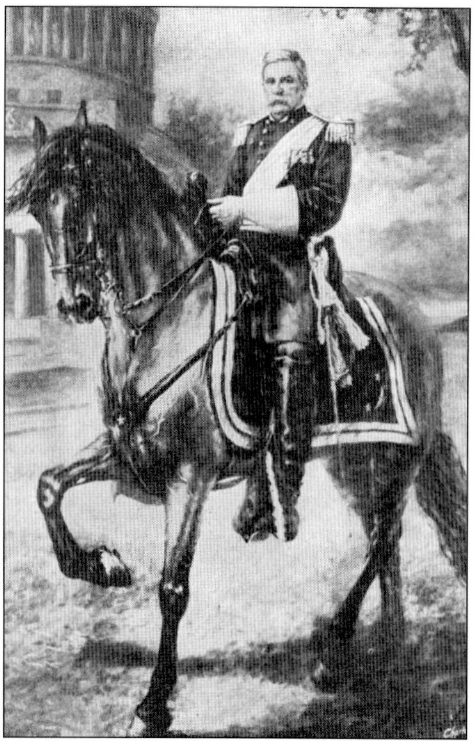

During the Civil War, the Fourth Iowa Infantry under Col. Grenville M. Dodge fought at the Battle of Pea Ridge in Arkansas. In this bloody engagement, the brigade's conduct was so heroic that it earned the admiration of a Confederate general, who stated, "The Fourth Iowa Regiment won immortal honors." Following that battle, the regiment met up with General Sherman in Vicksburg, Mississippi. John R. Kirk and Harvey and Henry L. Bradshaw, sons of Cass County pioneer Jeremiah Bradshaw, fought at both Pea Ridge and Vicksburg.

With the opening of the Civil War, Grenville M. Dodge was sent to Washington, D.C., to procure arms and equipment for volunteer troops in Iowa. In June 1861, he was commissioned a colonel in the Fourth Iowa Volunteers. For his gallantry at Pea Ridge, Dodge was promoted to brigadier general. He took part in Sherman's campaign in the South and was assigned the rank of major general. After the war, Dodge was instrumental in the development of the railroad.

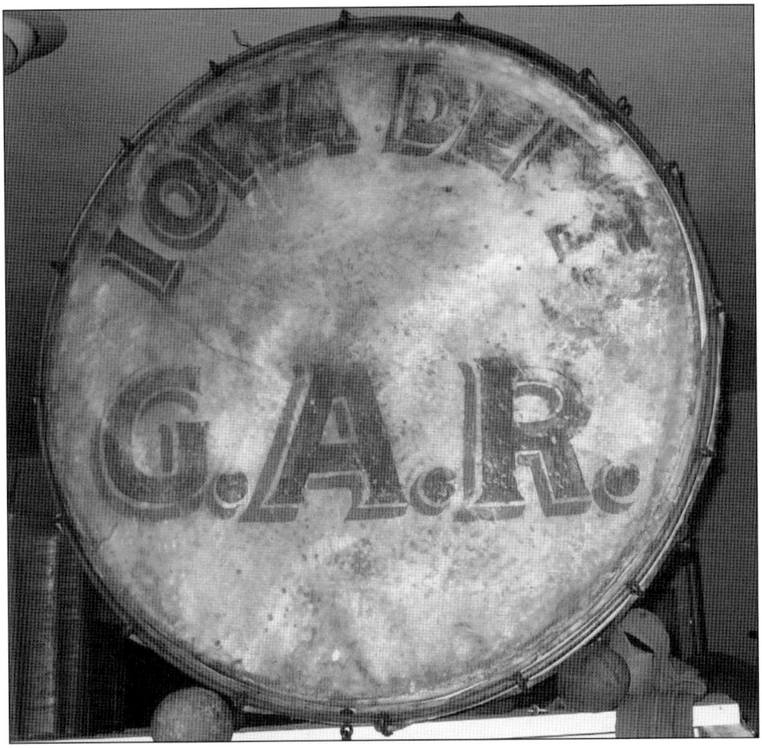

In the majority of photographs depicting the members of the GAR, a Civil War drum is prominently displayed. The drummer boy was often a young lad, some as young as 10 or 11. This drum is a prized artifact at the Cass County Museum in Griswold, Iowa.

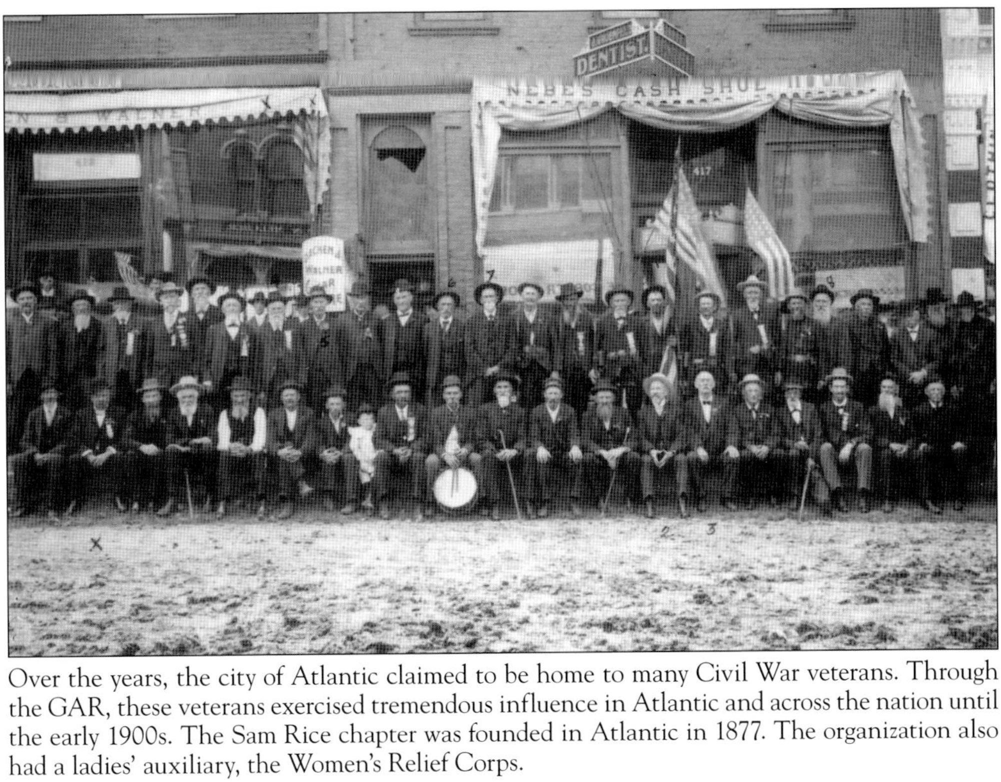

Over the years, the city of Atlantic claimed to be home to many Civil War veterans. Through the GAR, these veterans exercised tremendous influence in Atlantic and across the nation until the early 1900s. The Sam Rice chapter was founded in Atlantic in 1877. The organization also had a ladies' auxiliary, the Women's Relief Corps.

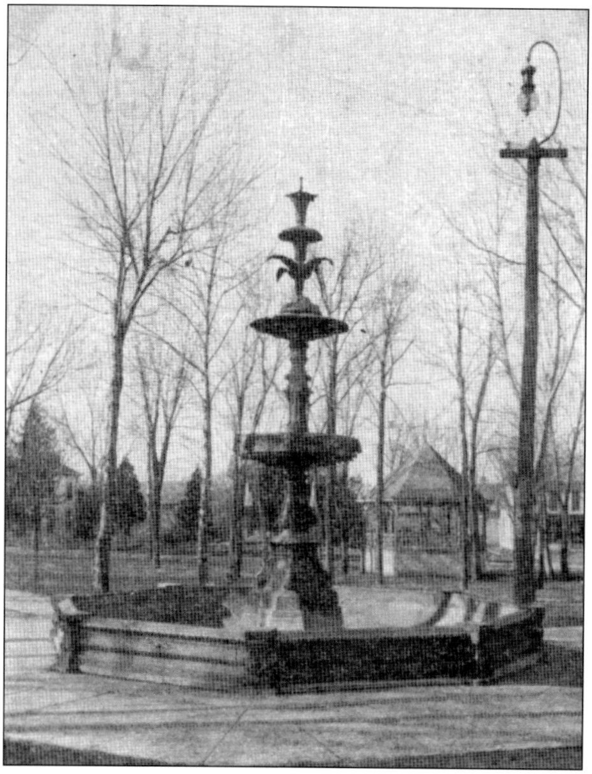

In the 1880s, the citizens of Cass County contributed $1,000 for the purpose of erecting a memorial to Ulysses S. Grant. A fountain was placed in the Atlantic City Park and had the distinction of being one of the earliest memorials placed in the area. It fell into a state of disrepair and was removed as a part of a government parks improvement project in 1933.

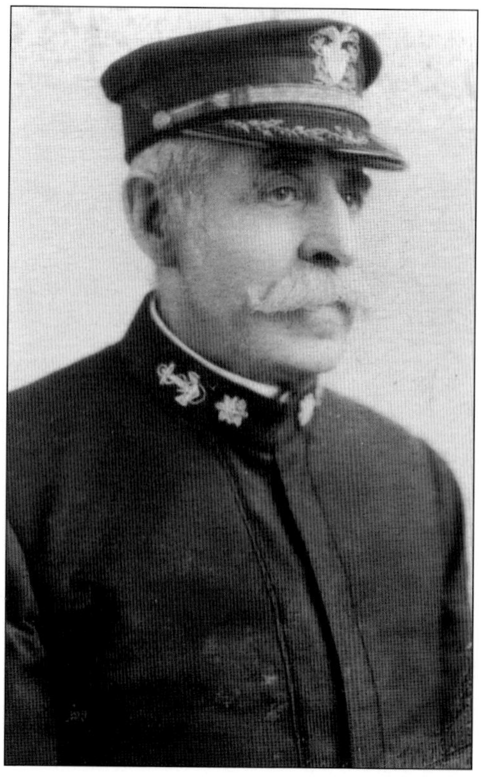

Comdr. George Stafford was Atlantic's first graduate of the United States Naval Academy in Annapolis, Maryland. He received his appointment in May 1873 and graduated with honors in June 1877. Stafford served under Commodore George Dewey and saw action in the Battle of Manila Bay in May 1898. Stafford was known in Atlantic as a great dancer and quite the ladies' man. He was a descendant of Atlantic pioneer families Hawks and Osborne.

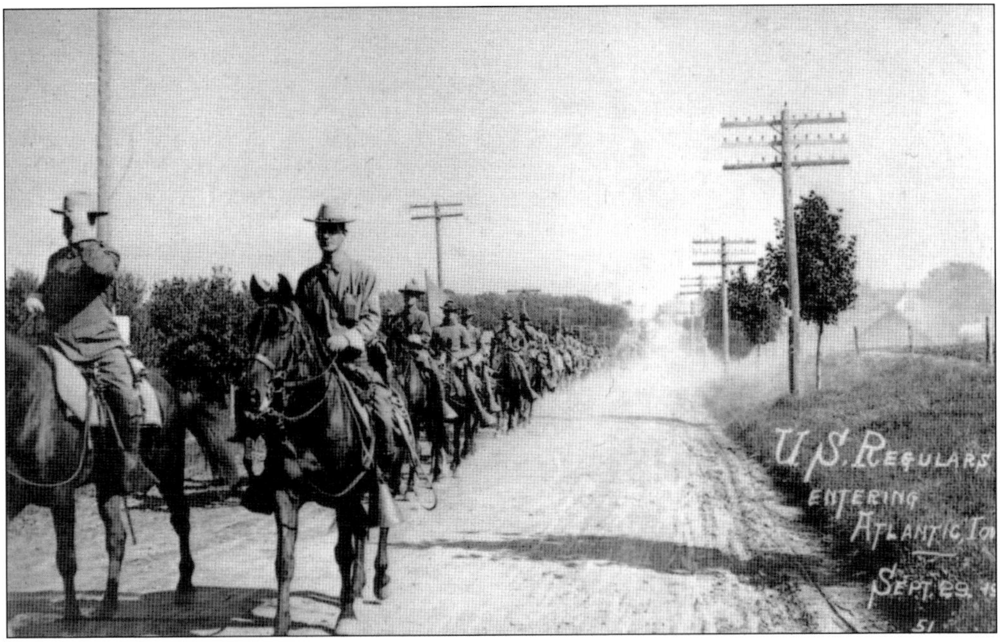

On September 29, 1909, a cavalry brigade of U.S. regulars enters Atlantic (above) en route to Omaha. According to an article in the *Atlantic News-Telegraph*, the troops came into town with "a swish and a swirl, and the trampling of 800 horses and 1,500 soldiers. Their splendid horses were in prime shape; their trappings shone and glistened." It was reported that some of the soldiers were afoot, leading their horses, a punishment for insubordination. The group camped at the Cass County Fairgrounds (below). Men were allowed to spend time that evening viewing two moving picture shows at the Bacon Opera House and skating at the portable rink set up on Walnut Street. Their stay was marked by gentlemanly conduct and a high regard for the rights of others.

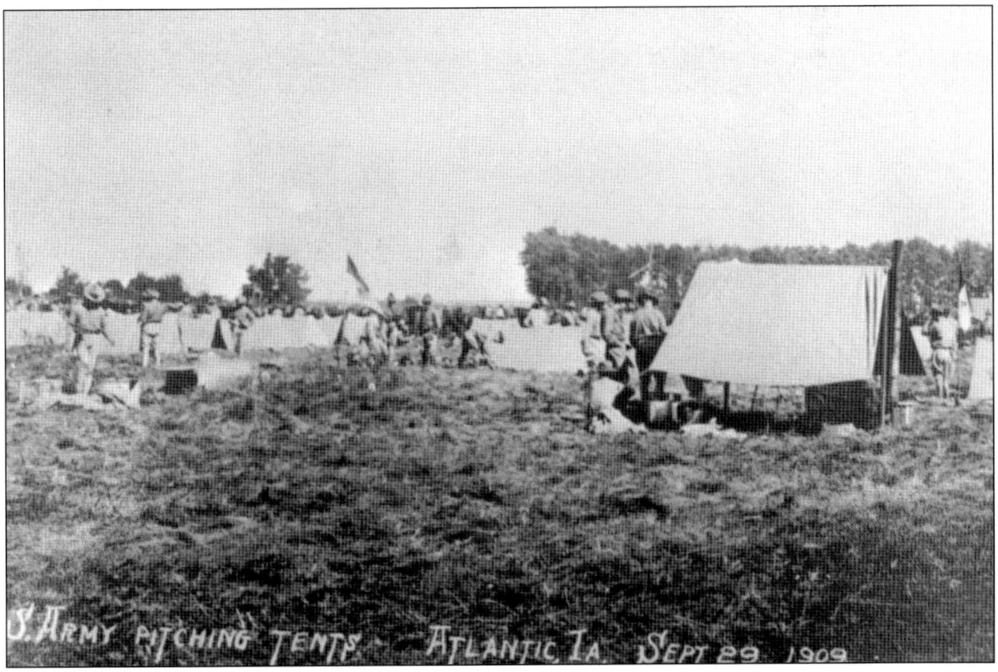

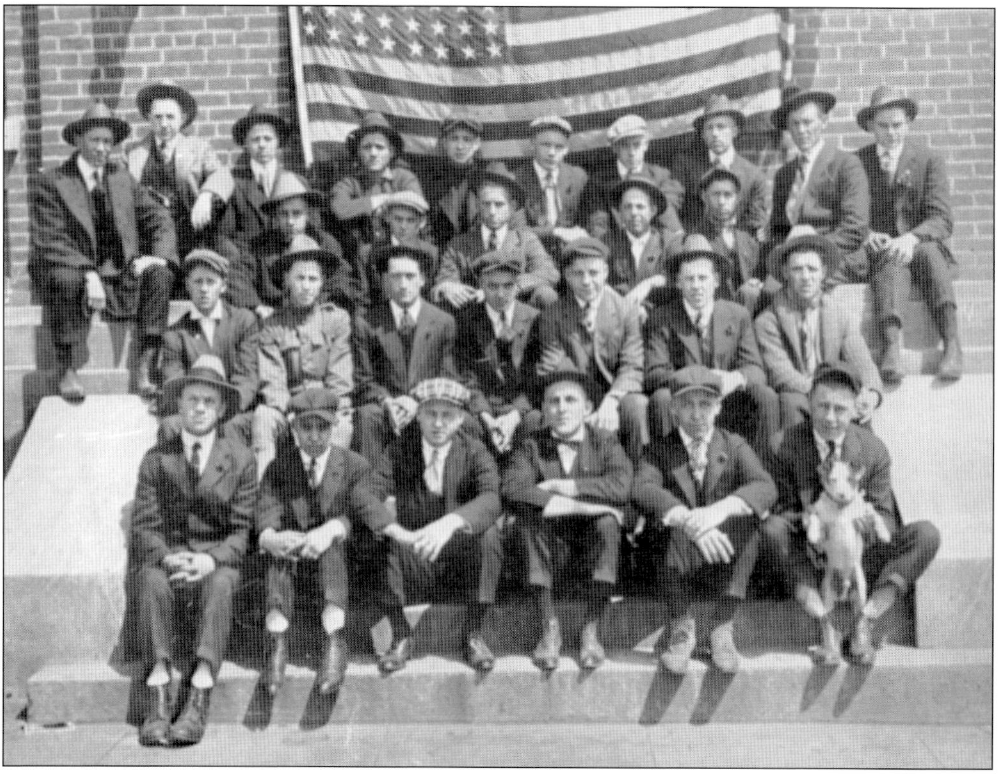

In March 1917, with the clouds of World War I on the horizon, many young Atlantic men decided to join the Iowa National Guard. The Third Iowa Regiment recruited heavily. The group of men in this image would become part of Company M. Raymond Coker was one of the young men who enlisted on April 4, 1917, two days before war was declared. On July 4, Company M was mobilized.

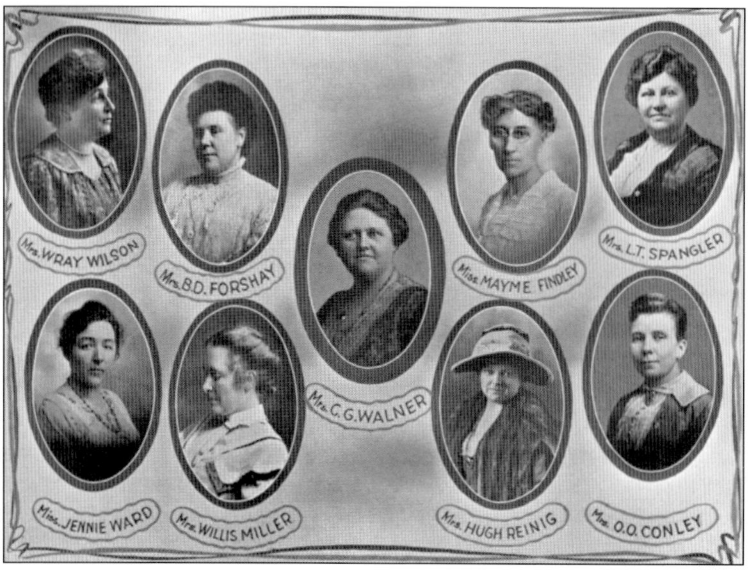

Early in 1918, American women formed the Women's Committee of the Council of National Defense. This group organized and aided in carrying out a program for national conservation of food. The Cass County chapter was chaired by Mrs. B. D. Forshay of Anita, Zeta Reinig of Griswold, and Mrs. C. G. Walner and Mayme Findley of Atlantic.

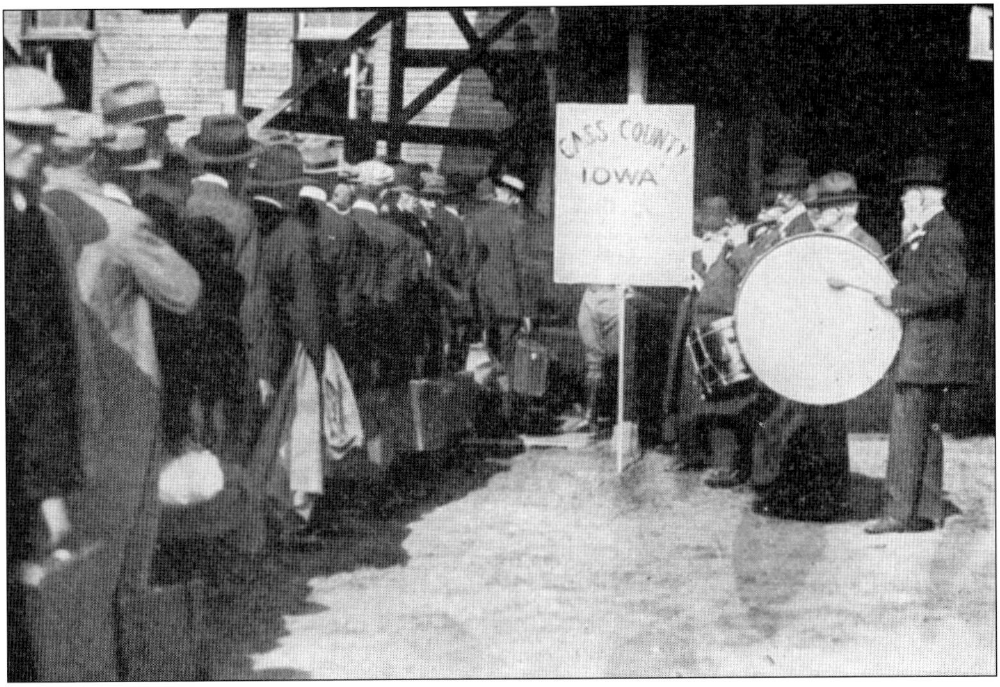

In 1917, Cass County men report to Camp Dodge in Des Moines, welcomed by a committee of Civil War veterans and a Cass County sign. Former Atlantic resident Eddie Rickenbacker became one of the most famous World War I ace of aces, credited with shooting down 26 enemy planes. Rickenbacker, who lived in Atlantic sometime between 1909 and 1916, sold Fords for the Herring Automobile Company and raced at many local fairs. He later won the Indianapolis 500 and became president of Eastern Airlines.

World War I took a heavy toll on the young men of Atlantic. On March 9, 1918, Company M of the 168th Regiment, Rainbow Division, went into battle in Baccarat, France. During the bombardment, Cecil Conley and Fred Turner of Atlantic were killed. The 168th has been heralded in the history of that terrible conflict. Cass County lost 30 men in World War I.

THE HONOR ROLL

Cecil M. Conley	Ray Enfield
Fred D. Turner	Joseph A. Baller
Irwin O. McConlee	James P. McCourt
Lloyd L. Morrill	Samuel L. Hazard
Max L. Hubbell	Sam A. Miller
Phil A. Brooks	Glen G. Blanchard
Norbert Wilson	Andrew M. Anderson
Charles E. Donohoe	Vernon Purvis
Oscar Henry Bartley	Louis C. Schuler
Guy H. Peters	George A. Stengel
Clyde A. Smeltzer	Edward M. Hansen
James Howard South	George A. Ihnen
Leo Jennings	Bernard W. Keffer
Clyde J. Harris	Carl J. Lechner
Frank H. Enfield	Frank Pieken

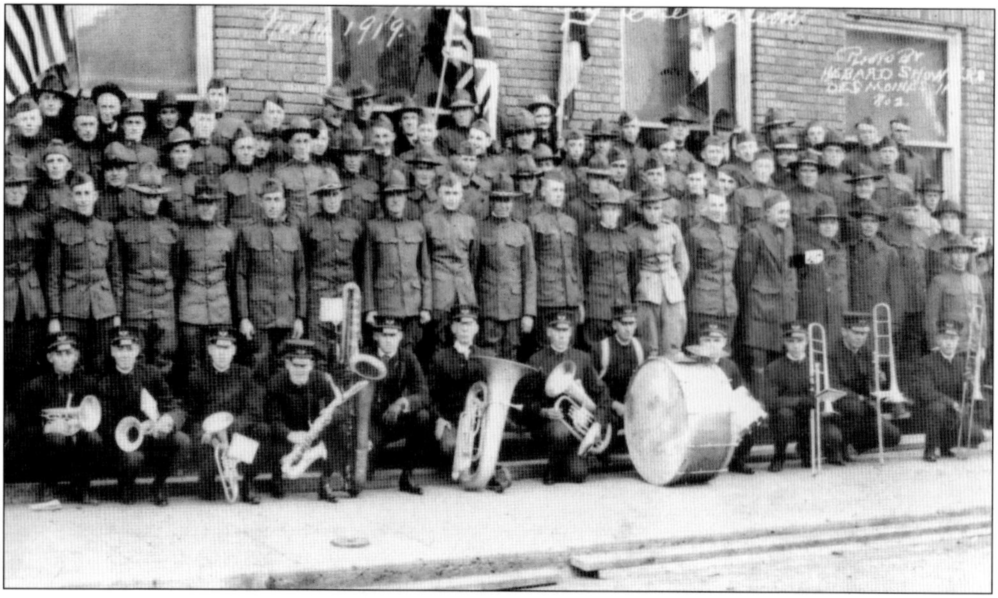

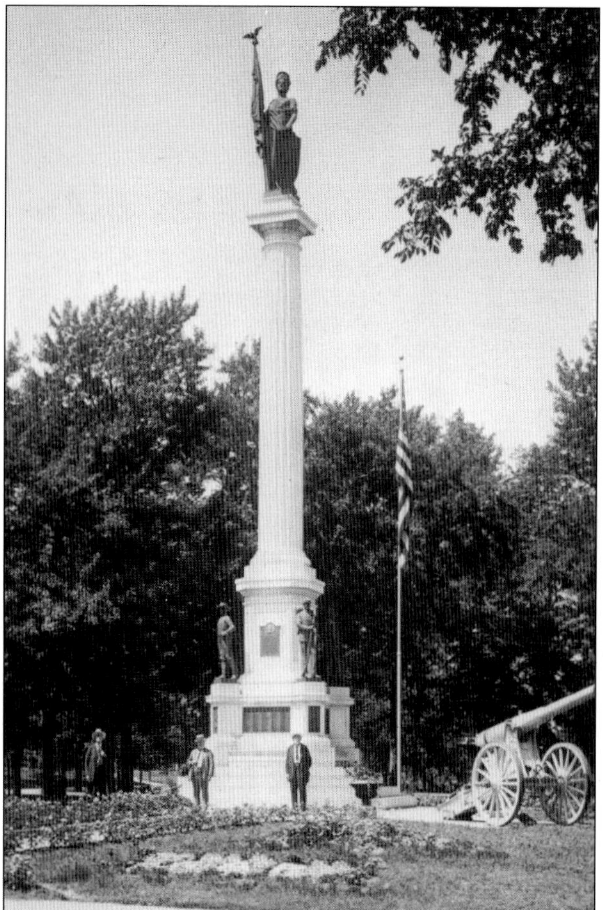

Following the cessation of hostilities in 1918, communities celebrated the end of the "war to end all wars." Armistice Day was celebrated throughout the United States. This Egbert Studio photograph, taken in front of the Atlantic City Hall on East Fourth Street on November 11, 1919, is labeled "First Annual Armistice Day Celebration" and captures a group of World War I area veterans.

The idea of the Cass County Soldiers' Monument originated with Civil War veterans Cyrus B. Osborne and J. S. Pressnal. Dedicated in the Atlantic City Park in July 1919, it bears the names of all Cass County Civil War veterans and cost $22,894. Buried in the base of the monument are the records of the various county GAR groups, a Springfield rifle, and a captain's sword. The monument is dedicated to veterans of all wars.

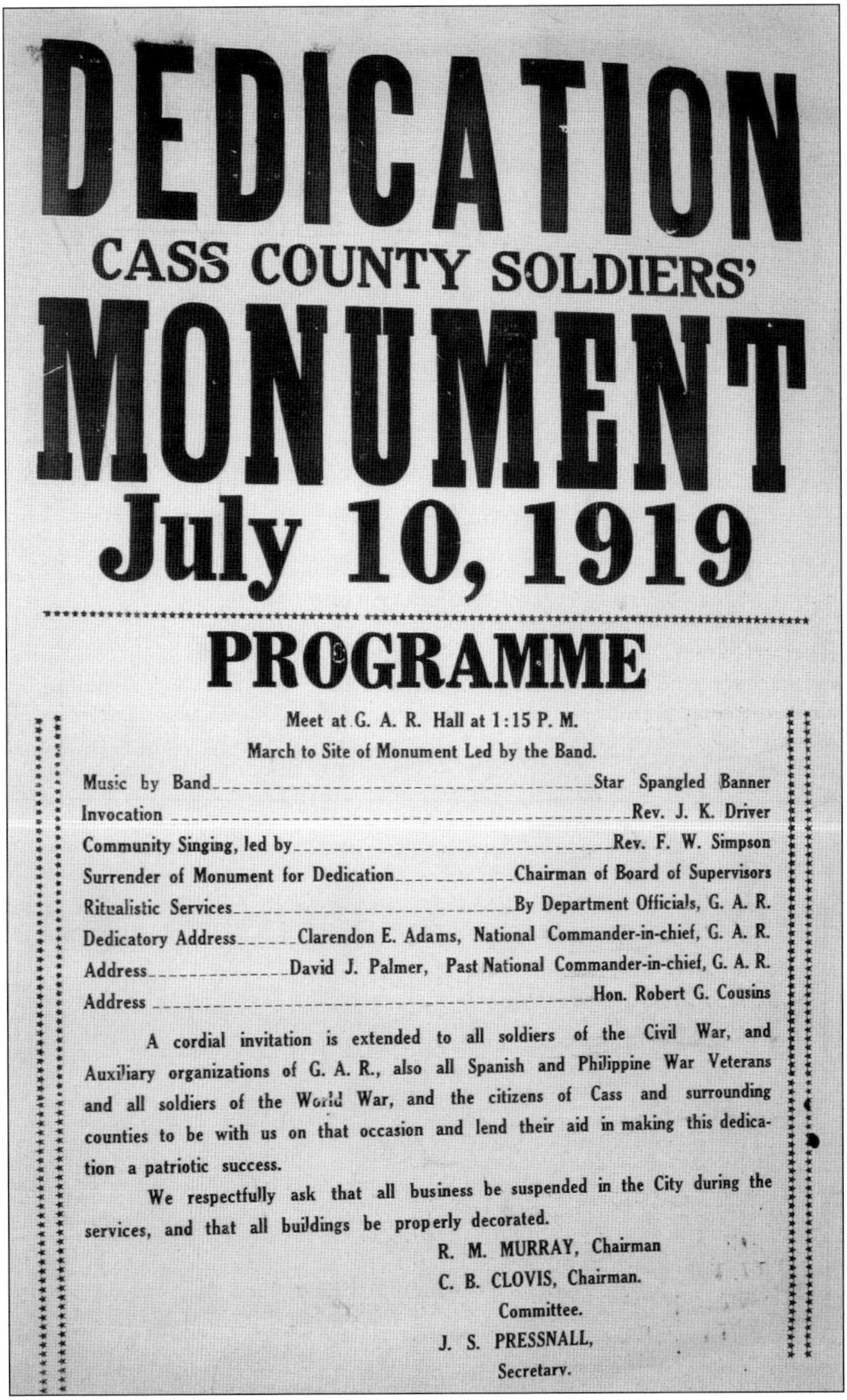

DEDICATION
CASS COUNTY SOLDIERS'
MONUMENT
July 10, 1919

PROGRAMME

Meet at G. A. R. Hall at 1:15 P. M.

March to Site of Monument Led by the Band.

Music by Band ---------- Star Spangled Banner

Invocation ---------- Rev. J. K. Driver

Community Singing, led by ---------- Rev. F. W. Simpson

Surrender of Monument for Dedication ---------- Chairman of Board of Supervisors

Ritualistic Services ---------- By Department Officials, G. A. R.

Dedicatory Address ------ Clarendon E. Adams, National Commander-in-chief, G. A. R.

Address ---------- David J. Palmer, Past National Commander-in-chief, G. A. R.

Address ---------- Hon. Robert G. Cousins

A cordial invitation is extended to all soldiers of the Civil War, and Auxiliary organizations of G. A. R., also all Spanish and Philippine War Veterans and all soldiers of the World War, and the citizens of Cass and surrounding counties to be with us on that occasion and lend their aid in making this dedication a patriotic success.

We respectfully ask that all business be suspended in the City during the services, and that all buildings be properly decorated.

R. M. MURRAY, Chairman
C. B. CLOVIS, Chairman.
Committee.
J. S. PRESSNALL,
Secretary.

This advertisement for the dedication service of the Cass County Soldiers' Monument was widely circulated throughout the county. The dedication date, July 10, 1919, was a countywide event and brought thousands to Atlantic. Clarendon E. Adams, national commander of the GAR, was the main speaker for the event.

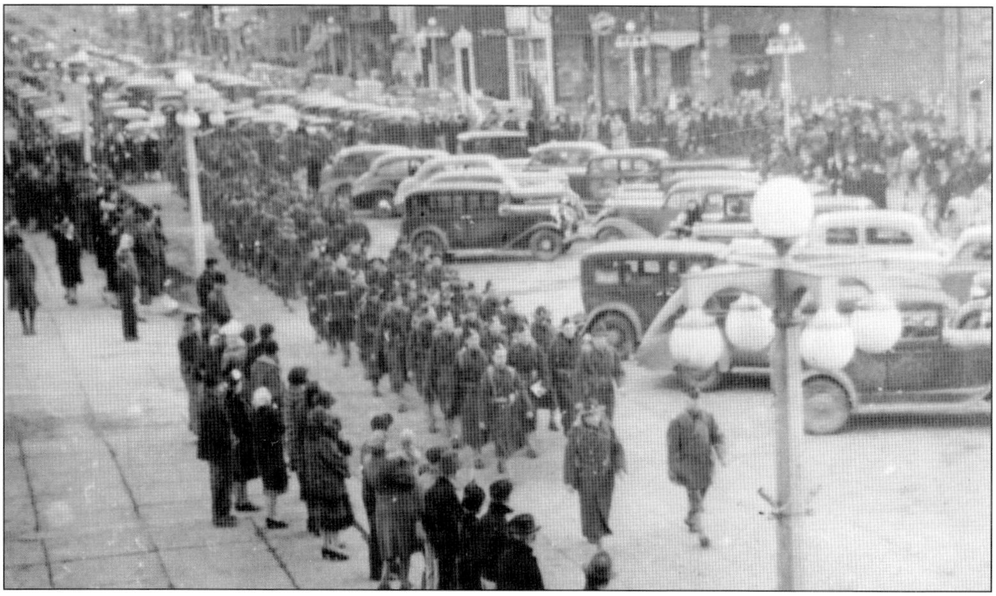

When World War II broke out, Atlantic maintained Company K, part of the Iowa National Guard's 168th Regiment. The company included many men from Atlantic. The group took part in the invasion of North Africa. On February 17, 1943, at the Battle of Faid Pass, Company K was surrounded, and the Germans took many men prisoner. Many Atlantic families received notification that their sons or husbands were missing in action. News finally arrived that all 44 men who had been unaccounted for were in fact prisoners.

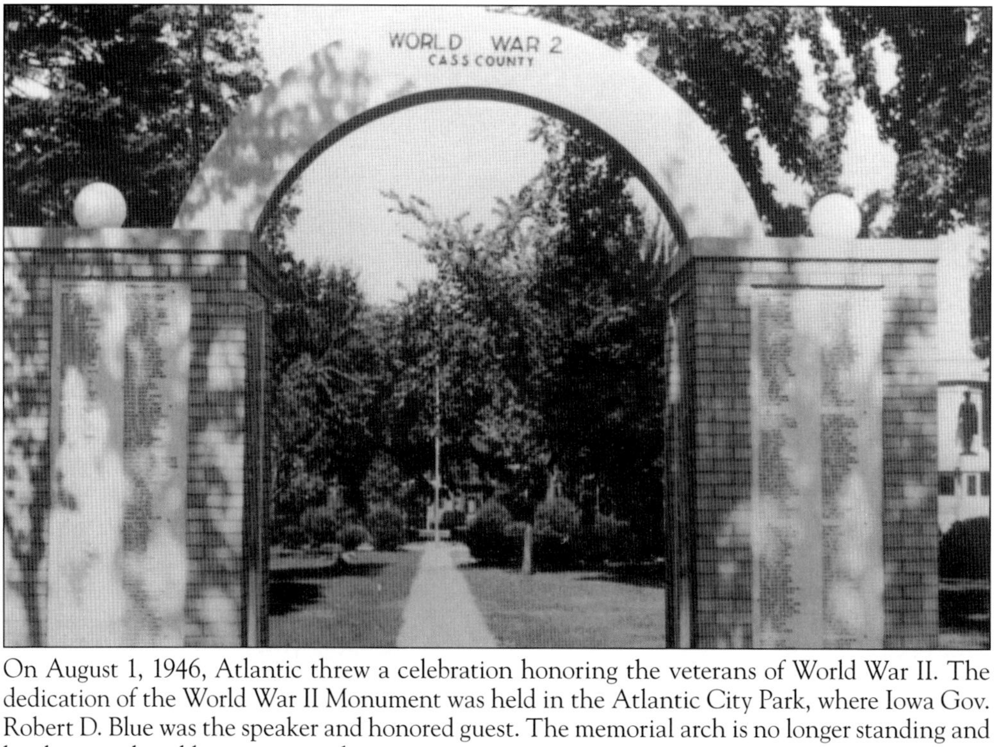

On August 1, 1946, Atlantic threw a celebration honoring the veterans of World War II. The dedication of the World War II Monument was held in the Atlantic City Park, where Iowa Gov. Robert D. Blue was the speaker and honored guest. The memorial arch is no longer standing and has been replaced by a stone marker.

Seven

Coming of Age

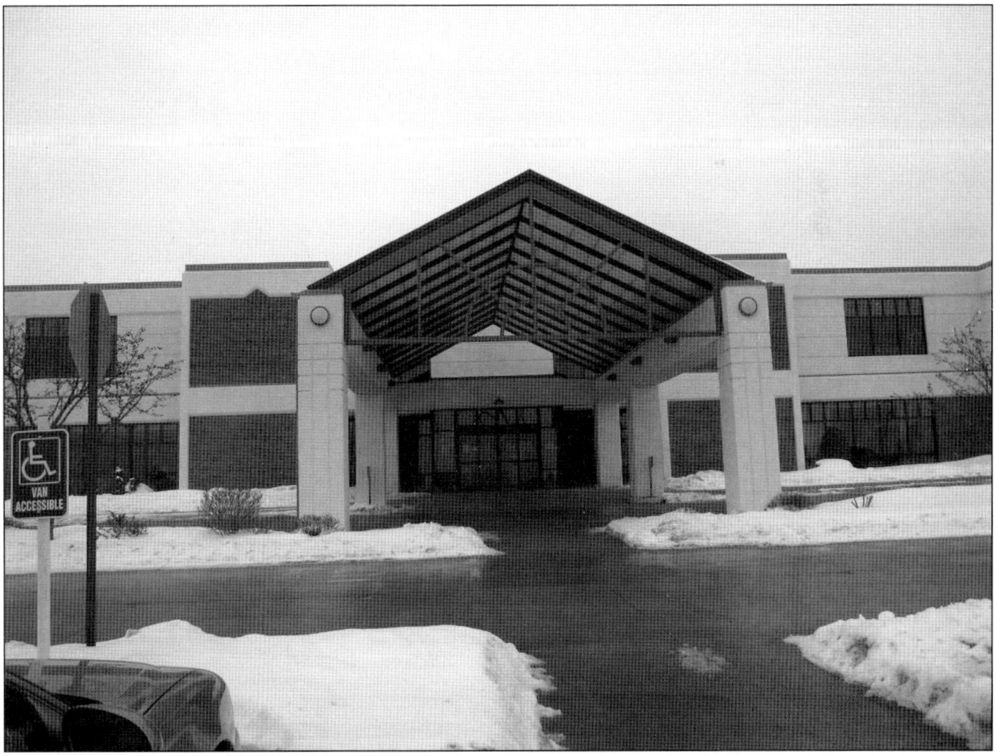

The new Cass County Memorial Hospital was completed in October 1968. It was built on a 25-acre site donated by the E. A. Kelloway family. Major expansions were carried out in 1974 and 1984. In 1998, construction was finished on an $8.6 million addition and renovation.

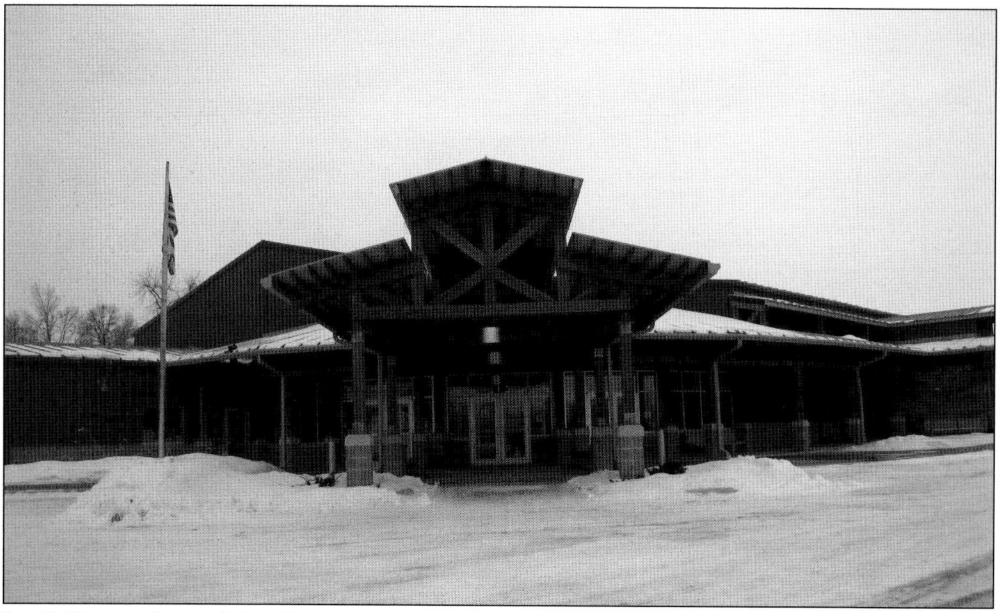

In 1998, members of the Cass County Agricultural Educational Association held meetings regarding the building of a community center for Cass County. Ground-breaking for the center took place on August 3, 2000. The new community building was complete in time for the 2001 Cass County Fair. It was officially dedicated on September 9, 2001.

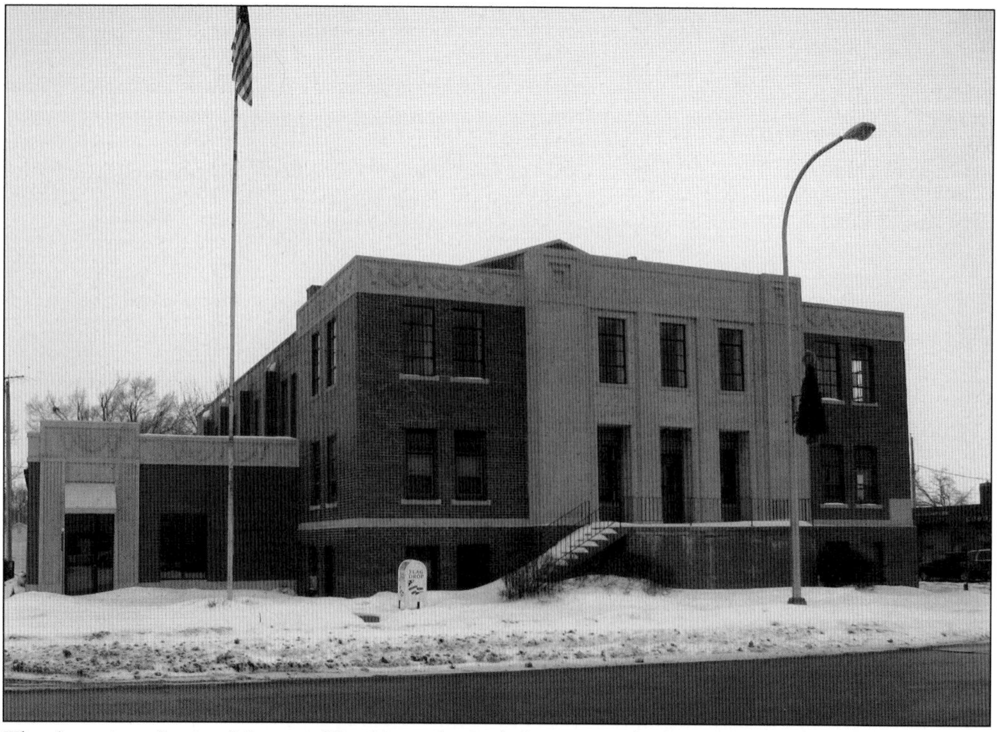

The American Legion Memorial Building, formerly known as the Iowa National Guard Armory, is the current project of ARISE (Atlantic Rock Island Society Enterprise). Plans include a museum, meeting rooms, genealogical area, and a place where various veteran's groups can meet.

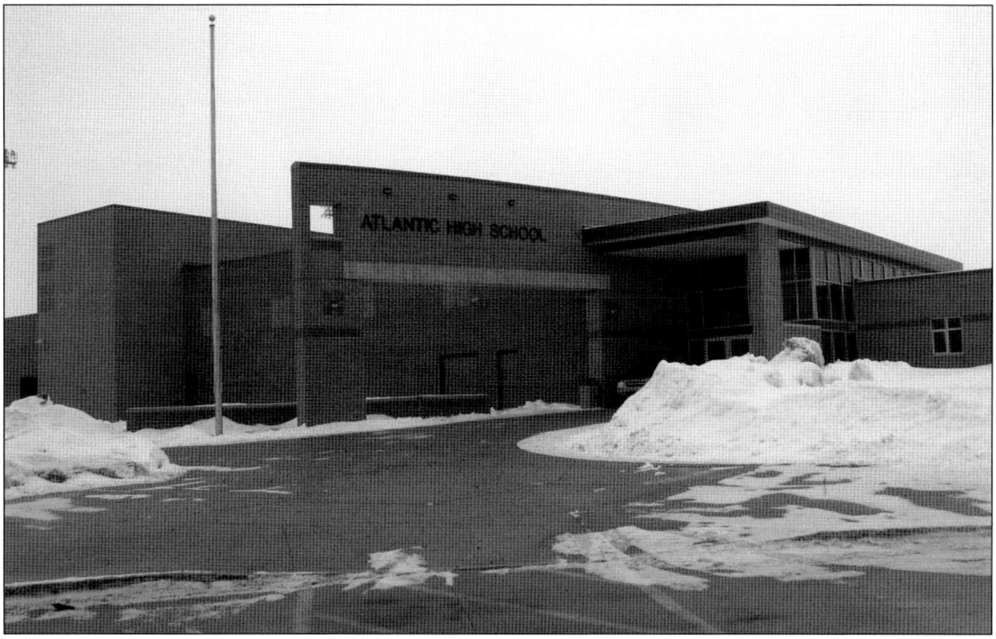

Atlantic has had a long and proud history of furthering education in the area. From the beginnings of East Side School in 1871, the community has continued to provide excellent facilities and opportunities for students. This new high school was completed in 1996.

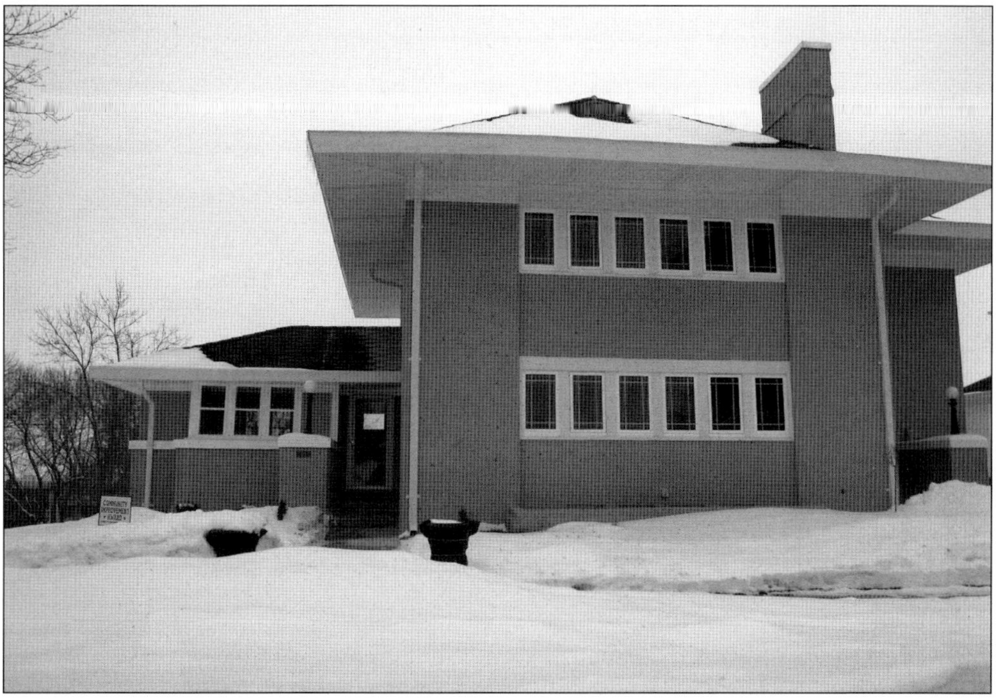

This Prairie style home is located at the corner of Ninth and Locust Streets. The Charles F. Chase family moved into it on November 1, 1915. In 1927, the home was purchased by Judge Whitmore. Bob and Judy Camblin have owned the property since November 2008 and have returned it to its original magnificence. The house is on the National Register of Historic Places.

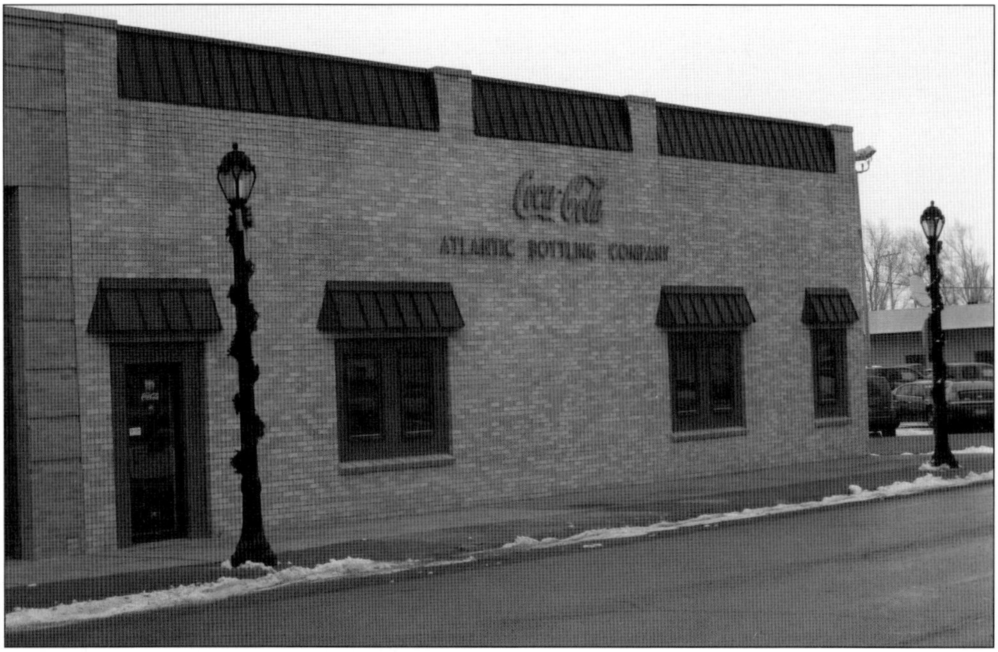

In 1929, Harry and Henry Tyler acquired the Coca-Cola franchise for the Atlantic territory. In 1949, Harry Tyler assumed sole control of the Atlantic area. His son James took over the management in 1958. Kirk Tyler, James's son, is the current president and chief executive officer. The Tylers have been leaders in the promotion of the city of Atlantic. Coca-Cola Days are celebrated in Atlantic each summer, and the event brings crowds of avid Coca-Cola fans from all around the country. In 2001, Atlantic was named the Coca-Cola capital of Iowa. (Below, courtesy of Sue Fischer Photography.)

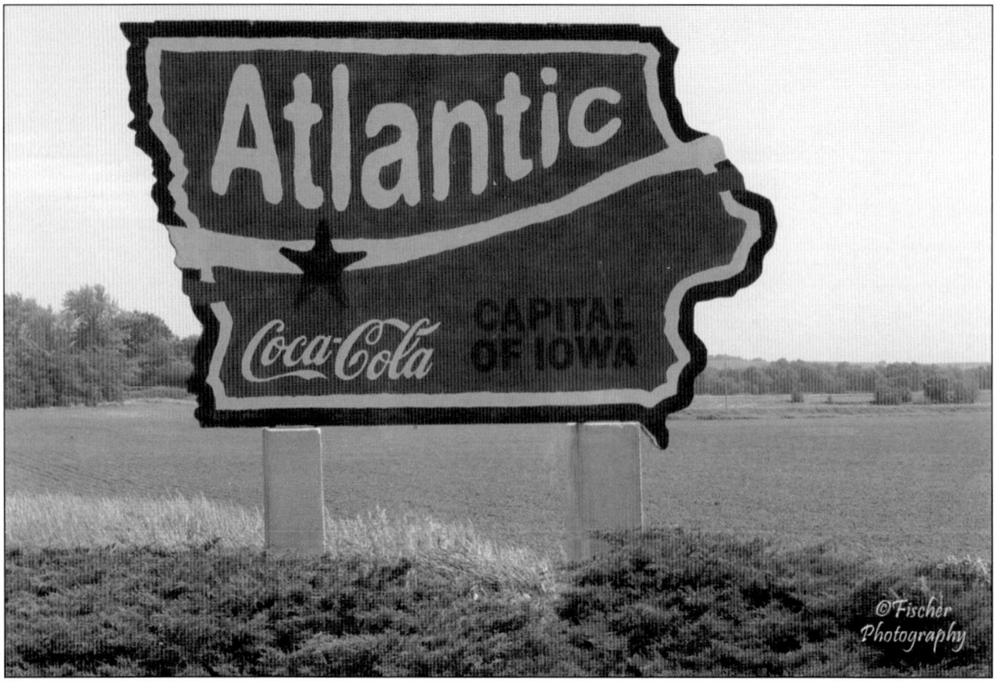

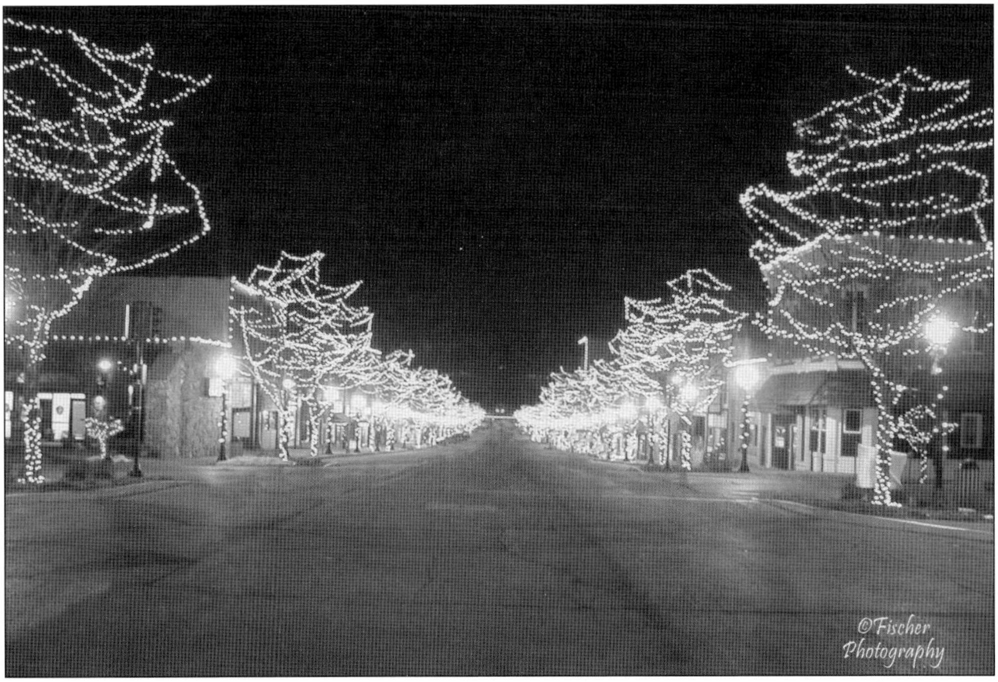

Residents of Cass County agree that there is no other city in the state as lovely as Atlantic at Christmas, as seen in this Chestnut Street photograph. Visitors come from miles around to view the lights display. The city park and streets are decorated with thousands of tiny white and colored lights, and there are Christmas scenes set up in the park. (Courtesy of Sue Fischer Photography.)

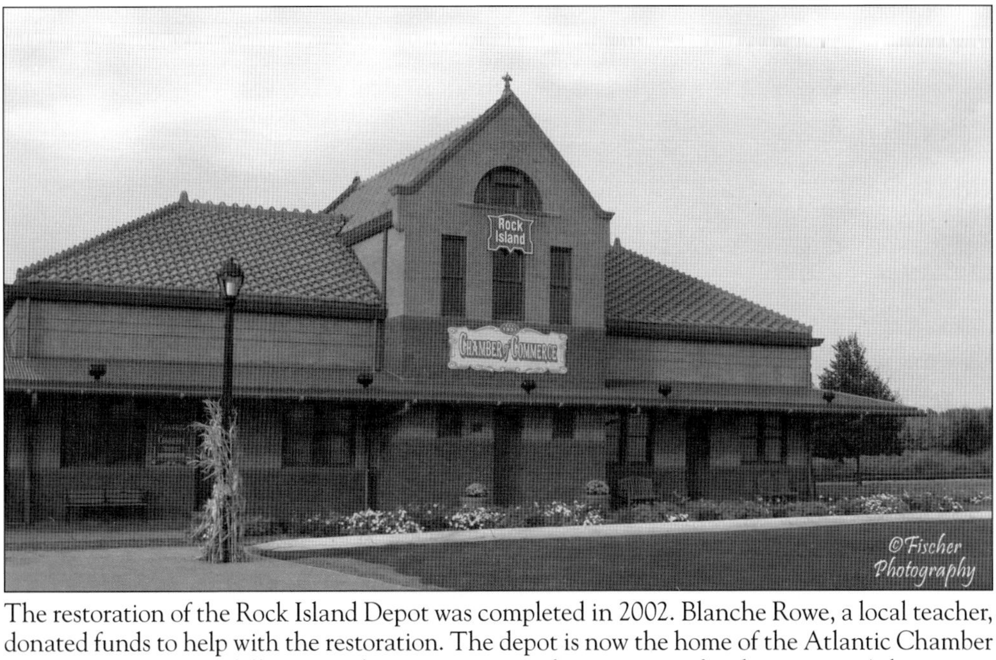

The restoration of the Rock Island Depot was completed in 2002. Blanche Rowe, a local teacher, donated funds to help with the restoration. The depot is now the home of the Atlantic Chamber of Commerce. Beautifully restored, it serves as a welcome center for the county. Atlantic was once the dream of Franklin H. Whitney; today that dream is alive in a vibrant, thriving, and proud city.

www.arcadiapublishing.com

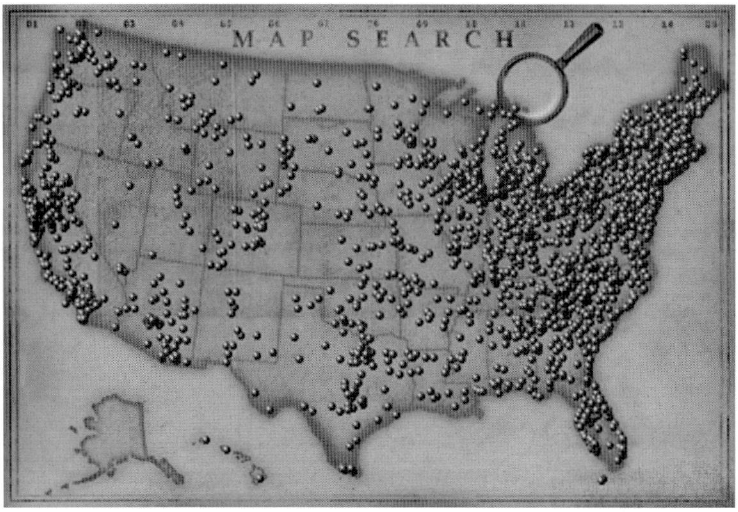

Discover books about the town where you grew up, the cities where your friends and families live, the town where your parents met, or even that retirement spot you've been dreaming about. Our Web site provides history lovers with exclusive deals, advanced notification about new titles, e-mail alerts of author events, and much more.

MADE IN THE USA

Arcadia Publishing, the leading local history publisher in the United States, is committed to making history accessible and meaningful through publishing books that celebrate and preserve the heritage of America's people and places. Consistent with our mission to preserve history on a local level, this book was printed in South Carolina on American-made paper and manufactured entirely in the United States.

This book carries the accredited Forest Stewardship Council (FSC) label and is printed on 100 percent FSC-certified paper. Products carrying the FSC label are independently certified to assure consumers that they come from forests that are managed to meet the social, economic, and ecological needs of present and future generations.

FSC
Mixed Sources
Product group from well-managed forests and other controlled sources

Cert no. SW-COC-001530
www.fsc.org
© 1996 Forest Stewardship Council

Find *Your* Place in History.